An Invitation to Slow

"Each of us would be wise to receive, consider thoughtfully, and yes, to ponder slowly the invitations put forth in the pages of *An Invitation to Slow*. The invitations to quiet, courage, gratitude, community, and more are rooted in the lives, work, words, and hearts of two people whose wisdom blends together to create not a loud, rushing river but rather a quiet, steady stream of insight that, when applied, will lead to greater human flourishing in the all-too-often cacophonous world we live in. Read. Reflect. Respond. Renew."

—**Jeff Crosby**, author of *The Language of the Soul: Meeting God in the Longings of Our Hearts*

"Mark and Lisa McMinn are veteran writers who connect with the reader through sharing their personal experiences and communicating their research in a way that is inviting and easily understood. They have also adapted the adage 'show, don't tell.' This means they invite instead of instruct. You will not be admonished to be slow to speak, fear, anger, judge, envy, consume, grasp, isolate. What you will receive are examples and evidence that will draw you toward enriched living."

—**Dan McCracken**, former publisher, Barclay Press

"In these crazy-fast times measured in nanoseconds by gadgets on our wrists that overload us with information, the McMinns have gifted us with an important call to a pace that more fits the speed of our souls. I especially appreciated the 'Pauses' interspersed throughout the text and the 'Slow Ponderings' at the end of each chapter. I think you will too."

—**J. Brent Bill**, author of *Holy Silence: The Gift of Quaker Spirituality*

"The speed of now and the invitation to slow are daily contradictions that frustrate our souls and wear out our bodies. In this gentle, practical book the McMinns use compelling facts and spiritual truths as invitations into a different pace with different values. Like quiet waters the book invites you into a more spacious life with yourself and God. Enjoy."

—**MaryKate Morse**, professor of leadership and spiritual formation, Portland Seminary

"With clear eyes centered on God and seasoned by thoughtful reflection, Lisa and Mark McMinn have gathered a path of wisdom. *An Invitation to Slow* brings together the painful realities of our twenty-first century lives and the ancient gifts of quiet, courage, empathy, humility, gratitude, generosity, contentment, and community. This book will meet you where you are and welcome you to transformation. For anyone who is longing for the slow and sacred way to Christ-centered wholeness, this is your book."

—**Lacy Finn Borgo**, author of *Faith Like a Child: Embracing Our Lives as Children of God*

"Mark and Lisa McMinn offer an invitation to slow down and pause amid the fast pace of life. Their writing is inviting—full of humor, relatable stories, and an authenticity that allows the reader to engage deeply in their own introspection. We get a sense of their own journey of allowing a slower and contemplative pace in their lives while recognizing the influences that swirl around us all that say it isn't possible. Along the way, they invite us to pause and reflect on what we are reading and how we are engaging with the words they have written. This book is a gift that offers an invitation along with practical ways of reflecting on our experiences and longings in life. What a true gift."

—**Kathi Gatlin**, executive director, Companioning Center, and spiritual direction educator

"At a time when too many of us feel frenzied, frustrated, hopeless, and isolated, *An Invitation to Slow* entices us toward a more humane way of being and one more fully in harmony with God. Take the title seriously as you reflect on the stories, collection of research, suggested practices, and queries. Rather than offering simple strategies for mastering some of life's vexing challenges, Lisa and Mark call us to ponder, reimagine, and reintegrate our way of being in the world. As a member of their community, I see them working on this daily and appreciate their willingness to share what they are learning with the rest of us."

—**Colin Saxton**, Quaker minister, stewardship theologian, and author of *Living the Eternal Promise*

An Invitation to Slow

Resist the Speed of Now, Make Space for Quiet, and Cultivate an Intentional Life

Mark R. McMinn *and*
Lisa Graham McMinn

CASCADE *Books* • Eugene, Oregon

AN INVITATION TO SLOW
Resist the Speed of Now, Make Space for Quiet, and Cultivate an Intentional Life

Copyright © 2024 Wipf and Stock. All rights reserved. Except for brief quotations in critical publications or reviews, no part of this book may be reproduced in any manner without prior written permission from the publisher. Write: Permissions, Wipf and Stock Publishers, 199 W. 8th Ave., Suite 3, Eugene, OR 97401.

Cascade Books
An Imprint of Wipf and Stock Publishers
199 W. 8th Ave., Suite 3
Eugene, OR 97401

www.wipfandstock.com

PAPERBACK ISBN: 979-8-3852-2351-0
HARDCOVER ISBN: 979-8-3852-2352-7
EBOOK ISBN: 979-8-3852-2353-4

Cataloguing-in-Publication data:

Names: McMinn, Mark R., author. | Graham McMinn, Lisa, author.

Title: An invitation to slow : resist the speed of now, make space for quiet, and cultivate an intentional life / by Mark R. McMinn and Lisa Graham McMinn.

Description: Eugene, OR: Cascade Books, 2024 | Includes bibliographical references.

Identifiers: ISBN 979-8-3852-2351-0 (paperback) | ISBN 979-8-3852-2352-7 (hardcover) | ISBN 979-8-3852-2353-4 (ebook)

Subjects: LCSH: Spiritual life—Christianity. | Digital media.

Classification: BV4501.3 I65 2024 (paperback) | BV4501.3 (ebook)

VERSION NUMBER 10/18/24

Unless otherwise indicated, all Scripture quotations are taken from the *Holy Bible*, New Living Translation, copyright © 1996, 2004, 2015 by Tyndale House Foundation.

Scripture quotations marked NIV are taken from the Holy Bible, *New International Version*,® *NIV*.® Copyright © 1973, 1978, 1984, 2011 by Biblica, Inc.®

Scripture quotations marked NRSV are taken from the New Revised Standard Version Bible, copyright © 1989, Division of Christian Education of the National Council of the Churches of Christ in the United States of America.

To those who gather at North Valley Friends Church,
who quietly and kindly became our people.

"Above all, trust in the slow work of God . . . and accept the anxiety of feeling yourself *in suspense and incomplete.*"

—Pierre Teilhard de Chardin

Contents

Acknowledgments | ix

Introduction	Fast and Slow	1
Chapter 1	Slow to Speak: An Invitation to Quiet	12
Chapter 2	Slow to Grasp: An Invitation to Contentment	30
Chapter 3	Slow to Fear: An Invitation to Courage	51
Chapter 4	Slow to Anger: An Invitation to Empathy	76
Chapter 5	Slow to Judge: An Invitation to Humility	98
Chapter 6	Slow to Envy: An Invitation to Gratitude	118
Chapter 7	Slow to Consume: An Invitation to Generosity	139
Chapter 8	Slow to Isolate: An Invitation to Community	164
Conclusion	Railway Stories	185

Bibliography | 193

Acknowledgments

A book, like a life, is a coming together of many hearts and minds. We will name a few here, even as we silently hold many more who have influenced, sustained, and encouraged us through our years of living and becoming.

Thanks to our early readers for your encouragement and suggestions: Jeff Crosby, Dan McCracken, and Paul Bock. Others have lent their support and good reputations as endorsers. When we look at your kind words we remember you with thanks.

Several courageous souls have permitted us to recount fragments of their stories in these pages, some unnamed, and some first-named: David, Carol, Karl, Ginny, Paul, Maureen, Bill, Mike, Ben, Emily.

A group of friends magically emerged in 2023. We gather, laugh, play pickleball and word games, pray, eat, celebrate birthdays, and support one another through daunting life passages. Thank you friends for being the sort of robust souls who give and receive, and for the joy, gratitude, kindness, and wisdom you offer to the world.

As mentioned in the introduction, we sit each week in silence with Friends who show up every week to do the work of waiting worship. Silence knits people together in weighty ways.

Always, we offer gratitude for our daughters, sons-in-law, and grandchildren. And for our siblings by birth and marriage, and our parents, deceased and living. You bring us wisdom, goodness, and joy.

To those who help us put the "semi" into semiretired—Lisa's directees and supervisees and Mark's psychotherapy clients—we hold you in respect and esteem for how you grow through the liminal places and passageways of life.

Thank you, too, for the professionals at Cascade Books who helped form this book. We appreciate your wisdom, guidance, artistry, and excellence with words.

Introduction
Fast and Slow

While it is undoubtedly true that smoke detectors save lives, far more often they scare the bejeebers out of people. If you're not entirely sure what bejeebers are, they have something to do with hearing the shrill, pulsing sound of all the smoke detectors in your entire house going off at 3:30 in the morning because your Airbnb guests burned a bagel before their early flight. That's when you discover what bejeebers are, just as they are being scared out of you.

That may have happened to us.

Inside each of our bodies we have a sympathetic nervous system that triggers a fight-or-flight response to stimuli. It acts as our inner alarm and blares whenever we see a rattlesnake coiled and looking in our direction, when we skydive, give a teenager that first driving lesson, or endure awful telephone music for hours on hold. And, it turns out, the inner alarm blares when the outer one does (as when someone burns their bagel). When this happens, don't expect to get back to sleep any time soon, because the sympathetic nervous system dumps adrenaline into the bloodstream, and adrenaline works well for those times in life when we need to fight or take flight. It's not good as a sleep aid.

Don't mess with the sympathetic nervous system. When we face a dire threat and need to reroute all our available resources to survival, our attention narrows, our hearts pump faster, we become self-focused, our pupils get bigger to let in more light, and blood vessels that supply muscles also dilate to get more oxygen where it might be needed as the bronchia in our lungs expand to collect all that extra oxygen. Thank

God for the sympathetic nervous system because it helped us survive earlier days when we encountered lions, tigers, and bears. Even now it helps us survive the worst moments of life.

Then, eventually, we calm down and get our bejeebers back. The parasympathetic nervous system is the yin for the sympathetic nervous system's yang. Our muscles relax, pupils contract (along with major blood vessels), heart rates slow, bronchia shrink, we start to notice others again, and we return to a normal state of calm and quiet. Thank God for the parasympathetic nervous system also. Otherwise we would be in a constant state of hyperarousal and fear. And that's no way to live.

The Speed of Now

An insidious sort of speed now carries possibility, peril, and hyperarousal into the human psyche moment after moment. The speed of electronic communication, which travels at approximately the speed of light (186,000 miles per second) to our handheld devices and laptops, reaches into our fragile self-images, influences our circle of friends, affects our cities, and touches every corner of the world.

The speed of now is attractive in many ways, giving us access to information and social interactions like we've never had before. We are now encyclopedic. How far is it from Chicago to Amsterdam? What organic gardening methods help tomatoes thrive? Where is the Bible passage about the good Samaritan? What will the weather be like today? Any of these questions, and billions more, can be answered in five seconds with the device we hold in our hand, carry in our pockets, or set down near us during the day and keep on our nightstands while we sleep.

It's not just information we carry in our pocket but also the capacity to interact with others. We have messaging, social media, networking apps, workplace sandboxes, and email continually chiming, dinging, vibrating, popping little red circles onto our retina displays, reminding us that someone out there is thinking of us or at least bidding for our attention.

One could argue this is the best of times for humanity. Because we can know almost anything within five seconds, shouldn't we be humming along in harmony as we identify the problems in our world and labor together to make them better? And with all this capacity for social interaction, it seems we would be deeply content, resting securely in a sense of belongingness.

But we are not. Since 2006, the Gallup organization has collected worldwide data each year about negative experiences, including pain, worry, sadness, stress, and anger and then converted the responses to a hundred-point scale called the Negative Experience Index. Though we might expect 2020 and 2021 to be high because of COVID-19—and they are—the trend over the entire past decade points disturbingly upward, long before the pandemic struck, and continuing upward after the pandemic subsided.[1]

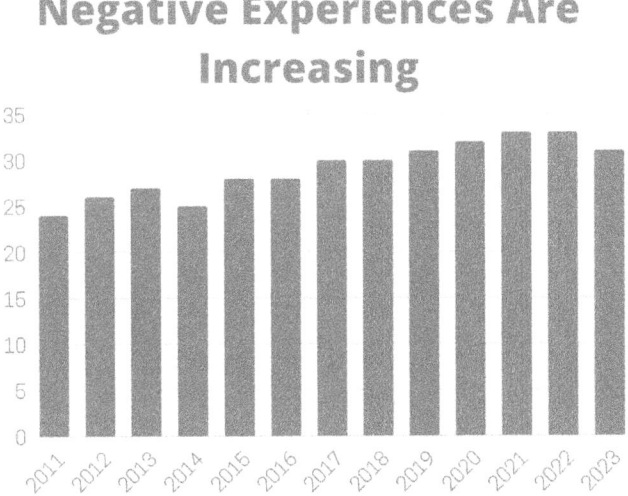

The twenty-first century had a rugged beginning. The millennium started with the bursting of the dot-com bubble, leading to economic angst, then a terrorist attack that shook our national confidence and sense of safety. Controversial military campaigns in Iraq and Afghanistan followed, and then the Great Recession. Then a pandemic landed, driving the world into isolation and fear. Parks and meeting houses became eerily quiet as we turned toward Zoom, Facetime, and Teams for consolation and community. As we write this book, we are enduring one of the most hotly contested and contentious presidential elections in US history, leading to hostility and division throughout the nation, the Russo-Ukrainian and Israel-Hamas wars are raging, gun violence punctures our collective

1. Gallup, *Gallup Global Emotions*, 8.

humanity monthly, and climate disasters show up regularly in the news cycle. Tragedies keep rolling in like storm clouds on the horizon.

There are reasons our sympathetic nervous systems have raced for twenty-five years now, and our most beautiful human qualities and our social connections suffer in response. When we feel threatened, we tend to think of ourselves first. It's probably unnecessary in preflight instructions to tell people to put their own masks on before helping others because when the moment of crisis arrives, that's what almost everyone will do. This is not a commentary on our sin nature; it's the reality of how the human body works in times of emotional arousal. The intentional quiet ways of being that make us most human and most attuned to one another get easily lost when we live in the flurry of stress, dissent, and tragedy.

> **Pause:** Take a breath. We know we're not telling the whole story, and we'll return to that. In fact, it's essential we do, and it's where we are headed with this book. But bad news is most of what we hear and read about. It activates our sympathetic nervous system and sometimes shuts us down. Becoming aware of that is part of this journey. Chronic sympathetic nervous system arousal is no friend to spiritual health or to wholesome relationships.

We have had difficult things to endure this century, as is true of any time in history, but things are not worse than ever. In many ways things are better, such as health care, sanitation, disaster relief, and global communication. But with all these advances, news travels faster than ever, and bad news more prominently than good.

Prior to electronic communication, bad news got announced by a messenger to the village, by a letter in the mail, or in the local newspaper. People would mourn and struggle, as people do in the terrible moments of life, and then they would regain a sense of hope before the next bad thing came along. Electronic communication brought bad news into our living rooms each day, initially with the evening news. Then 2007 brought the first iPhone, and the Android followed a year later. In 2015 came Apple watches, which can alert us to "breaking news" throughout the day with startling vibrations sent through the electronic appliance strapped to our wrists, moment after moment, with incredible speed. Bad news chimes at us as soon as it happens, popping into our awareness day and night, continually galvanizing our sympathetic nervous system. Today we carry the world's troubles around like a backpack filled with bricks, constantly added to by the latest news feeds and social media posts. Continually on edge, our anxious and angry souls ooze (or vomit) fear on one another in wounding ways.

Plus, the news we receive is increasingly polarized. When news was limited to a few broadcast channels, the networks were bound to the Fairness Doctrine, which meant newscasters were required to offer multiple perspectives on controversial topics. As channels proliferated with cable television, fairness could no longer be monitored, so the doctrine was jettisoned near the end of the twentieth century. We no longer have Walter Cronkite signing off with "And that's the way it is." Instead, we have hundreds of news outlets clamoring for our attention, many of them customized to the political leanings of those who subscribe. For these designer news outlets, objectivity is no longer a goal. It's about holding on to ratings and subscribers, and there is no better way to do this than evoking fear about what the "other side" is doing as we are lured into angry and oversimplified diatribes about the foolishness of those with different perspectives.

Truth, it seems, is now located in the eye of the beholder, something to be asserted, instead of something to be discussed, discovered, and discerned in wisdom communities. Maybe our longing for stability after a couple of decades of social, political, and ecological unrest inclines us to assert a shallow form of certainty because we can't handle more uncertainty. Blue and red spread increasingly further apart as society becomes fragmented and troubled beyond belief.

A bumper sticker we saw recently read "Heavily armed and easily pissed." Really? Is this who we have become?

Of course, we won't always agree with one another. People have always faced interpersonal rifts and strident disputes, and the church has been part of this. Christians not only went on crusades against the "infidels" but persecuted and executed each other over different theological views both before and after the Reformation.

What concerns us is not just how uncivil and unkind and agitated we can be to one another, but also how quickly we can now magnify our unkindness. While Christians no longer literally execute those we deem heretics, we sometimes do significant public damage to the reputations of those with whom we disagree, and our ability and tendency to damage one another has never been faster.

Like a blank slate onto which we project our entire human nature—both good and malicious—social media is a contemporary mirror of who we have always been. We connect, laugh, care, learn, and banter; we share sorrows, joys, and memories. But we also sometimes struggle to bring our best selves to that detached cyberspace, resorting to slander, rumor, oversimplification, unfair judgments, untimely anger, and bullying. Social media can bring us together, and it can tear us apart.

Humanity has always been a perplexing mix of virtue and vice, but now our opportunities to wound one another are easier and faster.

How do we listen to God in such a time as this? How do we steady and prepare our souls to respond well to one another? Where is the good news of a redemption that brings love, peace, and justice in our lives and communities?

> **Pause:** Stop, just now, and think of something good that still happens in your various communities as they bring faith, hope, and love to hurting people. Hold this contribution with gratitude and see it as a sign of God's continued faithfulness to use communities as the healing hands and feet of Christ.

James, in his New Testament epistle, suggests being "quick to listen, slow to speak, and slow to get angry" (Jas 1:19). Perhaps humanity has always tended to get this backward, to be slow to listen, quick to speak, and quick to become angry. How might we lean into the alternative path James offered two thousand years ago?

An Invitation to Notice

Now might be a good time for another breath—a deeper and longer breath. Despite all the anger, violence, and division, good things are also happening.

In the same Gallup polls where negative experiences have increased for the past decade, pollsters ask about positive experiences, such as getting good rest, being treated with respect, smiling, laughing, learning, doing interesting things, and feeling a sense of enjoyment. As our negative experiences have increased around the world, our positive ones have not decreased, and the positive ones are more prevalent than the negative.[2]

---

2. Gallup, *Gallup Global Emotions*, 2.

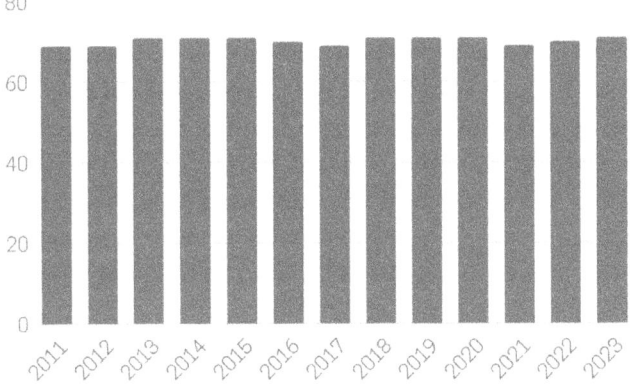

And did you notice in the earlier graph that negative experiences took a dip in the most recent year?

Good things happen around our world every day, bringing us delight and hope and drawing out the best of human nature. Not all our bumper stickers are angry. Some of them call forth love and goodness, inviting us to be the best version of ourselves. A popular one right now reads "Be Kind."

It's not just that we are stressed. We are also resilient.

We still love and work and play and laugh. We put gratitude apps on our phones so we can remember to be thankful, our kids laugh on the playground, and they play soccer for fun as parents and grandparents huddle around to cheer them on. Drivers are often courteous on the highways; families and friends gather for good food and conversation. We meet together, sing praise choruses, engage in meaningful conversation, offer loving acts of kindness to people we know and some we don't. People make homemade sugar cookies and sourdough bread and delight in wood-fired pizza.

In the past couple of decades we have seen the world work collaboratively to understand viruses and develop vaccines. Many have also continued to fight extreme poverty and hunger, racism, sex trafficking, and the challenges of a changing climate. Some do the good work of bringing health care to those without it, others of strengthening forest and ocean health and developing affordable renewable energy sources.

We still compose music, create art, plant apple trees and dahlias, heal the sick, clothe the naked, and visit the widow and orphan. We have continued, as it were, to pour ourselves out generously, mirroring God, whose generous outpouring of love keeps the world from coming apart.

Christian faith has deep treasures to offer us, which we will explore throughout this book. As humans made in God's image, we have choice as we move through our days, weeks, months, and years. How will we choose to live, and who will we choose to be in this highly charged era? How do we practice at living well, at forming ourselves to help us walk through hard things with resilience and grace? How do we return to the slow rhythms of calm and quiet? How can we create quiet space to slow down, breathe, see what needs to be seen, and to think deep thoughts while held in the loving gaze of God?

We live in a day of fast information, fast fingers, fast food, fast shipping, fast words, fast anger, and fast judgment. In the pages that follow, we invite you into slower, quieter, more intentional ways of being, exploring how these might attune us to—and help us trust—the slow work of God in order that we might love one another and the world as God does.

Drawing from our fields as former academics in psychology and sociology, and current practitioners in psychotherapy and spiritual direction, we explore the particularities of our time that shape how people feel, think, and act in frenzied, and often thoughtless and unkind ways. In the pages that follow, we weave together the pressured realities of contemporary life with how we might slow down, returning to rhythms of calm and quiet that help us attune to God, forming and transforming how we live. Our chapters pair a lure to be loud, grasping, fearful, angry, judgmental, envious, acquisitive, or self-sufficient with an invitation to be formed by choosing quiet, content, courageous, empathetic, humble, grateful, generous, and connected ways of being. By being slow to speak, we invite the possibility of quietness. Learning to be slow to anger calls us toward greater empathy. Growing in contentment helps us to be slower to grasp.

Ultimately, each of these invitations is a movement toward God.

That conversation starts, as all things do, with some sort of shared understanding of what it means to move toward God. We offer two considerations. The first begins with the early Christian understanding expressed by the apostle Paul: *we already are held in the heart of God*. Paul writes that "everything was created through [Christ] and for him" and that "he holds all creation together" (Col 1:16–17). Before Paul's time, ancient Hebrews also understood there was nowhere God was not. David writes, "I can never escape from your Spirit! I can never get away from your presence!" (Ps 139:7). We don't need to move toward God as God is already as close as our next breath and heartbeat. Our existence depends on Christ calling creation into being and then sustaining and holding it together. John's Gospel asserts that the Word (whom we call Christ) created everything there is. Life itself was in him, and this life gives light to everyone (John 1:3-4). "So the Word became human" and lived here on earth among us. "He was full of unfailing love and faithfulness" (John 1:14).

We do not have to move toward God because God, who is full of love, is already as near to us as God can be. We cannot choose or unchoose this nearness.

The second consideration, however, names that we can choose to ignore God's nearness or live awakened to it. Living awake puts us on a journey of discovery—experiencing what it is to abide with God in Christ—to have our minds transformed, renewed. As we become attuned to the proximity of God, we discover we are already abiding in Christ. Our everyday lives can become infused with God's goodness and love, God's love becoming perfected in us. We have a choice to live an awakened life, one that responds to a God whose love is extravagantly touchable—always. What if becoming transformed by God's love is our life's work?

We will be introducing (or reintroducing) practices intended to slow and quiet you, putting you in the path of God's love or, perhaps more accurately, attuning you to God's love, which already surrounds you. As you encounter practices in this book (and elsewhere in your faith journey), remember two things. First, as one might try a few musical instruments before settling on one to practice with intention, so you might do with some of these. But we encourage you to find one practice that resonates with you (and perhaps later one that challenges you) and to settle into practicing that one for a good while. Second, remember they are called practices, not proficiencies. Showing up with intention is all that is necessary. Achieving competency is not.

Dundee Bistro is a place we go for dinner on occasion. We travel there in one of two ways. Typically, we journey by car, which is hands down faster, more efficient, and more comfortable. However, at least once a summer we turn the late afternoon and early evening over to a long stroll, a ten-mile jaunt along country back roads that includes this delightful dinner break in the middle. We sup leisurely under a canvas canopy shielding us from the sun and head back home full and refreshed. Walking offers a different way of engaging our community. We see cows, pigs, sheep, and horses as the individuals they are, rather than as pieces of blurry (even if lovely) landscape. Sometimes we exchange moments of eye gazing, creature to creature. We pass vineyards and observe where the grapes are in the growing season. Can we see the grape clusters? Have the farmers pruned to manage the leaf canopy yet? We hear the old man in overalls working on his rig half a mile before we see him, because Johnny Cash keeps him company—on loudspeakers, it would seem, since we can hear Johnny from so far away. We pass The Good Life Preschool, remember two of our grandchildren who attended there, and think warm and grateful thoughts of the school but even more of our children and grandchildren. We ascend the Harvey Creek Trail, noticing how very low (or not) the water level of the creek is before zigzagging our way up the hill that takes us to the top of Dundee. From there we see the Willamette Valley before us—houses, farms, fields, forests, the highway, hills, and purple mountains in the distance.

We talk—of course we do—but not constantly. What we talk about will not often be remembered, but the sentiments, ideas, dreams, and questions we speak are threads woven into the fabric of who we are and have become over the course of our long journey together.

A gift of slow is available in some capacity in every moment. We cherish those moments when we choose them, even as we also wonder why we don't choose them more frequently. May this book's invitations inspire us all to unwrap and accept these moments more often.

Slow Ponderings

1. Looking back over the last day or two, when has your sympathetic nervous system been most activated, and for how long? During that time, what did attentiveness to others look like? Now think about times of slowing and calm over the last day or two. Was your attentiveness toward others different during these times, and if so, how?

2. How have electronic devices increased your speed of life in recent years? In what ways have they affected your relationships with others?

3. Where do you find slow in your life? How does it affect your relationships with others? What role does faith play in your efforts to slow down?

4. Reflect on your use of social media. How has it been helpful in building relationships? How has it not been helpful?

5. In this chapter we pose the invitation to abide in Christ that you might learn the way of love. How do you respond to the way it is described here? What stirs in you at the invitation to be drawn deeper into abiding that your love might be perfected, that you might be transformed?

6. What life circumstances are you currently facing that come to mind as you begin reading this book? What are you hoping to find in the pages ahead?

Chapter 1

Slow to Speak: An Invitation to Quiet

The fertile soil of Oregon's Willamette Valley was stolen from Montana, Idaho, and Washington. Not stolen, exactly, but that's where Oregon's Jory soil originated. Geologists point to a massive flood about twelve thousand years ago and a proglacial body of water that once held as much water as Great Lakes Erie and Ontario combined. Until it didn't.

A series of ice dam failures caused torrential flooding through land we call Idaho and eastern Washington, a force equivalent to sixty Amazon Rivers racing through Oregon's Columbia Gorge to the Pacific Ocean.[1] All that water deposited topsoil in this lush valley where 75 percent of all Oregonians now live. If you're from Walla Walla, Spokane, or Coeur d'Alene, thank you for your exquisite dirt.

Today, Willamette (pronounced will-AM-it) Valley farmers grow berries, hazelnuts, vegetables, Christmas trees, and grapes, most notably pinot noir grapes. As of 2024 the valley is home to 1,016 vineyards, many of which have tasting rooms with panoramic views of the valley and surrounding mountains—the Cascade Range to the east and the Coast Range to the west.[2] One of us is a wine drinker and the other is not, but we both like sitting in Adirondack chairs at local vineyards, enjoying leisurely talk and stunning vistas. Gratitude wafts in on the

---

1. Glacial Lake Missoula, "Short Story," ¶1.
2. Willamette Valley Wine, "Facts & Figures," ¶5.

breezes, and whispers of grace ease into our conversation and silence as we settle into a quiet, slow afternoon.

When one of our favorite vineyards offered a Valentine's Day event, we purchased tickets and eagerly put the event in our shared iCalendar. It didn't turn out to be the romantic evening we envisioned.

Chilly rain characterizes Oregon Februarys, so a too-large crowd assembled inside a too-small tasting room. Our dream of a quiet, romantic dinner for two faded as we were ushered to a big table populated by a boisterous group of friends gathering for a reunion. The conversation at the table seemed pleasant enough, but with each course of the meal came another wine pairing and liberal fill-ups in between. If alcohol is a social lubricant in small doses, it is a verbal laxative in large ones. Lisa had a glass with the first course, and Mark a glass of water. Sometime later Lisa had a second glass to soften her agitation at the mounting noise in the room. Mark, as the abstainer, had all his mental capacities intact to observe the escalating volume and rambunctiousness of the crowd. We gave up trying to talk because we couldn't hear one another anyway, nor could we hear the jazz pianist and vocalist attempting to sing love songs over the din.

A memorable Valentine's Day, for sure, though not one we'd recommend.

Sometimes sitting around a table with a group of others, music playing in the background, is a gift of rich, meaningful conversation. But at other times, such as this Valentine's Day brimming with too much wine, some people retreat into passive isolation while others dominate with careless words in a steady crescendo. Does it sometimes seem that our twenty-first–century Western culture caters to those who speak soonest and loudest?

> **Pause:** Also imagine the noise, sensations, and feelings that bounce around inside your head when you are entangled in an anxious, fearful, angry, regretful, and very loud conversation with yourself. Being slow to speak challenges both our external and internal worlds. Sometimes we need to accept an invitation to quiet the inner loudness every bit as much as the outer.

Christianity is countercultural and calls us to walk to a different cadence than what we observe around us. How can we be slow to speak in a fast-to-speak world? And how can we quiet the chattering inside our own heads?

In the Introduction we referred to words written in the epistle of James: "Understand this, my dear brothers and sisters: You must all be quick to listen, slow to speak, and slow to get angry" (Jas 1:19). We see comparable advice scattered throughout the Old Testament Proverbs:

> A truly wise person uses few words;
> a person with understanding is even-tempered.
>
> Even fools are thought wise when they keep silent;
> with their mouths shut, they seem intelligent. (Prov 17:27–28)
>
> A gentle answer deflects anger,
> but harsh words make tempers flare.
>
> The tongue of the wise makes knowledge appealing,
> but the mouth of a fool belches out foolishness. (Prov 15:1–2)

There is also the extrabiblical advice probably quoted more today than any of these Scripture passages: "It is better to remain silent and be thought a fool than to talk and remove all doubt."[3]

Quaker theologian Richard Foster captures the need to silence internal chatter as well with this prayer:

> I have, O Lord, a noisy heart. And entering outward silence doesn't stop the inner clamor. In fact, it seems only to make it worse. When I am full of activity, the internal noise is only a distant rumble; but when I get still, the rumble amplifies itself. And it is not like the majestic sound of a symphony rising to a grand crescendo; rather it is the deafening din of clashing pots and clanging pans. What a racket! Worst of all, I feel helpless to hush the interior pandemonium. Dear Lord, Jesus, once you spoke peace to the wind and the wave. Speak your shalom over my heart. I wait silently . . . patiently, I receive into the very core of my being your loving command, "Peace, be still." Amen.[4]

What's happening to make us talk so much, so loudly, so provocatively, and sometimes so foolishly—both in our heads and out loud? And how can we dial it back to be more like the people God calls us to be? To the first question, we'll explore two factors: disinhibition and

---

3. While this quote has been wrongly attributed to Abraham Lincoln and Mark Twain, it certainly makes a point.

4. Foster, *Prayers from the Heart*, 58.

polarization.⁵ To the second, we offer an invitation to quiet, as both noun and verb.

Disinhibition: Our Brains on Social Media

Most of us are blessed with a "think twice before speaking" part of our brain. When someone has bad breath or wants to know how their not-so-good haircut looks, this part of the brain works to keep us out of trouble. It tries to keep us from saying, "I told you so," "You're wrong about that," "You ate that whole thing?," or "Why can't you be more like your brother?" But we don't always pay attention to this somewhat subtle part of our brain, and these sorts of words sometimes dribble (or spew) out of our mouths anyway.

Brains are complicated with their eighty-six billion neurons, so it's not quite right to identify a single part of the brain that performs any specific function, but the prefrontal cortex has a lot to do with "think twice before speaking." Neuroscientists associate the prefrontal cortex with "executive functioning," which isn't about corporate suits sitting around conference rooms but the responsible activities that all of us hope to exhibit, such as self-control, emotional regulation, inhibition, planning, time management, working memory, initiating tasks, and setting priorities.

Ideally, our prefrontal cortex helps us manage complex emotions and impulses. *Inhibition* keeps us from saying or doing everything we think, while *disinhibition* is blurting out words we might regret and acting impulsively. Brain injury, dementia, and tumors involving the prefrontal cortex make us vulnerable to disinhibition. So do certain substances and social environments.

At that Valentine's Day fiasco, alcohol affected the prefrontal cortex and compromised healthy inhibition for those imbibing generously of the goods offered.⁶ The more alcohol people consumed, the more compromised their executive functioning became as words flew freely and loudly.

Disinhibition is not all bad. It can lead to spontaneity and freedom, to risk-taking and adventure, to letting go and easing up on our

---

5. We explore these two factors because this is what space allows. There are undoubtedly many other factors that contribute to our loud and impulsive communication.

6. Abernathy et al., "Alcohol." Also, Stephan et al., "Meta-analysis."

sometimes overbearing sense of responsibility, which is especially helpful if that responsibility keeps us aloof, stiff, and tied up in knots trying to be or be perceived as perfect.

The others around our table seemed to be having an uproariously good time because they were carefree and unbounded for a few hours of laughter, raucous storytelling, and mirth. They may have said a few things they regretted later—if they remembered them—such as the woman who spoke seductively to Mark while Lisa was using the restroom, which is a strange part of any Valentine's Day experience.

Online disinhibition is also a thing.[7] We are prone to be louder, ruder, and more aggressive online than we would be in person. In this regard, our brains on social media act quite a lot like brains influenced by alcohol. Even those who are slow to speak in person may be quite loud and aggressive online. But why?

The online world works differently than the person-to-person world. Let's say you order a southwest salad at a restaurant but instead the server gives you the Cobb salad. You mention the mix-up to your server. In the process, you look one another in the eye and exchange a few words of explanation, and then the server apologizes and takes the Cobb salad back to the kitchen. It's a bit of an extra wait, but you don't mind too much because you will at least get what you ordered. When the server returns with the southwest salad, you smile and say thank you, and once again the server apologizes for the mistake. At the end of the meal, you leave a nice tip.

Now take this experience online. Imagine a misunderstanding on social media over different political opinions or commenting on a YouTube video on a controversial topic. You have an opportunity to express your candid opinion, so you do.

Notice several differences in these two situations.[8] First, in the restaurant, you are known and seen by those who are dining with you and other guests and staff. Perhaps you frequent the restaurant and have interacted with the server before. You may come again in the future. Being known helps inhibit impulsive words you might be tempted to utter. With the YouTube video you may be almost entirely anonymous in the feedback you leave. Second, there is immediacy in the restaurant encounter, which is synchronous: you speak, the server speaks, you

---

7. Suler, "Online Disinhibition."
8. Stuart and Scott, "Measure of Online Disinhibition."

speak again, then the server, and the transaction is complete. Online interactions are asynchronous, so they may go on for hours or days, giving us ample time to stew about something controversial between our exchanges. Our internal narratives may easily slip away from reality so that we distort what the other person is saying. One person posts a *Hmm* emoji on a Facebook reply, and another person spends two hours feeling disrespected before replying, "You don't know what you're talking about," showing how conversation and human civility can slip with hours of private rumination. Third, our view of self and others appears to be different online than in person. People tend to develop more confidence, even hubris, with their online personas than in person. Those who have used dating apps tell stories about how people can make themselves seem different online versus how they actually are in person. Fourth, the nonverbal realities of an in-person encounter root us in greater civility. With the server in the restaurant, the two of you smile as you speak, and you look one another in the eyes. Seeing into an actual retina impacts our brains differently than looking at a retina display when choosing our words. In fact, Israeli researchers who looked closely at the differences between online and person-to-person interactions concluded the main reason for online disinhibition is lack of eye contact.[9] When we look another human being in the eye, our words tend to be softer and gentler than if we use the same words electronically.

> **Pause:** Finding this research on eye contact has encouraged us to be intentional about looking one another in the eye whenever we face disagreement in our marriage. Something about the intimacy of eye contact helps quiet the inner clamor in tense moments and keeps our words from being too strong or loud.
>
> You might consider trying this next time you are having a tense conversation with a partner, child, friend, employer, or customer.

Polarization: Get Loud!

If you're a collegiate or professional sports fan, you're likely familiar with *Get Loud* or *Make Some Noise* flashing on the jumbotron, and if you're a Kansas City Chiefs enthusiast, you may want to point out that the

---

9. Lapidot-Lefler and Barak, "Effects of Anonymity."

Arrowhead Stadium throng claimed the world record for loudest crowd noise in 2014.[10] At 142.2 decibels, Chiefs fans produced as much sound as a gunshot, fireworks, or a custom car stereo at its maximum volume.[11]

Quieting ourselves involves a degree of detachment, stepping back and looking from a different perspective. We'll discuss this more soon, but for now let's try to back up a step and consider what the "get loud" message on the scoreboard is asking us to do. Essentially, the message is "We're in a tight competition here, and if you—the home team crowd—get incredibly loud, it may help encourage our players and intimidate the visiting players so that our team can win. So let's *Get Loud*!"

Getting loud is about encouraging the home team, but it's also about intimidation and especially about winning.

This doesn't happen just in sports arenas and stadiums. So much of contemporary life feels like an ideological competition between political parties. Throughout the United States we have our symbols of conservatism and liberalism, traditionalism and progressivism. They show up as elephants and donkeys, red and blue, candidates for political offices, flags and banners, catchy phrases and logos, and texts and online posts in all caps, but beneath it all is a deeply divided country. Both sides feel like they're fighting for the nation. Both are in this competition to win, and both seem willing to get as loud as necessary to make it happen.

The Carnegie Endowment for International Peace recently published a report showing that political values in the United States are not as different as most people think, but we are becoming more and more emotionally polarized. That is, Republicans dislike Democrats more than ever, and Democrats return the favor.[12] Survey researchers invented something called "emotional thermometers" to explore this story.[13]

---

10. Janela, "Kansas City Chiefs Fans."

11. American Academy of Audiology, "Levels of Noise," ¶1.

12. Kleinfeld, *Polarization*, 21.

13. Graph data drawn from the American National Election Studies, *Time Series Cumulative Data*.

SLOW TO SPEAK: AN INVITATION TO QUIET   19

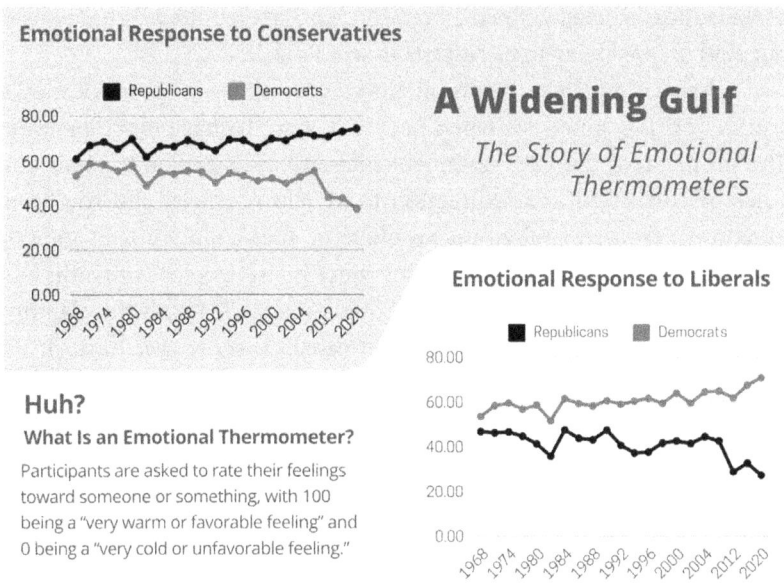

A Widening Gulf

The Story of Emotional Thermometers

Huh?
What Is an Emotional Thermometer?
Participants are asked to rate their feelings toward someone or something, with 100 being a "very warm or favorable feeling" and 0 being a "very cold or unfavorable feeling."

In 2024, the emotional thermometer toward the Republican Party was seventy-four when rated by Republicans and twenty-four when rated by Democrats—a whopping difference of fifty points. Emotional responses toward the Democratic party differed even more, by fifty-five points.[14] Eight in ten Democrats now believe the Republican Party has been taken over by racists, while a similar number of Republicans believe the Democratic Party has been taken over by socialists.[15]

Numbers and graphs tell part of the story, but this is not just about polling and statistics. It's about a growing chasm in civil discourse that runs through families and faith communities and shows up in classrooms, local school board meetings, yard signs, and recall petitions. How many people dread or avoid holiday gatherings, knowing that the dinner table will undoubtedly serve up hostility alongside the mashed potatoes? How many folks get "unfriended" in the metaverse or the in-person world because they zealously support a different political idea or candidate?

Americans have always held a variety of views, but now it's about winning. Getting loud is presented as a virtue because it will help our side win the election and reclaim the soul of this great, yet apparently fragile, nation. At some point we should raise questions about whether the soul

14. American National Election Studies, *Time Series Cumulative Data*.
15. Public Religion Research Institute, "Dueling Realities," ¶3.

of the nation is being defined by our loudness and conflict. What part of our soul are we losing in our efforts to win it back?

Christians believe in prophetic voices—those who speak God's truth at critical junctures when people or nations have lost their way. The prophets of the Old Testament offered God's loud and persistent voice of correction and redirection to Israel's northern and southern kingdoms. God still raises up prophets to speak the truth in today's world, and we still need to listen for these incisive voices of truth, but the problem is distinguishing the prophet's voice from all the clamoring voices surrounding it. Decades of research show that most of us perceive ourselves to be right about most things (a phenomenon called self-enhancement), and now we have immediate access to social media platforms where we can proclaim our opinions 24-7 to anyone who will listen. Instead of a lone voice crying out in the wilderness, today we all seem to think we're prophets.

Ours is an age of loud people, convinced they hold the truth, getting even louder to persuade others. One *Scientific American* blogger put it succinctly: "All of our egos are just too damn loud."[16]

As a White, educated, upper–middle-class male with quite a lot of privilege in my life, I (Mark) feel a particular need to quiet my ego. Some voices are un- or underrepresented in our world and have been historically ignored, which means I need to spend more time listening and less time sharing my views. It doesn't mean I have to stop talking altogether (hey, I'm coauthoring a book), but it does place responsibility on me to be quiet more and to encourage those who have been overlooked to speak. But all voices—including my overused one and those who have been disregarded for far too long—are clearer and stronger once we learn to balance loud with daily rhythms of quiet.

> **Pause:** Having just read about the polarization of our day, take a moment to notice your emotions and physical sensations. Where do you sense tension or agitation in your body? Sit with that a moment, and let yourself fully feel it. Reflect on how often you feel this sort of tension and agitation and what other kinds of conversations bring it about. How long does it linger? What helps ease it? In this next section, we invite you to quiet.

---

16. Kaufman, "Pressing Need," ¶2.

An Invitation to Quiet—Noun and Verb

Imagine, for a moment, a storyteller in a room full of children. She has now come to the intense part of her story. She lowers her voice, maybe down to a whisper. The children lean in to hear her, not wanting to miss anything, and she leans in as well, wanting them to catch every word. She speaks slower, looks her listeners in the eye, and holds their attention with a soft-spoken voice.

By *being* quiet, she *creates* quiet.

Sociologist Dennis Covington paints a similar picture as he ends his book exploring a faith community in the Appalachian Mountains and how they unexpectedly helped him redeem something of his own faith:

> It's late afternoon at the lake. . . . Most of the children in my neighborhood are called home for supper by their mothers. They open the back doors, wipe their hands on their aprons and yell, "Willie!" or "Joe!" or "Ray!" Either that or they use a bell, bolted to the doorframe and loud enough to start the dogs barking in backyards all along the street. But I was always called home by my father, and he didn't do it in the customary way. He walked down the alley all the way to the lake. If I was close, I could hear his shoes on the gravel before he came into sight. If I was far, I would see him across the surface of the water, emerging out of shadows and into the gray light. He would stand with his hands in the pockets of his windbreaker while he looked for me. This is how he got me to come home. He always came to the place where I was before he called my name.[17]

What if the way out of our polarizing, loud, competitive anger starts with hearing footsteps on the gravel as God comes to where we are, and a still, small voice inviting us to quiet ourselves (verb) and the freedom and peace quiet offers (noun)?

Taking a Step Back

Imagine a recent heated exchange you had with someone. You may or may not remember how it escalated, only that it did, and that it ended poorly, as these things often do. At some point you may have wondered how you landed here when you started off simply talking about who might take out the garbage or clean the kitchen.

17. Covington, *Salvation at Sand Mountain*, 268.

When you choose to pause temporarily (and it is both a choice and a learned skill), you are practicing *detached* awareness—a tool of contemplative mindfulness. This involves stopping your words, thoughts, and actions to distance yourself from a situation so you can think about it in a different way. You have not stopped thinking. Rather, your thinking shifts from being judgmental to taking a nonjudgmental, neutral perspective that stands outside the situation enough to reflect on your and/or the other person's behavior more broadly and deeply. You bring compassion for yourself and for the one with whom you are engaged, and sometimes from that compassion comes greater clarity.

If that sounds hard to do, that's because it is. Choosing to take a step back requires a concentrated effort right at the start to just stop talking.

Of course, silence can be its own weapon, as in, "I won't talk to you because I want you to know how angry I am." This is not that. Rather, this is a humble silence that requires the will to quiet our inner tirade, that sludgy place out of which our defensive and accusatory words spew.

For a lot of us, our inner dialog is pretty much nonstop. It's the voice in our head fueled by our fears, anxieties, embarrassments, anger, shame, pride, envy, jealousy, and simply a desire to be heard, understood, and loved. Our inner dialog gets us stuck on a hamster wheel where we rehearse the offenses of others or hold the same confrontational conversations over and over or stew over worst-case scenarios.

Here's an interesting fact: hamsters are motivated by the mere presence of wheels to run. They get an endorphin release that inclines them to run, even though they are not going anywhere or receiving any external reward for doing so. Perhaps it is similar for a lot of us. While not an endorphin release, the presence of our inner dialogue partner effectively competes for our attention, keeping us from being able to take a step back and move toward a place of quiet, detached, and thoughtful attentiveness.

Taking a step back requires trusting that there is a bigger story, even if you can't see it or imagine it. The bigger story is connected to your past and the past of whoever else is involved in your conversation (be it an internal one or one happening in real time). Taking a step back acknowledges that this encounter has been shaped by our and the other's wounds, successes, failures, values—the lenses we use to see the world and how we understand our place in it.

Hefty requirements, those. Unattainable even.

Yet we can learn to quiet our minds. Like any skill, detached awareness needs practice. Centering Prayer (which we will look at in more detail later in this chapter) offers one way to train our minds in this way. Based on an ancient Christian practice, it helps quell the constant monologue we keep with ourselves. While that isn't the goal of Centering Prayer, it is a by-product of adopting a regular habit of it. In Centering Prayer, we learn to quiet the monologues and dialogues. Centering Prayer teaches us to quiet and temper how we conduct conversations with others.

Over time and with practice, we discover we have befriended an inner witness who observes what is transpiring. This inner witness, who goes by different names (e.g., Holy Spirit, Present Teacher, observing ego), does important work in the instant between a provocation and our response (internal or external) by offering an invitation to pause, to take a step back, and to quiet ourselves. If we do so, our perspective softens and broadens, and we feel ourselves slow, at least enough to note we have a choice in where we go next.

Of course, often we choose not to listen, diving headlong over the falls anyway. Our inner witness knows we could have made a different choice but will greet us on the other side downstream—*without judgment*—as we trudge, dripping and battle-fatigued, to the shoreline. Over time we learn to trust our inner guide.

God's still, small voice offers us invitations to quiet ourselves. Not until we learn to better hear (even if we will not always heed) that voice can we hope to welcome more open and honest conversation rather than that which merely escalates noise and inflicts wounds. Sometimes the things we call conversations are really the absence of genuine conversation, while the stance of quieting, of saying nothing for a moment or two, makes space for real connection.

The Quiet of Belonging

Quiet—as a place—is free of disturbances, a resting place, a peaceful repose. Imagine, for a moment, such a place you have visited. Perhaps it is a favorite bench in a park, a climbing tree from your childhood, a hammock on your porch, or a chair by a window in your home.

These are likely places where you are alone, and we often associate quiet with aloneness. What would you say to our suggestion that our deepest quiet comes not from being alone but from our sense of belonging?

We imagine that you would at least consider it counterintuitive, and indeed it is. But stay with us a moment. What if our greatest sense of quiet comes from knowing we belong, knowing we are not alone in the universe, knowing we are not primarily responsible to make the most out of life? Does that comfort you or make you uncomfortable?

The point is, we are *not* alone. We can never be alone. When Jesus said, "I will be with you always" (Matt 28:20), he meant it literally. In chapter 3, "Slow to Fear," we will consider why the Bible says not to fear when there is so much around us to make us afraid. The only reasonable answer is that God is with us always, even when we are facing unimaginably large problems.

Our very existence is possible because we belong to God, we come from God, we return to God. The air in our lungs, the water in our muscles, our bones and blood are drawn from matter, from substances drawn from the earth that Christ, as the Word of God, spoke into being and holds together. We inhabit a living world created by God, held together by Christ.

Howard Thurman, an American Baptist preacher, theologian, and social activist of the twentieth century, spoke of it this way:

> The earth beneath my feet is the great womb out of which the life upon which my body depends comes in utter abundance. There is at work in the soil a mystery by which the death of one seed is reborn a thousandfold in newness of life. The magic of wind, sun and rain creates a climate that nourishes every living thing. It is law, and more than law; it is order, and more than order—there is a brooding tenderness out of which it all comes. In the contemplation of the earth, I know that I am surrounded by the love of God.[18]

What might change if we lived as though that were true—if we lived into an awareness that we are not alone but belong, that our life is not about us, but we are about Life? How might we function as families, communities, and nations if we saw ourselves as part of a "brooding tenderness" out of which all life comes rather than as autonomous selves?

Maybe we would be inspired to treat our near and distant kin with more kindness (a word that comes, after all, from the root *kin*). Maybe we would lean toward cooperative ways of being rather than competitive ones, toward ways that incline us to be slow to speak and quiet enough

---

18. Thurman, *Meditations of the Heart*, 210–11.

to listen to what is spoken softly, or even to not-yet-spoken words we can hear burbling beneath the surface in the silence.

In Oregon, creatures we encounter on our country roads are not deterred by rain. We have determined to join them in their resolved way of accepting what the day brings and taking our walk up the hill rain or shine. During one drizzly January walk, we noted a flock of European starlings—stocky birds that fly in large family groups. They settled on the ground of the vineyard we pass and conversed with squawking voices. Then in unison they rose in wet, velvety silence like a choreographed moving, swirling cloud to another part of the vineyard, descending back into the chatter of multiple loud conversations. In the five minutes it took to walk by them, they soared and descended several times—quiet movement in the air punctuated by loud chatter on the ground. We wondered where their cues came from and how they knew to bank left or right, up or down, so as to avoid airborne collisions. We wondered if navigating their way without catastrophic consequences was accomplished in silence.

Maybe our decisions as humans rising into action would be less catastrophic if we introduced silence into our processes—a deep quiet that recognizes and respects that we live in community and need to quell our conversations to attend to how our fellow members move left and right and up and down.

The skill of being quiet long enough to observe how we might participate gracefully, honestly, mercifully, and lovingly in the world calls for living out of quiet places. One such space for us has been what is known among Quakers as an unprogrammed meeting, what our church calls *waiting worship*. As we mentioned in the Introduction, every Sunday we sit with about a dozen other people who long for a place of waiting silence. We are mostly silent in the hour we sit together. We learn to enter a deep kind of quiet before speaking. We become attentive to what lives and moves beside, beneath, above, and within us.

God invites us into that kind of quiet—a counterintuitive and countercultural place characterized by love. Quiet is a noun, a place of rest and peace amid the storm. It is also a verb. As we learn to quiet ourselves, we become slower to speak and more attuned to the loving, gracious heart of God.

To quiet our voices when they tend toward polarization and loudness, we first need to quiet the inner noise. Quieting our mind does not turn it off or shut it down. We still think when we need to think, but we learn to keep our mind calm, to slow it down, to bear witness to conversations in our head and conversations we have with others.

The spiritual practice of Centering Prayer poses one way to train our minds to quiet. It offers a break from our constant inner monologue. It serves as a humble reminder for how consumed we often are with ourselves.

Centering Prayer

While relatively new to the Christian West, some histories of centering prayer lay the roots for it in Jesus' pattern of going to be alone with God before major events—his forty days of fasting in the wilderness before beginning his ministry and his night in Gethsemane before his crucifixion being perhaps the two most notable. The clearest roots emerge in the practices of fourth century desert mothers and fathers, whose prayer practices attempted to live out Paul's exhortation to pray without ceasing and offered Christians a place of humility and surrender to help them confront internal temptations and struggles. However, it was a fourteenth-century English monk (the anonymous author of *The Cloud of Unknowing*) who described a method of prayer that laid the foundation to what we use today.[19]

The history of Centering Prayer is interesting and useful, though perhaps more important is its theological significance. The prayer offers a kind of "mini-death" practice of dying to self. This dying to self that we might live in Christ is the theological root for centering prayer. Dying requires letting go of what we want in order to create space for God to lead us toward a truer way of being, of living in the world. We practice quieting our insistent and loud interior dialogue, our voice of fear and anger, our dreams and wants. As we practice letting go of our ego once or twice a day and entrusting ourselves to God's loving gaze, we might discover that we are living lives more attuned to God.

The form of centering prayer used today is largely modeled after the work of Cistercian monk Thomas Keating.[20] Generally practiced for twenty minutes twice a day, my (Lisa's) practice has been twenty minutes once a day. Most often I get out of bed in the morning, slip into a sweatshirt and pants, and head out to the barn with Oliver, our little dog. I love most of all the winter days when the stars are still visible in the night sky on my short trek. We climb the steps up to a prayer cabin

19. See Bourgeault, *Centering Prayer*.
20. Keating, *Intimacy with God*.

that sits above the goat barn and pray. Oliver sits quietly on my lap and models stillness, and maybe his attentiveness is his own form of prayer. Then we go down to greet, feed, and open the barn for Hazel and Clara, our Nigerian Dwarf goats, and their daughters, Oakley and Julian. The routine is grounding and centers me as I begin the day.

While Centering Prayer can put other kinds of prayer into a new and fuller perspective, it is not a replacement for prayers of gratitude, confession, lament, and petition. During Centering Prayer, we acknowledge and agree to God's presence and action within us. We practice relinquishing, surrendering, and being fully present to these moments with God.

Over time, contemplative prayer becomes a way of being and walking in the world. Our attention moves outward, our perspective broadens, and in that shift, we discover, as David does in Psalm 139, God's presence everywhere. We find our rumpled spirits quiet more easily and discover a greater capacity to extend God's love to others.

The following are suggested steps for engaging in contemplative prayer.

1. *Choose a word.* The word you choose becomes the symbol for your intention to acknowledge and agree to God's presence and action. While the word can be anything, avoid one that is loaded for you. Choose a word that is neutral yet comforting, such as *Love, Peace, Mercy, Silence, Stillness, Calm, Here/Now, Trust, Yes, Home,* or *Jesus.*

   Once you have a word, stay with it for a while. It is not magical, but treat it as sacred—a word to call you back to your intention. Change it if you find it distracting or unhelpful. A simple "gaze" on God may feel more quieting or less distracting than a word. In that case, you release thoughts by gazing on God, knowing God is gazing on you.

2. *Settling.* Find a quiet place to sit comfortably, set a timer, and close your eyes. "Sitting comfortably" means relatively comfortably—not so comfortably that you fall asleep, but comfortably enough to avoid thinking about being uncomfortable. A sitting posture that keeps your back straight will be helpful. You might start by reciting a prayer of consent or gratitude or acknowledging God's presence.[21] Silently repeat your word as an expression of your intention to consent to God's presence and action within you. Repeat

---

21. Contemplative Outreach has a variety of resources to assist with Centering Prayer, including prayers you might use to begin and end your time, and a timing option with various chimes you might use. See https://www.contemplativeoutreach.org/.

it slowly as you breathe, and as you do, release whatever is happening around and within you. Repeat your word slowly and gently, never forcefully, and so let go of thoughts.

3. *Regarding inevitable thoughts.* When you become aware of thoughts, gently repeat your word and release them. Thoughts include feelings, memories, insights, reflections, your to-do list, and the nearly ever-present monologue about this or that. These are expected and normal. Releasing them without judgment is your practice at letting go. Releasing is not emptying your mind of thoughts, but a practice that allows you to refocus. Note that the only activity you initiate during Centering Prayer is returning to your word when you become aware of thoughts.

4. *Ending your prayer period.* If you have set a timer, when it goes off, remain in silence with your eyes closed for a moment before opening them, getting up, and leaving this place of quiet to engage your day. End your time with a short prayer of intention and/or gratitude.

Thoughts of all sorts will bombard you. Your only task is to relinquish them once you become aware of them. Over time you will likely notice that as you say your word to let your thoughts go, your body sinks into a relaxed place. Besides ordinary wanderings of the imagination, you may think of things you imagine jotting down, psychological breakthroughs that you think you should keep thinking about because they are amazing. You will be distracted with thoughts like, *I'm doing great!, I'm doing terribly!, I don't feel anything!,* and *This is a waste of time!* Your only task is to let all these thoughts go. If something is important, you will remember it later.

Avoid thinking that this practice is productive. It is not. You are *being* rather than *doing*. You are choosing *slow*. Also avoid analyzing your experience, holding expectations of what you should experience and aiming at some specific goal. Don't think success means having no thoughts, or feeling peaceful or joyful, or feeling God's presence, or at least having some satisfaction that you have "achieved" a spiritual experience. None of that matters. This is not about success or feeling a particular way.

Resist thinking of Centering Prayer as a super-spiritual experience. While it is simply practicing quieting and releasing, it is also a discipline that fosters being attuned to God. It is an exercise of faith, hope, and love, a movement beyond *talking* to God to *communing* with God.

Slow Ponderings

1. What regrets do you carry about speaking too quickly or too loudly?
2. To what extent do you identify with the notion of inner chatter that we introduce in this chapter? Can a person be quiet on the outside and still loud on the inside?
3. What habits are you developing to keep your online voice civil and kind?
4. What is your reaction to the Centering Prayer practice? If something makes you skeptical about it, explore your assumptions about how prayer is supposed to happen and what it is supposed to look like. What makes you skeptical? If you are drawn to it, what is it that draws you?
5. Have you experienced the "inner witness" observing you during a conflict or confrontation? If so, what has been your experience? Is it a shaming witness or compassionate, one that cheers you on? Has it served you well or not so much? Do you sense an invitation in these questions?
6. Do you resonate with the idea of *belonging* being part of how we learn to be slow to speak? If so, how so? If not, what doesn't connect for you about that?

Chapter 2

Slow to Grasp: An Invitation to Contentment

A hand is "a prehensile, multi-fingered appendage located at the end of the forearm."[1] Biologically true, yes, but lacking the poetry that offers bigger and broader dimensions of a thing. Hands are also connected to the heart. Each day we have a choice to live with hands open and upward, giving and receiving with gratefulness and generosity, or to move about with fists clenched, clutching, knuckles pulsing. What we choose for our prehensile appendages on any given day must certainly be connected to the state of our hearts.

Before we ever *choose* to grasp, we do so instinctively and reflexively. The palmar grasp reflex is well known to any parent who has fallen in love with a newborn. Simply place a finger on a newborn's palm, and the infant automatically wraps their tiny fingers around yours. When put in terms of prehensile appendages, it sounds like this:

> The response of the reflex comprises flexion of all fingers around the examiner's finger, which is composed of two phases: finger closure and clinging. The latter occurs as a reaction to the proprioceptive stimulation of the tendons of the finger muscles due to slight traction subsequent to the application of pressure to the palm.[2]

---

1. Wikipedia, "Hand," https://en.wikipedia.org/wiki/Hand.
2. Futagi et al., "Grasp Reflex," ¶2.1.

When described in the language of the heart, the grasp reflex feels like a symphony of love, a tiny child clinging to warm connection, hearts melting in deep affection, bonds being formed for a lifetime.

The grasp reflex slowly disappears over the first year of life as the child gains voluntary control over when to grasp and when to let go. Yet even for adults, it seems, this requires a lifespan to learn. So often we grasp after things that need to be released, and we sometimes fail to hold firm to what matters most. The holy grasping that comes so naturally to an infant requires slow intention for grown-ups, best discovered in places of contentment.

Holy Grasping

Living requires some grasping. Blessed with opposable thumbs and precision grip, humans can pick up a fork to eat pasta, pluck a pear from a tree, or dig a carrot from the garden. We grasp to eat and eat to live.

Relationship requires grasp, though with more nuance than eating. We learn to hold on tight to those who mean much to us, even when times get difficult, and sometimes we must learn to let go when we least want to. Almost anyone who has enjoyed a long marriage or friendship will speak of times when tenacity and commitment helped them through difficult times, and almost anyone who has survived the heartache of divorce or widowhood will speak of the gut-wrenching pain involved in releasing the other. We also grasp on to our children when they are young and learn to gradually release them as they come into their own adulthoods.

Similarly, people of faith experience something like spiritual grasping at times. The psalmist writes,

> As the deer longs for streams of water,
> so I long for you, O God.
>
> I thirst for God, the living God.
> When can I go and stand before him? (Ps 42:1–2)

In times of deep struggle, lament, and spiritual questioning, sometimes grasping for God feels like our only option.

As the infant grips a loving finger, so we cling to God, or maybe just to our hope in God, in the most demanding and difficult times of life.

We grasp for justice in a world where power rules, where discrimination and oppression persist, stubbornly resisting efforts for rightness, for fairness. We grapple for peace when one country invades another and millions of refugees flee their homes and loved ones for an unknown future. Our hearts ache for a better way.

Hope is elusive in some seasons of life, but still, at best, we cling to it. When loved ones get sick and die, when loneliness or depression cloaks us like thick, daylong fog, when the world bends under the weight of a pandemic and its aftermath, when we hear the earth groan for redemption, we still wake each morning, swing our legs over the edge of the bed, wrangle a foot into each shoe, and take one step at a time, imagining possibilities of walking toward a day when the sun shines brighter.

Holy grasping reminds us that greed and grasp are not synonyms. Yes, grasping can regress into greed, but holiness can live there too. Contentment is not the absence of grasping but the process of learning to pay attention to how our hands and hearts come together in our desires, dreams, aspirations, and relationships. Later in this chapter we offer three principles and three practices as an invitation to contentment, and in their various ways each of them calls us to pay attention to our hearts before telling our hands what to do.

On the fourth Thursday of every November, most of us living in the United States celebrate a day of Thanksgiving. Our grateful hearts beckon our hands to mash potatoes, slice apples for pie, unfold napkins, and pass the gravy. These same hearts and hands may embrace family and friends and perhaps join together in prayer as we lift up our soulish bodies to God in gratitude and holy contentment.

And after Thursday, Friday comes.

Greedy Grasping

At 5 AM on Black Friday in 2008, Jdimytai Damour—a thirty-four-year-old Haitian immigrant—was trampled to death by a Walmart crowd in Long Island, New York.[3] One of the main incentives impelling the throng was a deal on a forty-two–inch television for $598. The same size television sells today for less than half that price.[4] On that same fateful day in 2008, two women started arguing in a Toys "R" Us in Palm Desert,

---

3. McFadden and Macropoulos, "Wal-Mart Employee Trampled," ¶4.
4. Dubner, "Who Killed Jdimytai Damour?," ¶2.

California, and the men with them drew weapons and killed each other.[5] Three years later a woman used pepper spray in her quest for a deeply discounted video game, or perhaps to defend her teenage children after other shoppers wanted the same game.[6] In 2012, two people were shot outside a Tallahassee Walmart after a heated dispute regarding a parking spot.[7] Another shooting and death occurred in 2016 over a parking spot at a Reno Walmart.[8] The list goes on and on. There's even a macabre website that keeps track of Black Friday deaths and injuries.[9]

Admittedly, these are extreme examples, but notice the vivid contrast. The same hands that rise in thanks on Thursday are capable of greedy grasping on Friday. Our hearts, like our hands, are complex and multifaceted, inclined toward both the holy and the greedy.

We'll explore the deadly sins in chapter 6, where greed shows up along with envy. They belong together. Envy is greed's first cousin. People prone to greed experience more malicious envy than others, and when they coincide people experience less satisfaction in life.[10]

Though ordering the deadly sins is no longer in style, many throughout history have taken literally the apostle Paul's warning to Timothy that "the love of money is the root of all kinds of evil" (1 Tim 6:10). Religious scholar and author Phyllis Tickle observes that "greed, by any name, is the mother and matrix, root and consort of all the other sins."[11]

Greed is bigger than loving money, just as rushing through stores and fighting off mobs on Black Friday is about more than balancing the checkbook. When Dutch and American participants were asked to identify the core elements of greed on a 1–8 scale, money made the list, but it ranked sixth behind some other troubling and more generic qualities that show up in abundance on Black Friday.[12]

---

5. Bermudez and Vives, "Store Reopens," ¶1.
6. Gray, "Black Friday Pepper Sprayer," ¶2.
7. Associated Press, "Two People Shot," ¶1.
8. ABC13, "Shopper Opens Fire," ¶1-5.
9. "Black Friday Death Count."
10. Crusius et al., "Dispositional Greed."
11. Tickle, *Greed*, 15.
12. Seuntjens et al., "Defining Greed."

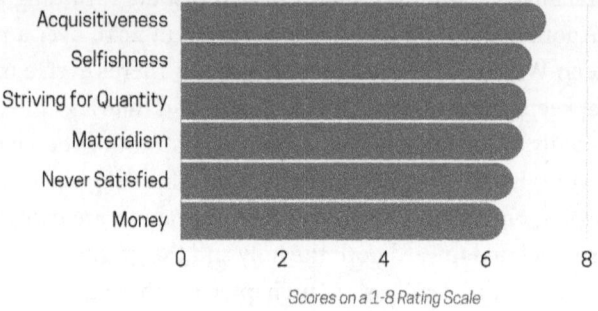

Acquisitiveness tops the list, and while this can certainly involve money, there are plenty of other ways to be acquisitive in an anxious quest for more. In a fascinating series of studies, researchers showed that being inclined toward greed is related to eating the whole bag of chips once opened, having many sexual partners, always acquiring the newest model of your preferred smartphone, and getting as many friends as possible on social media.[13] If four hundred Instagram followers makes me feel good, wouldn't eight hundred be better? And if I post something to Facebook on a Thursday afternoon, might I get more likes than if I post on a Sunday night? And if we can get to you to nod and smile at these examples, might we sell a few more books and get a higher Amazon sales ranking?

This is convicting to me (Mark) because I can't have Oreos in the house without eating the entire package in two days. And I need to have all the recent research articles on greed in front of me before writing a chapter such as this. Early in my academic career, I recall lying awake at night and counting all the publications I could muster by the end of the year. Sometimes I have clung too tightly to my idealism, to deadlines, to approval, to high expectations, to friendships that needed to be reconsidered or released. I am both capable and guilty of greedy grasping.

---

13. Seuntjens et al., "Dispositional Greed."

When Enough Is Not Enough

Imagine sitting in a cubicle at a research university, putting on a pair of headphones, and listening to relaxing classical piano music. Here's the twist. If you choose, you can "work" to earn some chocolates while you're sitting there. "Working" involves pressing a key that interrupts the music and blasts unpleasant white noise for a fraction of a second. You choose how often you press that key, but you also know that the more you work, the more you will be rewarded with chocolate. Do you sit comfortably and enjoy the music, or do you endure the unpleasant white noise for the sake of doing something worthwhile, like earning a tasty treat?

You have five minutes to listen to music (or earn chocolate), and then you have five more minutes to eat the chocolates you earned. It's possible to overearn, meaning you could earn more chocolates than you are able to consume in five minutes.

When this study was conducted, those who scored highest on a greed scale were also the highest chocolate earners and the most likely to overearn chocolates. The authors of this innovative study titled it well: "When Enough Is Not Enough."[14]

When is enough ever enough with chocolate? Or chips? Or Facebook friends? Or Oreos? Or earnings?

Each year the Economic Policy Institute publishes a report on the compensation of chief executive officers for the largest 350 companies in the United States. In addition to overall compensation, they report the ratio of the CEO's compensation to that of the average worker in the company.[15] In 1965, when the Rolling Stones were singing, "I can't get no satisfaction," CEOs were making twenty-one times what the average worker in the company earned. By 1978 the Bee Gees were singing "Stayin' Alive" and CEOs were doing so by making thirty-one times what their average workers made. The ratio grew to sixty-one when Bobby Brown recorded "My Prerogative" in 1989. By the turn of the millennium, CEOs were making 365 times what the average worker made, and this ratio has stayed quite steady throughout the twenty-first century.

It's striking to see the compensation ratio of CEO to average worker (remember, this is not the least-paid worker) move from twenty-one to one in 1965 to over 350 to one in just a few decades. If the average worker makes $30 per hour, the CEO makes over $10,000 each hour! The latest

---

14. Zeelenberg et al., "When Enough Is Not Enough," 110155.
15. Mishel and Kandra, *CEO Pay*, Table 1.

ratio at Walmart, where so many of those Black Friday incidents occurred, is 933 to one. It's even higher at Coca-Cola, at 1,883 to one.[16] The image comes to mind of a CEO sitting behind a desk piled with mountains of overearned chocolate, thousands of times more than could ever be eaten in five minutes or five years. Overearning has become a marker of value and status in corporate America and an example of our cultural comfort with greed resulting in gross inequality.

To be fair, this unfathomable increase in compensation is not just the responsibility of CEOs. These companies have boards with an explicit responsibility to make money for stockholders. By design, stockholders demand that companies be as profitable as possible, even if it means scrambling to get the top CEOs by paying outrageous salaries, bonuses, and stock options while paying other workers as little as possible to maximize profits and compete in the marketplace. In this sense, anyone with a pension or retirement plan that invests in stocks is complicit in the pay ratio imbalance. It may be good to reread that last sentence and sit with it, as uncomfortable as it may be.[17]

Remember that greed is not just about money but also about the strivings that make us feel successful and complete. George Goodman, the iconic author and broadcaster who wrote under the pseudonym Adam Smith, had this to say in *The Money Game*:

> The irony is that this is a money game and money is the way we keep score. But the real object of the Game is not money, it is playing the Game itself. For the true players, you could take all the trophies away and substitute plastic beads or whale's teeth; as long as there is a way to keep score, they will play.[18]

We ingeniously find ways to keep score. For Barry Bonds and his many fans, it was home runs. Bonds, one of the greatest baseball players of all time, had his career tainted with long-standing allegations of using prohibited performance-enhancing drugs, although Bonds denies knowing the drugs he got from a local laboratory were steroids.[19] Computerized models estimate that Bonds would have hit only 551 career home runs

---

16. Salary.com, "Browse Executive Salaries."

17. There are responsible investment options and finance companies that focus specifically on ethical investing. Everence is one faith-based example that offers solid returns on investments and contributes to making the world a more just and flourishing place in the process.

18. Smith, *Money Game*, 20.

19. Fainaru-Wada and Quinn, "Not as Great," ¶9.

instead of 762 if it weren't for performance-enhancing drugs. The scandal has kept him out of the Hall of Fame, at least for now.[20] Lance Armstrong and his followers kept score with Tour de France victories. Armstrong had seven consecutive wins after surviving testicular cancer, but all seven were eventually stripped because of performance-enhancing drug use.[21]

Winning can be addictive. Winning promotes our sense of entitlement and increases our inclination to be dishonest to gain advantage over others.[22] Maybe we shouldn't push for blue ribbons for our children. Maybe we would serve our children, our communities, and ourselves better to value and learn how to cooperate with others rather than compete with them. This is not, of course, a new thought.

Even if we like the idea of cooperating, often our greedy grasping comes from an inner heart space where we don't feel we *have* enough or *are* enough. We think more will help us feel better, so we drive ourselves to acquire more money, power, notoriety, success, experiences, and approval. But fast drivers often hit unexpected speed bumps, dangerous curves, and pockets of dense fog. We are left to make sense of our crashes, failures to arrive, or more simply, our burned-out selves.

> **Pause:** Can you identify with enough not being enough? Chocolate and Oreos may seem like trivial examples, but sometimes small things mirror bigger and deeper yearnings to have enough, to be enough.
>
> Can you imagine that some of your grasping comes from a sense of inadequacy, feeling that you are not enough? If so, what emotions, feelings, and thoughts stir around this for you? Take some time to sit with them, perhaps to write about them.

Trickle-Down Greed

A disturbing story about greed sits deep in the Old Testament, in the time of Elisha the prophet. Naaman, the commander of a competing army, suffered from leprosy, so he loaded up his animals with 750 pounds of silver, 150 pounds of gold, and ten sets of clothing and set out to find Elisha in Samaria. One of us (we'll let you guess which one) is a spreadsheet geek,

---

20. Guardado, "Bonds Misses HOF," ¶1.
21. Cohen, "Timeline," ¶2012.
22. Schurr and Ritov, "Winning a Competition."

so we know that in today's dollars, this would be about $5 million, plus whatever ten pairs of jeans and ten shirts cost. Both the king of Aram and the king of Israel got involved in the drama before Naaman eventually found Elisha. After a bit of grumbling and seven dips in the muddy, murky Jordan River, Naaman was cured. Grateful, Naaman offered a gift to Elisha, but Elisha turned him down and sent Naaman away in peace.

Who needs that much money, anyway? Elisha's servant, Gehazi, who overheard the conversation, was pretty sure Elisha (or maybe Gehazi himself) needed at least a fraction of it. Perhaps Gehazi, who had been a faithful servant to Elisha, convinced himself that surely God would want them compensated for doing God's work. As Elisha's servant, Gehazi would have been tasked with procuring their provisions and gathering whatever he could when they didn't have enough, which was likely often, especially given that this story takes place on the heels of a famine. So maybe Gehazi thought Elisha was being unnecessarily humble in his refusal to accept any payment for services rendered. Whatever his motivations, Gehazi chased down Naaman, requested some of the silver and clothing—allegedly for Elisha—and came home $60,000 richer.

The story ends badly. When asked by Elisha where he had been, Gehazi lied and suddenly came down with leprosy. One wonders if the story might have been different had he not lied. But lie he did, and Elisha declared that Gehazi's descendants would also suffer from leprosy, making for a tragic ending to a harsh story (2 Kgs 5).

This story serves as a poignant reminder of greed and its generational consequences. Feeling a lack of something in life, a dis-ease, we reach out to grasp something we expect might make things better. But at the end of the day our frantic efforts at pain relief only make it worse. Dis-ease leads to selfish ambition, which—as we read in the epistle of James—leads to "disorder and evil of every kind" (Jas 3:16). Those who score highest on greed tend to show less concern for others, see the world as unfair, and be less likely to assist others who need help.[23] Tragically, these disordered priorities trickle down through generations, and our greedy grasping is picked up by our children and our children's children.

Here are a few examples from social science research showing how greed and privilege worm their way into our social structures and classes, slithering from one generation to the next.

---

23. Bao et al., "Dispositional Greed."

- People tend to be generous toward others after being the recipients of generosity, but an even stronger tendency is seen with greed. That is, those who are taken advantage of by greedy others tend to become greedier themselves in future interactions.[24]
- Children from less affluence behave more altruistically than those from wealthy families.[25]
- Individuals from lower-class families demonstrate more compassion for suffering than those from upper-class families.[26]
- Those from lower-class families are better able to read emotions accurately than those from higher social classes.[27]
- In laboratory studies, those coming from lower-class homes are more generous, charitable, trusting, and helpful than those from upper-class families.[28]
- Those from wealthier homes experience the positive emotions of contentment, pride, and amusement more than those from lower social classes. In contrast, those from lower social classes experience compassion, love, and awe more than those from wealthier backgrounds.[29]
- Those from lower social classes tend to engage more in behaviors that benefit others, while those from higher social classes engage more in behaviors that benefit themselves.[30]
- Upper-class individuals report a greater sense of entitlement and narcissism—and they look at themselves more in the mirror—than those from lower social classes.[31]
- Those driving expensive cars are most likely to cut off other drivers at four-way stops and most likely to disregard pedestrians in crosswalks.[32]

24. Gray et al., "Paying It Forward."
25. Miller et al., "Roots and Benefits."
26. Stellar et al., "Class and Compassion."
27. Kraus et al., "Social Class."
28. Piff et al., "Having Less, Giving More."
29. Piff and Moskowitz, "Wealth, Poverty, and Happiness."
30. Piff and Robinson, "Social Class."
31. Piff, "Wealth and the Inflated Self."
32. Piff et al., "Higher Social Class."

These examples are poignant, but it is important to keep in mind that not all wealthy people get their money through greed. Sometimes it is some combination of good fortune, social position, and hard work. Still, there are costs when people become accustomed to wealth because money can make us less like the people we hope to be, and these stunted human capacities then trickle down to future generations.

If, when tempted to grasp, Gehazi had remembered how God had provided for Elisha and him during the famine, and if he had known the consequences of his choice, surely he would have chosen differently. What about us today? Can we choose differently?

Opting Out

Eight decades ago, Mary Gertrude Anderson and her husband, Lloyd Anderson, avid mountaineers, had to buy expensive imported ice axes from their local shops to facilitate their adventuring. They wanted to find a way to help other climbers acquire the gear they needed at a more reasonable cost, and REI was born.[33] Recreational Equipment, Inc., a Seattle-based company, is a cooperative that encourages people to engage the natural world playfully and exploratively.

In 2015, REI created a bold, countercultural alternative to Black Friday by launching #OptOutside. Giving up one of their largest sales days of the year, the company decided to pay their fifteen thousand employees to spend the day outdoors with friends and family. #OptOutside has become a visible alternative to the competitive clamor of Black Friday. As we write this book, REI has now offered #OptOutside for ten consecutive years and shows no signs of stopping.[34] Hundreds of other companies have joined the effort, especially those selling outdoor recreational equipment.

These companies are likely reaping business benefits for their countercultural idea, and they are also promoting social, environmental, and physical well-being. A 2020 study found connections between time outdoors and reduced materialism. People living in states with more wilderness and national forests bought fewer big diamonds and spent less money in general on luxury brands. Just having participants stand for one minute and look at a grove of trees caused them to score

---

33. REI Staff, "REI History," ¶1–7.
34. REI Co-op, "OptOutside."

lower on a materialism scale when compared to those who stood in the same spot but looked in a different direction and stared at a building instead.[35] Being in nature evokes a sense of awe, where we feel we are part of something bigger than ourselves, and when we experience awe, we also show gains in compassion, generosity, and caring for others. Our sense of self gets smaller (in a good way) as we become less entitled and feel connected to something vast and powerful.[36]

The day after next Thanksgiving, we all face a choice. Do we enter the marketplace with its acquisitive grasping for parking spaces and discounted merchandise, or do we opt outside, where we see God's handiwork and locate ourselves in the mosaic of a vast and beautiful creation?

Opting out is bigger than one November day each year. Each of us will confront liminal moments in life where we make choices to move upwardly, laterally, or downwardly. These important decisions carry implications for our career, economic stability, family life, health, and spiritual vitality. We often have more choice than we may presume. The pressured messages all around us tell us to keep ascending, grasping for the next rung on the proverbial ladder, tirelessly moving upward. Sometimes this is good, calling us to challenge ourselves, exercise our gifts, or provide for our needs. And sometimes we are climbing just to climb without assessing the cost to ourselves and to others impacted by our choices.

I (Mark) worked too hard climbing in my early and middle adulthood, and it came at a cost to me, to Lisa, and to others. There are no rewind buttons in life, so I can't go back and change those choices now, but I can admire and encourage those on a wiser path.

Emily and Ben and their three young children—Matthew, Bekah, and Nathan—joined us one evening last strawberry season. Strawberry shortcake is always delicious, especially with freshly picked strawberries, homemade shortcake, and cream whipped up just before serving—and when enjoyed with good company. Emily had completed her doctorate in clinical psychology several years earlier, meeting and marrying Ben along the way. By the time she finished her degree, starting a family had more appeal than embarking on a career. She could have done both, as many people do, and she speaks highly of those making such choices. But Ben and Emily opted to put her giftedness and training to work inside their home instead. It means one career (and paycheck)

---

35. Joye et al., "Diminishment of Desire."
36. Piff et al., "Awe, the Small Self."

as Ben provides their family income working as a computer scientist remotely from home. They joked about being on the slow path toward paying off Emily's student loans, but not with any hint of resentment or regret. Both affirmed the goodness of their choices, their delight in family, and the spaciousness a single career allows them to enjoy. They described various pleasures in the life they have chosen—eating three meals a day together, bird-watching, one-on-one time with each child, seeing friends often, learning new things together and individually, and having less stress than most couples with young children they know. It's a countercultural choice, and not one every couple can make, but Dr. Emily speaks of her deep contentment with staying on the current rung of a ladder she may or may not choose to climb later. Ben is supportive and equally content with her choices.

John Woolman, the eighteenth-century Quaker abolitionist, faced a choice about opting out early in his career as a merchant. After moving from his childhood home, he began working as a storekeeper, which led to several offers in business. At the same time, he felt increasingly convicted about devoting himself to simplicity, ministry, social justice, and growing in spiritual wisdom. Woolman is best known for his autobiographical journal, published posthumously, which has been a literary and spiritual classic for almost 250 years. Over thirty years ago, a Quaker scholar wrote this about Woolman's journal:

> Time and again readers have noted the relevance of Woolman's insights to their own times. Especially in our day, his ethical convictions, rooted in religious experience, speak directly to the major issues of racial equality, economic justice, and the responsibility of the individual toward military and political authority.[37]

Notice how these words continue to resonate. Racial equality, economic justice, political authority—these remain enduring ethical issues. Woolman chose to organize his life around moral and spiritual ideals rather than economic security or social mobility.

Woolman wrote in his *Journal*, "My mind through the power of Truth was in a good degree weaned from the desire of outward greatness."[38] He observed that success in earning seemed to come along with desiring more earnings, often distracting a person from growing

---

37. Moulton, ed., *Journal and Major Essays*, 3.
38. Moulton, ed., *Journal and Major Essays*, 35.

in virtue.[39] Desiring to free himself from financial grasping, Woolman apprenticed as a tailor, taking a step down on the socioeconomic ladder from his family of origin.[40] He made this difficult choice even as he recognized at times a desire for "something greater."[41] Woolman built a simple house, planted an orchard on eleven acres, and supported his family modestly with self-employment income from tailoring and growing fruit. The orchard became more glorious than the house as John and his wife, Sarah, tended it with care.[42] Woolman opted out in one regard, though he opted into something richer, better.

Woolman's life, like Emily and Ben's, provides an important pivot as we turn toward an invitation to contentment. If we equate contentment with permanent vacation—sipping the beverage of our choice on a Caribbean beach—then Woolman is not our exemplar. His life was difficult in various ways, his fervor unsurpassed, and his work ethic robust. But let's look at contentment as a place of attunement, where heart and hands align, where the unnecessary and superficial strivings of a materialistic age fall away, where we feel the slow, deep satisfaction of knowing our purpose and calling, where the holy longings of our life align with God's care for a beautiful, broken world.

An Invitation to Contentment

The following three principles—paying attention, remembering, and mellowness of heart—offer an invitation away from our tendency to grasp greedily after what we think we need to be satisfied.[43] Think of this invitation nudging you to a place of quiet stillness knowing that you have enough, resting in the *enoughness* of what is. Like a weaned child no longer needing to thrash about trying to satisfy her hunger every time she's near her mama's breasts, imagine this as an invitation into comfortable beingness, satisfied and contently resting in your mama's arms (see Ps 131:2).

---

39. Woolman, *Word of Remembrance*, 5.
40. Slaughter, *Beautiful Soul*, 125.
41. Moulton, ed., *Journal and Major Essays*, 35.
42. Slaughter, *Beautiful Soul*, 191.
43. Lisa wrote a book on contentment some years ago: McMinn, *The Contented Soul*.

Paying Attention

In her young adulthood Mary Oliver accepted a calling to pay attention to the world and then to write about what she noticed—not in a reporting sort of way but with the expansive, expressive empathy of a poet. She lived a minimal sort of life so that she could afford to do this work. In a rare interview with Krista Tippet in 2015, Oliver said, "Somebody once wrote about me and said I must have a private grant or something; that all I seem to do is walk around the woods and write poems. But I was very, very poor, and I ate a lot of fish, ate a lot of clams."[44] One of the many who wrote of Oliver after her death in 2019 said, "Oliver lived a profoundly simple life: she went on long walks through the woods and along the shoreline nearly every day, foraging for both greens and poetic material."[45]

To avoid a life dictated by the demands of a boss to whom she sold her labor, who would then determine where she had to be, when, and for how long, Oliver patched jobs together. She'd teach a poetry seminar here and a writing course there and published poems as she could, which she did rather profusely, gaining an avid following of readers drawn to the way she guided them into the wonder and awe of paying attention.

Oliver's work, she said, was paying attention to the world, keeping her mind on what matters, which was not whether her boots were old and coat torn. Paying attention to the world meant "standing still and learning to be astonished" at all she saw, including pastured sheep, and even the pasture itself, which Oliver says, "is mostly rejoicing."[46]

Oliver had all she needed physically, and her contentment with "enough" gifted her with time and space to feast on, to join in praise with, to feel a connection to and to be grateful for all that is alive in the world and living out its own precious existence alongside hers.

I (Lisa) don't remember for sure who introduced me to Mary Oliver, though likely it was Allison, my earth- and word-loving student and teaching assistant from our Wheaton College years. Allison left notes and drawings, poems and quips on my desk, taped to my walls, slid under the door. I vaguely remember an Oliver poem among them, Allison rightly discerning that I'd resonate with her words. Oliver brings her full attentiveness to the almost invisible ordinary in front of us. Maybe what she brings is *kindness* to what is in front of her, a kindness born out of a

---

44. Tippett and Oliver, "I Got Saved."
45. Syme, "Mary Oliver helped us stay amazed," ¶2.
46. Oliver, *Thirst*, 1.

sensed kindredness with the world she inhabits. Her words subtly invite readers to stop scrambling and grasping for more and instead to stand still, maybe to squat down or lie down, to bear witness to and savor the gift of life we share with—well, grasshoppers, for one, who live out their lives in the green patches outside our doors.

At Fern Creek, which is what we call our little farm for reasons to be disclosed later, we are never sorry when we drum up the energy in an evening to trek down to the gazebo by the creek, light a fire in the firepit, and listen to rain pattering on the roof (often enough—this is Oregon, after all), the fire crackling, the creek burbling, and sometimes (when it is *not* raining) the conversation of great horned owls sending messages across the woods to each other. We savor life in these moments, and our place together in them—resting and still, weaned children in the bosom of God.

What if life is primarily an invitation to be attuned to the astonishing gift of life itself so that gratitude burbles up from our heart, mingled with joy in recognizing we are held—have always been and will always be—by a God who loves and holds us all? What kind of redemptions and restorations might be possible if we, then, came to love the world as God does? Attunement to the astonishing gift of life is the first principle of contentment.

> **Pause:** The invitation brings our full selves to *this* present moment. Just now you are reading these words. Pause, and notice what such an invitation stirs inside you. Perhaps set this book aside for a moment, step outside to see and feel what there is to see and feel, whether night or day, rain or shine. Give your full attention to what you see, hear, smell, feel on your skin. Let your attunement to this moment quiet background noises, such as stewing over some past moment or worrying about some future one. Stay awhile. Let yourself fall into this moment and notice whether gratitude and contentment burble up and spill over.
>
> Once you have experienced it, remember that it is always there. You can always return and touch this place of contented rest again by attending to your present moment.

Remembering

Contentment is rooted in remembering who we are and whose we are. We are persons who belong, and in remembering we find ourselves held by God, who called the universe into being and loves and sustains it. There is no place where God is not holding, loving, sustaining, and drawing creation to an irresistible, ultimate consummation.

The task of remembering weaves a persistent thread throughout Scripture. With the Passover, Israel remembers the faithfulness of God rescuing them from Egypt. They remember God's faithfulness during their forty years in the wilderness with the Festival of Booths. They built altars to commemorate moments when God stepped in to save them, wore *tefillin* (passages of the Torah in leather boxes) that reminded them of key precepts, and gathered regularly to hear a recounting of their history and God's faithfulness. The Psalms often call forth remembering God's faithfulness in the past when the day is dark and dangerous.

Contentment is also rooted in remembering our story—created, loved, forgiven, and redeemed. Remembering that we belong to this loving, faithful God makes it possible to accept an invitation to hold life, relationships, and possessions loosely, hands open, living out of a place of quiet contentment that invites, welcomes, and calms those who draw near.

The thorns and thistles of our existence make living from a place of contentment challenging. Of course they do. We live in a cultural milieu where grasping for comfort and pleasure, where seeking to escape hardship, is presumed to be our duty when confronted with discomfort. We have come to value what a consumer-driven market offers, a market dependent for its own health on shaping our desires and replacing contentment with insatiable hunger. Instead of living souls, we became avid consumers of experiences, achievements, and stuff.[47]

Remembering helps return us to the center. What if in remembering God's lovingkindness, we learn to love as God loves? What if our thirsting for God involves seeking justice for the oppressed and mercy for the orphan, the widow, the imprisoned, and the sick?

---

47. McMinn, *Contented Soul*, 21–34.

Mellowness of Heart

My (Lisa's) father looked for silver linings in gray clouds. He always encouraged us to look for hope or focus on something positive when days became disappointing, dark, or difficult. I've learned that this is not always a good thing, but it served him well and has served me well enough too. When Dad received a terminal cancer diagnosis at sixty-eight years of age, he fought the fight as well as he could. I saw him confront loss after loss quickly over two years. He went from an active, energetic life to needing a cane, then a walker, then a wheelchair, then needing help with all his transitions. He went from breathing on his own to needing oxygen, from manageable pain to pain that could not be managed without sending him into a foggy stupor.

When Dad finally conceded that he would not win this battle, I asked how he coped with the mounting losses. He paused and looked out the window before saying he figured it was God's way of helping him let go of his hold on life, because, as a newly turned seventy-year-old, he wasn't ready to stop living yet. A silver lining, yes, and also a mellow heart.

Once he accepted that living would end soon for him, simple things brought him joy. Until his last couple of days, every morning we'd transfer him from his bed to his wheelchair and roll him to his desk, where he spent time with God in front of his Bible. He would sleep there when he couldn't read anymore, and I imagined him napping in the arms of God. Dad spent much of the day on the couch and took simple pleasure in looking outside at rural Pennsylvania beauty. We sensed that he was going to places and memories inside himself that seemed to bring him peace.

Mellowness of heart, according to Catholic friar Ronald Rolheiser, is being openly receptive to God so that our lives lean toward a posture of grace, thanksgiving, blessing, and goodness.[48] Sometimes that means looking for silver linings in gray clouds, relinquishing our effort to control and grasp, and choosing to enjoy one day and moment at a time, accepting hardship as the pathway to peace.

We are, all of us, co-sojourners on this life adventure. Mary Oliver ends her collection *Thirst* with a piece by that name. In it she notes waking with thirst for the goodness she does not have. She walks to the pond and all the way sees that God has given her beautiful lessons and asks for

---

48. Rolheiser, *Holy Longing*, 66–68.

more time. She speaks of how her love for the earth and for God are having a long conversation, and speculates that in the end, she will be told to pack nothing for what lies ahead "except the prayers which, with this thirst, I am slowly learning."[49]

Contentment extends an invitation to live out of a centered place in God, a relational place. It begins with remembering that we belong to God and that our opportunity to live is an exquisite gift. We practice gratitude and staying awake to life, loving it all as God does. We remember God's faithfulness as we encounter joy and sorrow, personal, social, political, and environmental troubles and achievements—all of it touched by divine love.

May we learn to be content to pack only, in the end, our prayers. Perhaps the following practices can help us imagine what that looks like.

Three Contentment Practices

1. *Pay attention to the ordinary.* Choose an ordinary daily moment and take a week to practice being mindful to it. Perhaps attend to eating breakfast mindfully. What does your food feel like in your mouth? What does it taste and smell like? How does it feel as you swallow it? What do you notice as you become mindful of each bite? Or maybe pay attention as you walk from your car into your place of work, ministry, or vocation. What do you see, hear, and smell along the way? How does the air feel on your skin? What emotions emerge as you exit your car and then walk through the door of the building you are entering? Perhaps sit somewhere where you can observe the sunrise or sunset every day for a week. What happens internally as you pay attention to any of these ordinary moments—food from mouth to stomach, jaunt from car to building, Earth's daily turning on its axis as it journeys around the sun?

2. *Remember.* Set aside five minutes to "sink into your heart space." Sit comfortably, eyes closed, and remind yourself, "I belong—heart, soul, and body—to God." Repeat this several times, until you feel settled. Once settled, recall a time you felt peace and contentment. Walk through it, reexperience the details. Notice where you were, what you were doing, perhaps why you were doing it. Sit there awhile, recounting, remembering, re-feeling. After a few

---

49. Oliver, *Thirst*, 69.

moments, consider what burbles up as you recount that experience now. What does any of this suggest to you? Does it raise any questions? Is God inviting you to something? Try this each day for a week or so and note what comes.

3. *Let go.* Choose one way you push back natural limits to get more time, energy, or comfort, and let it go for a day, a week, or a season. Maybe leave your phone at home on weekend days, maybe choose somewhere you usually drive and walk that route for a time, maybe use candlelight at night instead of electricity. What struggles emerge in relinquishing this comfort, this control? What unexpected gifts or silver linings come from doing so? Where does God's provisioning or care or comfort show up for you? Does anything shift in what you begin to desire? Journal your thoughts before you begin, along the way, and at the end of the time you have allotted to set something down, including what choices you have moving forward and what inclines you to make them or not.

Contentment comes and goes in life, just as moods and perspectives vary from day to day. These practices encourage and welcome contentment but cannot force it. Practice helps, of course, but none of us feel continual contentment in our lives. Try these practices as you are inclined and notice what happens to your sense of contentment. Be patient with yourself, recognizing that good comes from practices such as these, even if you don't discern lasting change in your state of content or discontent. Change takes time and practice.

Slow Ponderings

1. Give some thought to the idea of holy grasping. When in your life have you felt most confident that you are grasping for something God would deem good and beautiful? How did this experience change and shape you?

2. Now give some thought to greedy grasping. In the Old Testament book of Isaiah, we read:

   > Is anyone thirsty?
   > Come and drink—
   > even if you have no money!
   >
   > Come, take your choice of wine or milk—
   > it's all free!
   >
   > Why spend your money on food that does not give you strength?
   > Why pay for food that does you no good?
   >
   > Listen to me, and you will eat what is good.
   > You will enjoy the finest food. (Isa 55:1-2)

   Can you identify with seeking food that doesn't really satisfy? Think about this both literally and metaphorically. What might accepting this invitation look like for you?

3. Do you find it ironic that John Woolman, who gave up his desire to climb upward, ended up writing one of the most enduring literary classics of recent centuries (though he never knew it because it was published after his death)? What life lesson do you find here?

4. Which of the three principles of contentment do you resonate with the most (paying attention, remembering, mellowness of heart)? Which do you resonate with the least? What stirs inside you in how you answer these questions?

5. What are the greatest obstacles to contentment that you experience in your day-to-day life?

6. We began this chapter with the idea of holy grasping, reaching out our hands and holding firmly to our search for God. How might one (or more) of the suggested contentment practices help you with holy grasping?

Chapter 3

Slow to Fear: An Invitation to Courage

Umbria lies in the heart of Italy, home of dense forests, Lake Trasimeno, truffles, fine wines, and the valley of Tiber. On the southeastern edge lies Norcia, traditionally known by its Latin name, Nursia—the birthplace of Saint Benedict around 480. The son of a noble, Benedict was sent to Rome to study but didn't care much for that life, so he retreated into the countryside, where he lived in a cave for three years as a hermit.[1] Some nearby monks invited Benedict to serve as their abbot, but his revolutionary and strict regime didn't mesh with their more relaxed approach. In fact, they wanted to be rid of him enough to poison him. The attempt to kill him failed, and Benedict forgave them, but he determined he was not the father to guide them and returned to hermithood.

The history gets fuzzy at this point because his biography, written by Pope Gregory I, is mostly about signs and wonders evident in Benedict's life. We know he started numerous small monasteries, was again the target of a poisoning attempt, and eventually established a rule of life followed by monks living collectively. There are now more than 1,400 communities of men and women living under the 1,500-year-old Rule of Benedict.[2] The Rule is not a theology of what to believe but rather a practical document for how to live a steady and serene life with

---

1. Gregory I, *Dialogues*, ¶1.
2. Chittister, *Rule of Benedict*, 17.

others, initially most relevant to monastics whose days involved work, prayer, and contemplation.

Sister Joan Chittister is a Benedictine nun with a doctorate in speech communications from Penn State University. Her books are winsome and inviting, and several of them explore how the rule is still applicable. She explains the role of the porter, one who stayed ready near the door of the monastery to respond to any who might come knocking day or night, in calm or storm, in plenty or famine. Chapter 66 of Benedict's Rule reads,

> At the door of the monastery, place a sensible person who knows how to take a message and deliver a reply, and whose wisdom keeps them from roaming about. The porter will need a room near the entrance so that visitors will always find someone there to answer them. As soon as anyone knocks or a poor person calls out, the porter will reply, "Thanks be to God" or "Your blessing, please," then, with all the gentleness that comes from reverence of God, provide a prompt answer with the warmth of love.[3]

Chittister observes that how we answer the door is very much like how we treat the world. The porter is to be always available, prompt, warm, and full of gentleness. Come any time you want to the monastery, and someone will be waiting for you to provide a helpful welcome that stems from a heart of love.[4]

Try putting yourself in the place of a travel-weary stranger, perhaps hungry, likely fearful, and uncertain about what lies ahead. You come to a monastery and dare to hope you might find a place of safety rather than danger. You muster the nerve to knock on the weather-worn wooden door, having no idea what might happen next. As the door creaks open, you see a kindly old man on the other side—the porter—who offers you a blessing from God, showing uncommon gentleness to calm your fears. You are ushered to the abbot, who prays with you, washes your hands, offers you food that is set aside especially for guests, and shows you to the guest quarters.[5] You later continue your journey as one who has been seen, nurtured, and bolstered in love, all in the name of Jesus.

Isaac and Megan Wardell had a vision such as this when they founded The Porter's Gate Worship Project in 2017, with a mission "to

---

3. Chittister, *Rule of Benedict*, 169–70.
4. Chittister, *Rule of Benedict*, 170, ¶3–4.
5. Kodell, "St. Benedict Teaches Us."

be a 'porter' for the Christian Church—one who looks beyond church doors for guests to welcome."[6] Their collaborative endeavor involving theologians, musicians, pastors, and Christian leaders from a variety of worship, cultural, and racial traditions considers how the church can be hospitable and welcoming to the stranger, the pilgrim, and the refugee, thereby loving God and neighbor in a complex and diverse world. The Wardells gather people for several days at a time to engage in meaningful conversation and ultimately to compose new worship songs.[7]

At a fragile time in our lives, one of our pastors passed on a song from Porter's Gate that can still bring tears to our eyes when we hear it. "Nothing to Fear" features the evocative voice of Audrey Assad, assuring us "there is nothing to fear, nothing to fear, for I am with you always." These words call to mind that kindly porter, welcoming us into community, graciously understanding the complex and messy ways that people live, and reminding us of a deep and abiding love that reaches into our doubts, quenches our deepest thirst, and calms our fears. For a moment, at least, we can lay down our burden and settle into gracious hospitality, and there is nothing to fear.

Yet that's not completely satisfying, is it? We can sing, "There is nothing to fear," but it seems there is *always* something to fear. How can we hold these two realities close together?

So Much to Fear

Each year a team of faculty and students at Chapman University surveys United States residents about what they fear. There are many things to fear, and we are good at finding them. Items on the fear survey include zombies, death of a loved one, insects, deep lakes, terrorist attacks, identity theft, climate change, pollution, White supremacists, Antifa, reptiles, muggings, medical bills, sharks, running out of money, clowns, hurricanes, earthquakes, tornadoes, and so much more.[8] Fear is everywhere. How then can we believe that there is nothing to fear?

Words are slippery, sloppy things, so exploring this paradox of fear requires some unpacking—and a few drawings along the way.

Fear begins with threat, especially if the threat is beyond our control.

---

6. Ford, "Artist Profile," ¶2.
7. Contemporary Christian Music Magazine Staff, "Healing Mission," ¶6.
8. Rapoport et al., *Methodology Report*, 10–18.

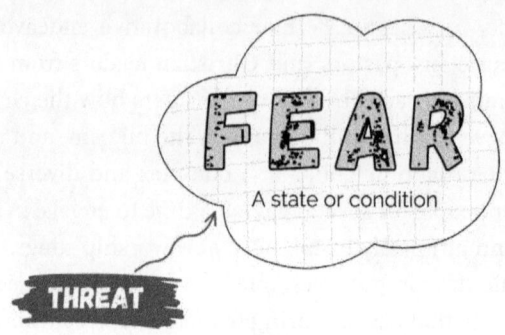

Goats are notorious escape artists, so before bringing Nigerian Dwarf goats to Fern Creek, I (Mark) constructed a robust fence to keep them close to home. Driving a T-post into the ground, I unwittingly hit an underground wasp nest. Before I knew what was happening, the wasps had me surrounded. The first few stings alerted me to threat, and I had no control over what the wasps were doing. At that point (and this all happened almost instantaneously), I responded in fear.

Biologists argue that fear is not exactly an emotion, but more like a state or condition.[9] Almost instantly, even before I could feel much emotion, I knew something was amiss as my brain and body figured out how to respond to agitated, stinging insects. Running and yelling were both involved, and then, once out of danger, I was sitting, feeling afraid, shaking, counting stings until I gave up trying, and maybe hyperventilating a little. Perhaps you have had a similar experience with a close call on the highway. You respond instantly by braking or swerving, and then a few seconds later you started to quiver and encountered the emotions that come with fear. The state of fear is like an alarm system telling you that something needs to be done to escape or avoid, the sooner the better.

---

9. Adolphs, "Biology of Fear."

When we experience a state of fear, certain things happen. Notice two arrows pointing out from fear. One arrow points to behavior because we instinctively know to escape or fight, or to die trying. The other points to emotion because fear reminds us that we are not in control of the threat we face, which makes us feel afraid. We only have two arrows emerging from fear in the diagram, but this oversimplifies matters. The diagram would get too complicated if we added all the arrows that belong. In addition to emotions and behaviors, fear affects our focus, triggers old memories and creates new ones, narrows our concentration, sways our reasoning abilities, influences our motivational systems, and so on.

When Christians say, "Do not fear," are we saying that we shouldn't have our normal built-in biological reaction to threat? No—we have no more control over this than the bird that flies away when a cat approaches. The state of fear is a biological reality, a gift to keep us from harm in the face of threat. But fear works best when it starts and ends quickly and when we have help from those around us. It took only a few seconds to get away from those wasps, and then the threat was over. Lisa brought me some Benadryl to help with the swelling, along with some empathetic, soothing words to help calm my rumpled emotions. Before I knew it, my body settled, and I was back driving more posts into the ground, though adorned with my bee suit in case I encountered another wasp nest.

The problem with fear comes when the feelings persist after the threat is gone. If fear is fleeting and adaptive, helping us get away from threat, then anxiety is more enduring and less helpful. It sticks with us like the pitch that gets on our hands when handling lumber or like gum on the bottom of our shoes. Anxiety untethers itself from reasonable threat, taking on a life of its own, visiting and revisiting us, waking us up at night, caging us in, festering into long worries that rob us of the peace and joy we might otherwise experience as we try to figure out how to gain control over whatever it is we fear.

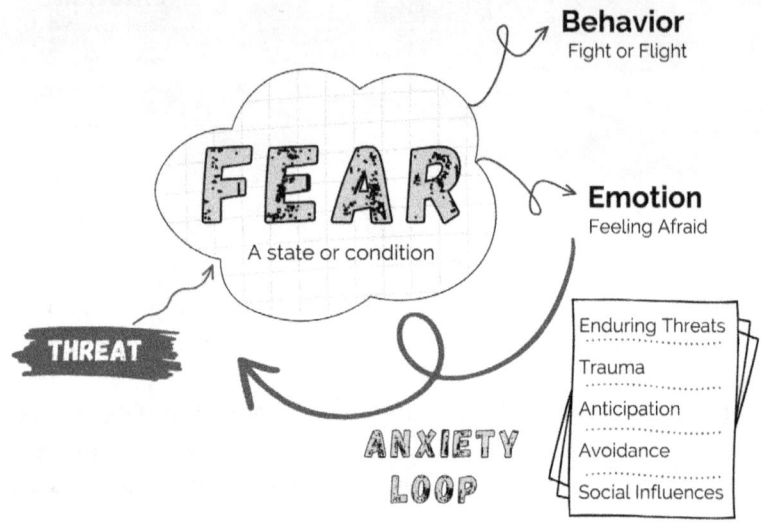

If fear is intended to come and go quickly, why do we find ourselves looped in anxiety? Entire books could be written on this question, and have been, so we will mention just a few reasons here.

Enduring Threats

The example of wasp stings is picking low-hanging fruit. It's easy to see how well our sympathetic (fight-or-flight) nervous system works when a threat comes and goes quickly. But what happens when the threat or our perception of threat persists?

Think about the abused child who lives with a repeat abuser. Or the first responder who encounters danger repeatedly on the job. Consider the family facing food insecurity, the person who lives in a high-crime district, or the person with a terminal medical diagnosis. Imagine the soldier marching or patrolling into harm's way week after week. Ongoing threat leads to persistent, sometimes disabling, anxiety.

During the years of COVID-19 we felt worldwide calamity settle around us like a dense fog, disrupting life as we knew it. In the wake of the pandemic, most counselors, clinical social workers, and psychologists had waiting lists as social, economic, spiritual, and physical disruption from the virus persisted longer than we ever imagined at the beginning. Anxiety and depression rates tripled in the months after the COVID-19 pandemic began.[10] The mental health consequences of the pandemic may linger for years.

Our collective wonderment about this century being the worst time of human history *ever* led some science and history folks to explore that question. They concluded that no, as troubled as the start of the twenty-first century has been, it's not as bad as it has ever been. The year 536 earned the Worst Year Ever title and began the worst year to be alive.[11] A major volcanic eruption in Iceland likely caused the troubles that followed,[12] bringing a persistent fog over the Northern Hemisphere—Europe, the Middle East, and Asia. The fog was so opaque that it created a perpetual winter, like a total eclipse of the sun that lasted eighteen months, making a dull version of the sun visible just a few hours each day as it cast only a "feeble shadow."[13] Tree ring evidence shows the devastating effects on plant life, resulting in famine, disease, and death. It truly was a terrible, horrible, no good, very bad year, exacerbated by another major eruption four years later and then one more seven years after that *and* the first outbreak of the bubonic plague.

At the beginning of this chapter, we invited you to imagine being a travel-weary stranger coming across the door to a monastery, but now we can add some texture to this imagination. The year 536 is just a few years after Benedict's Rule is written. You're sojourning through fog and famine, witnessing death constantly, wondering if the sun will ever return, if plant life and food sources can ever be redeemed. Each day you limp through a wasteland, looking for hope. Monasteries dot the Italian countryside, and those following the Benedictine Rule have a porter stationed near the door, ready to greet you, to offer you the "gentleness that comes from reverence of God."[14] You are ushered inside and treated as hospitably as Christ would be treated, offered food,

---

10. Twenge and Joiner, "U.S. Census Bureau-assessed Prevalence."
11. Gibbons, "Why 536." Also, RadioLab, "Worst. Year. Ever."
12. Little, "Worst Time in History."
13. Arjava, "Mystery Cloud," 78–79.
14. Chittister, *Rule of Benedict*, 170.

lodging, and respect. Can you imagine the comfort of being seen and cared for in such a gracious way?

> **Pause:** Notice how much we need the presence of another amid enduring fear—a kind porter, a hospitable community, an available psychotherapist, a spouse with Benadryl and comforting words, a caring pastor, a loving parent or child, a faithful friend, a thoughtful neighbor, a gracious God.

Trauma

Fear feelings might also linger because the threat is so intense as to be considered traumatic. At age fifteen, Kaiden found his mother dangling from a noose in the garage along with a terse note about the hopelessness of life. In one regard the threat ended a few hours later, when his mother's body was put in a black bag and driven down the road, but this sort of event can never really end. His mother's suicide ushered Kaiden into a long tunnel of despair and anxiety and into many years of therapy to help him cope with trauma, loss, and fear. Similarly, when a person endures combat or childhood abuse, the feelings may not resolve once the threat ends. The feelings may reverberate for months, years, or decades after the event is over.

While "aces" commonly refer to high-ranking playing cards, people who excel at a particular thing, or stellar tennis serves, the term has also become a well-known acronym for Adverse Childhood Experiences. These include emotional, physical, or sexual abuse, alcoholism or illegal drug use in the home, a household member with mental illness or suicide attempts, or having a member of the family go to prison. ACEs came into sharp focus in 1995 when the Center for Disease Control partnered with Kaiser Permanente in California to explore how childhood trauma might predict future health problems. The results were striking, and hundreds more studies ensued. Early trauma exposure increases risk of later depression; drug abuse; alcoholism; heart, lung, or liver disease; and cancer.[15] A likely reason for the connection between childhood trauma and later problems is *toxic stress*, which relates to the overarousal of the child's fight-or-flight nervous system during formative years of brain

---

15. Felitti et al., "Relationship of Childhood." Some researchers raise questions about whether ACEs is the most useful way to consider the effects of childhood trauma. See Lacey and Minnis, "Practitioner Review."

development.[16] Fear is meant to be temporary, and our bodies pay a price when trauma persists over a long time.

The Two "A" Words

Fear festers into anxiety when we begin thinking about threats in advance, before they happen, and then go out of our way to prevent or avoid the thing we fear.

The first A is anticipation.

If you watch television or movies, you've probably encountered shock scenes where a person is driving happily down a road, humming along with the music or having a warm, jovial conversation with another person in the car, when suddenly an SUV crashes into the side of the car. You gasp—a reaction the director hoped to elicit—because it keeps you engrossed in the story.

Fear enters suddenly, does its work, and then leaves. The scene changes, your heart rate goes back to normal, and the story continues.

With enduring anxiety, the order of things gets mixed up. A tragic event is no longer required to trigger fear. Anxiety comes first as we rehearse and imagine what bad thing might happen, even when the tragic event may not happen at all. Our lack of control over something we think we *should* be able to or *want* to control keeps us in a state of anxiety.

Freda dislikes public speaking, but her job requires her to make conference presentations twice a year. Her anxiety sometimes begins days before these speaking events, keeping her awake at night and distracted during the day. She often runs to the bathroom to vomit a few moments before her talk begins. Anticipating a threat can evoke a strong fear response, as Freda well knows. Twice a year she imagines making a fool of herself in front of a large group, and twice a year she does a reasonably good job with her presentations. It's what some people might call a waste of a worry, but to Freda this fear is intense and seemingly inescapable.

The second A is *avoidance*.

Freda likes her job, but twice a year she weighs the pros and cons of resigning and finding work that requires no public persona. Nelson once had a panic attack at a Chinese food restaurant, so now he stays away from all Asian foods. Beverley had a serious car accident several years ago, and now she stays away from driving whenever possible.

---

16. Harvard, "ACES and Toxic Stress."

Avoidance is a common response to anxiety, and it helps in the short term by asserting some form of control that keeps the fearful feelings at bay. But in the long run it gives fear enormous power over our lives, keeping us caged in anxiety.

Social Influences

We also get caged with our fears because of social influences. It almost goes without saying that our friends' and family's responses will influence our levels of anxiety before, during, and after difficult times. Similarly, there are large sociopolitical trends that can keep us locked in fear.

In the Chapman University survey we mentioned earlier, the top item—chosen from a list of possibilities—is corrupt government officials.[17] This is hardly surprising in a highly polarized time when political battles show up in our yard signs, newsfeeds, and social media posts. The other highly feared items include financial collapse, war, terrorism, and pollution. Each of these are genuine fears, no doubt, but ones that are shaped and perpetuated by the daily news cycle. Fear is contagious, and it is the stuff that makes news media compelling and profitable.

Aleksandr Solzhenitsyn, the Russian novelist and Christian who spent part of his life in the United States after being expelled from the Soviet Union, once gave a hard-hitting commencement speech at Harvard University where he spoke critically of the Western media. Solzhenitsyn observed that the press is more powerful than any of our branches of government yet has no accountability to monitor its impact on people. If a president or senator messes up, we can choose to elect someone else next time around, but there is no similar check on the media.[18]

Next time you view the news, look for the message behind the story. On the surface, the story is about someone's house burning down, a local robbery, international conflict, a regional drought, wildfires raging out of control, a coming blizzard, a corrupt politician, a fallen minister, or any number of other scandals and disasters. These are all things to fear. *Be afraid* is the subtle message. Beneath the surface, fear captures viewers and drives ratings and advertising sales.

If this works well, then we feel stressed and curious enough to stay tuned in or browse again next hour to see what new information is

---

17. Chapman University, "Top 10."
18. Solzhenitsyn, "World Split Apart," ¶7.

available about the unfolding trouble of the world.[19] Soon fear gives way to habits that feed anxiety.

Social media further adds to our anxieties. As a goat chews her cud, so social media allows us to regurgitate the fearful events from news outlets and to ruminate on them for days. However, cud chewing in goats suggests a relaxed, contented state, and the regurgitating and chewing of cud is a rumination process that integrates food so that it offers nutritional benefit. The metaphor doesn't travel very far for humans because our cogitating is seldom integrative, helpful, or calming and generally leads toward more and greater angst. A systematic review of twenty-three studies involving almost fourteen thousand participants shows that problematic Facebook use is positively correlated with psychological distress, including depression and anxiety, and inversely related to psychological well-being.[20]

What do we normally do when experiencing distress, such as anxiety? We reach out to others. Social support is one of our best tools to manage distress. But transpose this to a digital world and ask yourself where we are most likely to reach out for social support now. For many, it's social media. This can create vicious cycle where problematic social media use becomes a habit feeding our anxiety.

---

19. McCall, "Media Spread Fear," ¶2.
20. Marino et al., "Associations."

Looking for social support on social media doesn't always work. A recent study showed that real-life social support helps with anxiety and depression but support on social media typically does not.[21]

Even so, we'll be offering an example soon that reminds us that real-life support can happen on social media, and in ways that are beautiful and good.

> **Pause:** Have we made you anxious? We're feeling it too, so we know it's time to turn toward something more hopeful and invitational. Take a moment to reflect on what you hope to find in the rest of this chapter.
>
> Now take another moment and imagine the relationship between fear and courage. Explore it for a moment, and then we invite you to read on.

An Invitation to Courage

Fear is a slippery thing to describe, and so is courage. Coupling fear with an invitation to courage reflects their pairing throughout human history, from Aristotle's virtue ethics and the ancient Enneagram to Old and New Testament Scriptures,[22] though courage can easily be confused with loud, fast things.

If we think fear is something to be mastered and conquered through sheer willpower, then courage takes the shape of bravado, much like a testosterone-infused action movie where the protagonist walks into the flames with an automatic weapon in each hand. We expect our hero to walk through fire, vanquish all foes, and emerge victorious enough to star in a sequel a few years from now. Sometimes the stars show up in so many sequels that it seems they have triumphed over aging itself.

The No Fear clothing line appeared in the late twentieth century, founded by several extreme sports enthusiasts, then peaked around the turn of the century. The company also sold energy drinks in case you needed a "mother lode" of caffeine (the name of one No Fear beverage). A 2011 bankruptcy and 2021 relaunch make the brand less prevalent than in previous decades, but the not-so-subtle sentiment of having "No

---

21. Meshi and Ellithorpe, "Problematic Social Media Use."

22. For example, see Deut 31:6; Josh 2:11, 7:5b; 2 Sam 4:1, 13:38, 17:10; 1 Chr 22:13, 28:20; 2 Chr 32:7; Matt 14:27; Mark 6:50; John 7:13.

Fear" on a skateboard or motocross shirt remains: be fast and tough and conquer whatever stands in your way.

Wear "No Fear" on your T-shirt if you want, but that's not what *we* mean. Our invitation is to a slower, quieter sort of courage.

Look for two things in the pages that follow distinguishing our invitation from an action movie. First, we're not assuming courage conquers fear. Life brings its share of fear, and sometimes we can't outrun or conquer it. In these moments courage calls us to walk forward, knowing we lack control over uncertainties, dangers, and failures. One of our students recently referred to courage as walking ahead with wobbly knees. That's the invitation we offer, preferably with someone walking alongside you.

Second, we suggest the best pathway to courage is not willpower or muscularity but love. Love has a way of showing up everywhere for those who follow Jesus, as it shows up everywhere in the Bible. The apostle John writes that "perfect love expels all fear" (1 John 4:18). Love may not be our first thought when we think of fear or courage, though this is our invitation—to glimpse how love leads to a quiet, peaceful sort of courage that outlasts and outshines even our greatest fears.

Walking with Wobbly Knees

Some days carry fear, even for those who write books about being slow to fear. Sometimes those difficult days morph into sleepless nights, where old conversations and new imaginings ricochet fiercely inside the brain. When sleep finally comes, the ricocheting doesn't exactly stop, which leads to restless sleep and restive mornings. Then, once in awhile, those edgy mornings include a scheduled kayaking outing with one's spouse, which just doesn't sound very appealing to an agitated man without much sleep who is carrying around unresolved worries. (Okay, we're talking about a real person here.)

On this very real morning, after loading our twenty-five-year-old blue Dagger kayaks in the pickup and starting down the road, the gray Oregon clouds opened and spilled all over our windshield. For whatever reason, the impulse to turn back toward our warm home didn't win, so we ventured onward despite my grumpy reluctance. After backing down the Dayton Landing ramp, unloading the Daggers, and adorning ourselves and our dog with life jackets, we launched into the quiet flow of the Yamhill River. And almost immediately, the clamor quieted. The rain stopped. Birds sang in harmony with the quiet sway of the water as Lisa and I paddled gently downstream. We moved silently forward in the gentle breeze at first, but then we began to speak our thoughts. We wondered about a strange parasitic growth at the top of a towering Douglas fir. We remembered the history of our old kayaks and all the times we have found comfort in their shells. We noticed the soaring hawks overhead and joked about how our little dog thinks he protects us when it is very obviously the other way around.

This story of going on our planned kayaking excursion despite rain and grumpiness may not sound like a description of courage. Yet this quiet, slow sort of courage is the kind that we can find any day we choose to move forward into the rainy uncertainty of a new day, carrying our anticipations, troubles, and questions as we continue our long journey toward faith, hope, and love.

Courage begins by honestly seeing and naming our fears, recognizing we cannot outrun them.

The courage the disciples mustered in the aftermath of Jesus' death and resurrection set the world afire—but they didn't know it would turn out that way. They paced the room where they were staying with fear and without clarity, cloaked in uncertainty about all they had known and believed during three years of ministry with Jesus, and with profound questions about their own futures. Something changed when Jesus showed up in the room, not because he explained everything to their satisfaction or offered reassurance about what would happen next, but just because—against all odds—he stood in their midst. The disciples went on to transform the world with news of a loving God who is ever present in our suffering and fear and whose love nudges the world, keeping it moving toward God's ultimate end. As they initially feared, most of the disciples died as martyrs, and they did so having walked courageously and faithfully into the unknown.

Most of us won't change the world as the disciples did, but we all face questions, uncertainties, and fear.[23] Facing death may be the most fearsome walk of all, and it awaits each of us.

Early in the writing of this book, our friend David went with his wife, Carol, to the emergency room because of pain in his left knee. David assumed it was a problem with his cruciate ligament, but within

---

23. Moore and Williamson, "Universal Fear of Death."

twenty-four hours David and Carol were staring at a much more serious diagnosis—terminal Acute Myeloid Leukemia (AML).

There is nothing particularly unusual about dying, but right away we noticed something unique about how David and Carol faced this deep sadness. David, a former college professor and a technophile, kept his extensive network of friends, family, former colleagues, and students informed by Facebook. Whenever anyone would post words about his healing, David replied with kind, clear words of finitude. A friend posted, "Hope that healing will be fast and complete!" David replied, "Unfortunately, healing is not in my future. With this leukemia the prognosis is about one year." Another friend posted, "Play your trombone for the other patients! That would be a blast." David responded, "It would be, but I'm afraid my trombone playing days are over. I could play some good trombone music from my playlist." A few weeks later, David gave the Selmer Paris tenor trombone his parents bought him in high school to another musician, describing it as a "hard but necessary goodbye."

Even amid hard goodbyes, David steps forward, living fully into each day. He walks with Carol or their son, Steve, every day. He follows sporting events, especially those involving Baylor University, where he once taught. He released a new book based on his many years of journal editing. He celebrates his dear family and the friends who have journeyed with him through life.

David agreed to talk with me (Mark) about courage, but being with people is difficult when one has a terminal disease that degrades the immune system. One Wednesday afternoon two months after diagnosis, we each logged in to Zoom and had a candid conversation about living and dying. I asked him about his sturdy way of facing death, and David reminded me that one doesn't suddenly become a different person when faced with a terminal diagnosis. We die as we live, and for David living has always involved facing hard realities with courage and honesty, all the way back to his family roots on Chisel Finger Ridge in Appalachian West Virginia.

> Stuff happens, and you deal with it. And there is a Christian faith behind this, but not the kind that says, "Oh, God's going to fix this." Bad things do happen to good people. So in dealing with this news, it's a blow, but it's not so much a fear of death, per se, but the reminder of the preciousness of people.

David takes the necessary risks to see family, and he stays connected with others through phone and social media. If we are hard on social media at times in this book, it's important to remember that it plays an important role in our world too.

Carol, a nurse educator and an artist with words, posts frequently on Caring Bridge about this season of walking with David. Her posts are wise and courageous:

> I am always surprised and stunned at how averse to speaking honestly about nearly everything we are. We seem to fear the possibility that someone will truly see us. See our foibles, our fears, our doubts, our anger. So we cover up so many things.
>
> I am also stunned by our euphemisms for death. Passed, gone to glory, graduated up, resting in the arms of God, joined the church triumphant. They are endless. What keeps us from sharing the truth? For those of us who have lost someone it is a void, an emptiness. For the person who is dying it is the anticipation of the loss of all that they know and love. None of that is easy, lovely, flowery. Yes, for the Christian there is the assurance of life beyond this life. But folks right now this is the life I have. . . .
>
> Life is wonderful but it can also be raw and painful. I think we are called to see it in its fullness. To share ourselves with others in our fullness. To not deny others the benefit of being able to benefit from our struggles. To keep working at being as fully human as we can be.

Carol and David are walking the journey of death, as we all will someday. None of us will escape this plight, even if contemporary Western culture has worked to keep it mostly invisible. We're generally uncomfortable talking about dying, and, with aid from medical institutions, usually choose to postpone it at almost any cost.

Fortunately, we get some practice dying. Unless we die suddenly, how we face the fears associated with our endgame will be shaped by how we have faced smaller deaths along the way, such as the loss of a relationship, an affiliation, our health, our sense of who we thought we were, or the life we imagined we would live. The fear that comes with each loss emerges from the uncertainty of what lies ahead, facing into the unknown of something that may be worse than what we have comfortably known.

We are all on wobbly kneed journeys toward giving up dreams and fantasies, toward seeing ourselves honestly as flawed and fragile creatures, toward making peace with disappointments, and ultimately toward dying. Courage is the thread that runs through each of these journeys, offering hope for whatever step is required next.

Love as a Pathway to Courage

If the loud, fast courage of our time has the superhero walking into the flames, it's almost always a male walking alone. The slower, quieter courage we have in mind often involves having someone by our side. Carol bears witness to this in a Caring Bridge entry:

> When I had my breast cancer 9 years ago, I had to go to St. Vincent Hospital (where David is now going for his chemo) five days a week for six weeks. David went with me every time except one when he was out of town. Now that it is his turn to go for treatment for something quite serious, I have gone with him. We are capable of going by ourselves. The extra person really plays very little role in what actually happens while there. Yet we never questioned going along. In the Indigo Girls' *The Power of Two* there is a phrase about hard times being easier when you multiply life by the power of two. I know that not all folks I love and care about have that luxury, but it struck me what we are doing, dealing with the hardness by just sitting beside each other in the car.

Carol rightly names that many people don't have caring spouses for times such as this, but we hope for, maybe even ache for, someone—a friend, neighbor, pastor, mentor, family member, spiritual companion, or therapist—to walk alongside us in life, especially in the most difficult seasons.[24] As we noted before, Jesus' disciples developed and maintained courage in a fellowship of love, a sense of belonging and connection that kept them from feeling alone in their fears.

So also today, we find strength in knowing we're not alone in the fearful moments of life. Some in our Friends tradition describe this as *turning*: "Living in the Spirit within a supportive, faithful fellowship gives us courage and guidance to let our lives speak, even when we are afraid, and helps us turn toward each other and toward the Light."[25]

---

24. David moved in and out of remission with his leukemia before dying on June 8, 2024. The word "courage" showed up often during his memorial service. Carol now bravely walks her arduous journey of grief.

25. Friends Bulletin Corporation, *Faith and Practice*, 98.

Fellowship offers a place to turn in our most fearful moments, toward one another and toward God, touching our deep longings to know and be known.

I (Lisa) sat with Marcia, one of my directees, who had acquired the leadership of a team of engineers. COVID-19 challenges, unrest in the organization, and stormy political and social winds contributed to the turmoil in her department. Extra responsibilities fell to Marcia as people flailed in their own efforts to stay afloat. Marcia is a strong, courageous woman who can (and does) hold a lot together, evidenced by the full support she has from her superiors. For the first time since her daughter nearly died some years earlier, I saw her fearful, unsure she could do what was necessary to keep herself from unraveling and to meet the expectations of her job. When I asked what she needed most in this moment, she paused before replying, "To not be—to not feel—alone in this."

Marcia didn't need or want to be rescued, and she didn't need or want to quit, but she knew she needed to turn toward fellowship, that supportive and friendly affiliation with those who share our interests. She needed to know she was not alone.

Maybe courage is more about harmony than singing a stunning solo, about being collaborative and communicative rather than strong and silent. Perhaps courage flows out of love more than bravado, through joining others in dark and dangerous times.

Master storytellers often weave fellowship and friendship into the tapestry of their epic tales. In *The Lord of the Rings,* J. R. R. Tolkien's tale of Middle Earth, hobbits Frodo Baggins and Samwise Gamgee (a small people who prefer tending gardens and drinking ale to fighting), get swept into a battle for the fate of Middle Earth. They are chosen not because of their strength or swagger but because of their fortitude and friendship.

The depth of Frodo and Sam's friendship and love keeps readers rooting for them. Fans of this tale know that friendship keeps them persevering despite the calamities they encounter, their constant fear of what is ahead, and their longings for home. The task of destroying the ring of power is primarily Frodo's, whose utter disinterest in power makes him the only one able to carry it. But Frodo's disinterest in power, along with his fortitude and courage, are not enough. He needs companions—a fellowship, as it were: eight others who begin the quest with him, bringing him near the doors of Mordor. In the end he has only the steady presence of Sam, and Sam is enough.

At one hopeless moment in the movie, Sam offers a heartrending monologue about darkness always eventually passing and the good in the world being worth fighting for. An Internet search will show how popular the words have become in memes and artwork. But in Tolkien's original passage, Sam doesn't offer quite as much optimism. Tolkien, an Englishman who fought in World War I and lived through the Great Depression and World War II, wrote as one who had not only lived through dark times when you don't know how the story—and your part in it—are going to end, but saw people choose to live courageously and keep walking toward hope, toward turning a thing around in spite of the odds. That takes fortitude and courage, made easier with a companion. At a particularly dark moment in Frodo and Sam's journey, they have the following conversation:

> "I don't like anything here at all," said Frodo, "step or stone, breath or bone. Earth, air and water all seem accursed. But so our path is laid."
> "Yes, that's so," said Sam. "And we shouldn't be here at all. . . . But I suppose it's often that way. The brave things in the old tales and songs, Mr. Frodo: adventures, as I used to call them. I used to think that they were things the wonderful folk in the stories went out and looked for. . . . But that's not the way of it with the tales that really mattered. . . . Folk seem to have been just landed in them—their paths were laid that way, as you put it. But I expect they had lots of chances, like us, of turning back, only they didn't. . . . We hear about those as just went on—and not all to a good end, mind you; at least not to what folk inside a story and not outside it call a good end."[26]

Frodo and Sam came to expect that they would die, even if, against all odds, they were successful in their task to Mordor. Courage and fortitude kept them from turning back. It did not keep them from experiencing fear.

When you walk into fear, even with wobbly knees, having another person with you provides mental and emotional strength—head and heart strength—that empowers your knees to keep going when outcomes are uncertain. Yes, sometimes we must walk stretches of that path alone, but fear is more easily faced in the company of a friend or two.

---

26. Tolkien, *Two Towers*, 320–21.

At one time or another we all find ourselves in a fearful story. When that happens, bravery and pluck will help, but the center of the story is love. Again, from our Friends tradition:

> Courage is a fundamental act of faith.... As we continue letting go of our fears and following the motions of love, we are led into a new, more abundant and joy-filled life. Although this life is not always free of pain, it is graced with a courage that will endure any adversity.[27]

The phrase "motions of love" may be confusing at first, as if we're merely going through the motions of something rather than deeply experiencing it. But this has a particular meaning emerging from the work of the eighteenth-century Quaker John Woolman, whom we introduced in chapter 2. As Woolman embarked on a peacekeeping mission to speak with Native Americans in 1763, he felt compelled by God's motion of love to better understand indigenous life.[28] Love is no passive emotion but a compelling force that moves us to action. Love changes us, and it changes the world.

One of the most compelling exemplars of this turn toward love is Julian, the fourteenth-century English anchoress of Norwich (one who lived in seclusion in a cell attached to a church and dedicated herself to prayer and devotion) and the first woman known to publish a book in English, which she wrote out of deep suffering. She lived her entire life during the Hundred Years' War (which lasted 116 years) between England and France. She survived several bouts of the bubonic plague in her village and likely lost her family, perhaps a child and husband, during one of them.[29] During an illness that nearly killed her, she had the visions that became her life's work. Part of her vision involved hearing God say, "I may make all things well, I can make all things well and I will make all things well and I shall make all things well, and you shall see for yourself that all manner of things shall be well."[30]

The repetition is intentional.

Her hearing "all manner of things shall be well" emerged out of her pressing questions about sin and its destructive consequences. She came to a humble recognition that God will make something good and

---

27. Friends Bulletin Corporation, *Faith and Practice*, 100–101.
28. Kershner, "(Com)Motion of Love."
29. Frykholm, *Julian of Norwich*, 21–28.
30. Earle, *Julian of Norwich*, 87–89.

redemptive of sin, that God's love is far greater than the most horrible sin. She gained confidence that the worst evils against humanity, creatures, and creation itself would be redeemed and made well.

Julian's confidence came from an assurance that all creation had been brought forth in divine love, was sustained by that love, and would, in the fullness of time, be brought in love to unity under Christ.[31] Her work reflects the teachings of Paul, perhaps most clearly expressed in his letter to the church of Ephesus: "He [God] made known to us the mystery of his will according to his good pleasure, which he purposed in Christ, to be put into effect when the times reach their fulfillment—to bring unity to all things in heaven and on earth under Christ" (Eph 1:9–10, NIV). The church, over the centuries, has recognized and validated Julian's work.

God's love is the center of every story, even the most frightening and difficult ones. This radical claim of the good news seeks to remind us that all begins and ends with God's love, declared first in the teachings of John and Paul, and carried throughout the teaching of the church.

I (Lisa) remember a conversation with my friend Laura, on the porch of a vacated house where her family was staying temporarily when Oregon fires drove them from their home. I brought some fresh produce from our gardens, eggs from our hens, a jar of flowers, and some homemade jam, knowing their inadequacy to fill any real need but knowing enough to hope such a gesture might offer another kind of sustenance. Through masks intended to stave off COVID-19 (though not the fires' smoke), we talked of literal fires and the figurative political and social ones. How could we not? We were in the home stretch of 2020, wondering what our nation would look like when we crossed the finish line.

Laura lives deeply, and I have touched that depth in my friendship with her. As I left, I said, "I know that all will be well," and she paused until I looked her in the eyes, and then she said, "All *is* well." I held her gaze, nodded, and repeated, "All is well," and we touched the deep truth of it together for a moment—that exquisite existential truth that already all is well—though it is a hard truth to hold, and even touching it for a moment requires a fellowship of two, not one, to embrace the mystery of things being very much not well while acknowledging in a deeper place things already are.

The struggle to hold that tension rightly feels wobbly. Yet this struggle, too, is part of our journey from fear to courage.

---

31. Earle, *Julian of Norwich*, 22.

God does not promise to remove the circumstances making us fearful, nor to remove the fear itself. What God guarantees is twofold. First, God promises that we are never alone. God is as present to us as our heartbeat, our breath. God is above us, beneath us, around us, and within us. God experiences our fear with us, including all the firings of our sympathetic nervous system that keep us on high alert. God holds us and our fear and will not let us go. Yes, it helps to have another human walking with us. That's what David and Marcia needed, and Laura and you and me. We are made for relationship, and a cord of three strands is not easily broken for a reason. We have a cloud of witnesses who have gone before us and are cheering us on. Even when we feel alone, we are not alone. The transcendent God of the universe, who created it, is also immanent, present everywhere. The Word who spoke it into being holds it together and is ever with us in it.

Second, God promises that indeed, all shall be made well. It can't help but be so. Bonaventure, the thirteenth-century Italian theologian, spoke similar words as Julian's a hundred years before her. He summarized God's movement in the universe in three steps: From out of God's love all things are brought into being. Since all things emanate from God, all things are a manifestation of God, reflecting and expressing something of God. Finally, all things will return to God, from whom they have come.[32] This is a long and optimistic view of history. It allows for the unfolding of tragic eras and ones that blossom with goodness, the comingling of suffering and joy. Because all shall be well, we can, with courage and fortitude, choose to lean into the long arc of history as we walk the short bit that is ours to traverse and say, yes, all is well. Wanting that and doing it are, of course, two different things, which is why we practice at a thing.

Remember the standardized test questions from school that would ask you to read a passage and then identify the main point? We began this chapter with the Porter's Gate song "There is nothing to fear, nothing to fear, for I am with you always." What is the main point of this chorus?

A. There is nothing to fear.

B. I am with you always.

Answer A is bound to disappoint because we can always find plenty of things to fear. Sometimes they may seem so overwhelming that it feels

---

32. Rohr, *Eager to Love*, 166.

difficult to breathe. Answer B carries the promise of love because if God is with us always, then even the circumstances and threats evoking fear are not as powerful as we might imagine. If we see answer B as the main point, then there truly is nothing to fear and all will, indeed, be well.

Two practices come to mind. One is *simply* (though not *simple*) the practice of fellowship and friendship, the forging of ties with others who will walk with us when the way is dark. Much more could be said about that, and whole books written on it. We are enormously grateful to have forged friendships with people who walk with us, and have allowed us to walk with them, when our paths have been bleak and hard. And we'll leave it at that.

The second is a practice of relinquishing control where our presumed need or desire for it is to manage fear. If we are in control, we can hope (falsely) that we will not be abandoned or hurt or lose anything that matters to us. But letting go of control is counterintuitively a way to release fear's power over us. Doing so acknowledges that we do *not* have the control we think we do. In choosing to release our perception of control, we can find ourselves held in the arms of God.

Relinquishing Practice

The Relinquishing Practice is a cousin of the Welcoming Prayer,[33] which we introduce in the next chapter. Consider this a precursor, with a focus on relinquishing.

1. *Quiet.* Put yourself in a quiet place and begin by taking some deep breaths. Perhaps when you inhale, imagine God saying, "I love you," and when you exhale, say, "I love you" back to God. Feel yourself settle into your chair as you exchange "I love yous."

2. *Invite.* When you have quieted, name your fear and welcome it to this moment. Speak to it: "I see you, cancer" or "I feel the weight of you, debt." Perhaps it is a fear regarding your work, a broken or breaking relationship, the consequences of an addiction, or crises in your township or the world. Allow yourself to fully feel and experience what comes as you name your fear. Does your chest tighten? Your throat? Your jaw? Do you feel shaky, teary, jittery? Sit with those fears and feelings and acknowledge them.

---

33. Contemplative Outreach, "Welcoming Prayer."

3. *Relinquish.* Thomas Keating suggests reciting the following four statements.[34] After saying them all, note if one resonates more with your situation and stay with that one. Repeat it slowly. Watch yourself letting go. Imagine what would be different if you let go.

- I let go of my desire for security and survival.
- I let go of my desire for esteem and affection.
- I let go of my desire for power and control.
- I let go of my desire to change the situation.

You do not relinquish a thing once, but over and over. If this is helpful, consider making a practice of it. Perhaps begin or end your day with it. After a while you will find your relinquishment statement accompanies you throughout the day, serving as an invitation to let go when you feel yourself getting tangled up yet again in fear.

It's okay if your knees wobble a bit. That's what knees do in fearful times.

---

34. Godspace, "Focus—Welcome—Let Go," ¶3.

Slow Ponderings

1. We began the chapter telling the story of a song that declares, "There is nothing to fear, for I (God) am with you," which comes from an Old Testament promise to a people in captivity (Isa 41:10). Now that you've made your way through the chapter, does it make any more sense that there can there be nothing to fear when there is so much to fear? How does God's promise to be with us help to reframe our fears?

2. Think of a time when your fear persisted even after the threat subsided. What kept the fear going, and what eventually allowed you to release it? Or have you?

3. Reflect on your use of social media and news outlets on the Internet. How do they impact your experiences of fear and courage?

4. Does the optimism of Julian of Norwich and Bonaventure resonate with you or feel like escapism from real pain? If the latter, what is it that makes their optimism seem unrealistic to you?

5. Do you have friends who can walk with you no matter which fear hounds you? If not, where do you find your courage, and what compensates for an absence of a supportive "fellowship"? What steps might you be able to take toward trusting someone with your fear?

6. When you imagine approaching the end of your life, what will courage look like for you? What practices might you engage in now to help you face death with courage?

Chapter 4

Slow to Anger: An Invitation to Empathy

Steve Bartman sat in Section 4, Row 8, Seat 113 at Wrigley Field on October 4, 2003, when he instinctively reached for a foul ball. If you've ever been to a baseball game and seen a foul soaring in your direction, you realize that Bartman did what most of us would have done—in some blur of excitement, disbelief, and self-protection, he reached out to catch the ball. But on that fateful day, as the Cubs were ahead 3-0 in the eighth inning and five outs away from their first World Series in fifty-eight years, left fielder Moises Alou might have caught the ball if it weren't for the fans in Section 4, Row 8. Alou showed his frustration, and the television crew zoomed in on Bartman. The Cubs went on to lose the game, and they were later eliminated from the National League Championship Series, perpetuating the mythical curse against the Cubs. The supposed curse started in 1945 when a local tavern owner tried to bring his billy goat into the game and was denied, leading to the tavern owner declaring, "The Cubs ain't going to win no more."

Billy goats and curses aside, Bartman's life would never be the same. His picture instantly flashed everywhere—the wire-frame glasses, blue Cubs hat, green scarf to shield him from the October Chicago chill, headphones so he could listen to the game as he watched it, and the face of a genuinely remorseful, deeply loyal Cubs fan who couldn't believe what had just happened. But people weren't interested in his remorse or sincerity because they were looking for a scapegoat even more than a billy goat. Security officers escorted the suddenly infamous Bartman from the field as fans threw beer and yelled obscenities at him. Disgruntled acquaintances posted Bartman's name and address online, and angry fans, well, fanned one another's vitriol, sending hate mail and death threats. Police guarded Bartman's home, and after issuing a heartfelt apology, Bartman went into deep silence, though not into the witness protection program, as the Illinois governor mockingly suggested.

One can't help but wonder how Bartman's life might have been different if he hadn't been vilified for a reflexive thing that any of us might have done. Pat Looney knows. He was sitting close to Bartman, and Looney had already determined that if he could get the foul ball, it would go to his firstborn child (Looney's wife was pregnant). But his grasp fell two inches short. The ball and ensuing infamy ended up deflecting to Bartman instead.[1]

Bartman's story reminds us how quickly anger can erupt and how easily it becomes unfair, impulsive, and damaging. If this were the full story about anger, then living well would entail shutting off our anger completely. But living well is more complicated than this because anger, like speaking and fear, is inevitable, necessary, and good in some situations. To suggest otherwise would be to oversimplify the complexity of human experience.

A case can be made for anger, as we are about to do. Still, we live in a day so accepting and welcoming of anger that we might easily overlook the potential damage it causes. After making a case for anger, we will argue for slow. Then we will consider how challenging and valuable it can be to move from angry self-interest toward empathetic awareness of others.

The Case for Anger

Poet and philosopher David Whyte describes anger as a form of compassion that points us toward what we value. Anger breaks into awareness when we can see something is not right.[2]

Shortly after Easter in 1944 a fifteen-year-old high school student delivered a speech in Dublin, Georgia, titled "The Negro and the

---

1. Drehs, "Almost Famous," ¶2.
2. Whyte, *Consolations*, 13.

Constitution" as part of an oratory competition sponsored by the Elks. Later that evening as he returned victorious to Atlanta, the teenager and his teacher, Sarah Grace Bradley, were told by a White bus driver to give up their seats for White passengers boarding the bus. Bradley and her student must not have moved quickly enough because the bus driver began shouting obscenities at them. Reluctantly, they stood for the ninety-mile trip back to Atlanta. The student later described that long trip home as "the angriest I have ever been in my life."[3]

Any of us might feel annoyed in a situation like this—being asked to stand so another can sit—but for Martin Luther King Jr., this was about justice more than personal inconvenience. Each day he rode a bus across Atlanta to attend Booker T. Washington High School, where Blacks were to sit in back and Whites in front. Even in the absence of White passengers, those front seats were to remain empty, which meant many Black passengers had to stand in the aisle at the back of the bus, leaving empty seats at the front. King writes, "Every time I got on that bus I left my mind up on the front seat. And I said to myself, 'One of these days, I'm going to put my body up there where my mind is.'"[4] Throughout his life King demonstrated that anger could serve as a moral emotion pointing toward justice and equity.

The notion of a *moral emotion* requires explanation. Research psychologists have developed many theories and taxonomies to explain our daily encounters with emotion. One recent study suggests we have twenty-seven different types of emotions, and the lines between them are more fuzzy than clear.[5] When something threatening happens around us, we typically experience either fear or anger. As described in chapter 3, fear causes us to retreat, escape, or avoid a situation. Anger causes us to stand our ground and fight back.

But in many ways anger is more complicated than fear because it has a moral dimension. Moral emotions help us monitor and maintain principled standards as individuals and as a society. Inward-facing moral emotions such as shame, guilt, and embarrassment help us manage our own behaviors as we experience or anticipate what we might feel if something about us were widely known.[6] Outward-facing moral emotions such

---

3. Carson, ed., *Autobiography*, 10.
4. Carson, ed., *Autobiography*, 9.
5. Cowen and Keltner, "Self-report."
6. Tangney et al., "Moral Emotions."

as anger, contempt, and disgust help us construct a civil society where people treat one another with respect, justice, and honor.[7]

Imagine the driver in front of you texts through most of a green light, causing you and those lined up behind you to miss the light and be delayed. In response, you feel angry, mostly because something you feel entitled to has been taken from you and perhaps because you intuitively know that bad things happen in a society where others selfishly ignore the needs of those around them. In response, you honk for a long time and yell and make hand motions. A few minutes later, as you pull into your driveway, you notice your new neighbor's car matches the one you just encountered, and you feel a sudden surge of embarrassment for how you acted. In the first case, you experienced an outward-facing moral emotion based on how the other driver behaved, but now you are experiencing an inward-facing moral emotion based on how extremely you responded.

Is anger wrong in this example? Well, no. It's just what happens when something seems selfish and unfair. It shows up for the sake of personal and collective good. Is your reaction justified? That's a more complicated question because we live in a constant tug-of-war between self-interest and concern for others. Sometimes our perspectives can be quite shallow, such as wanting our team to win the baseball game, whereas other times our values can be quite noble, such as treating all human beings with dignity regardless of their skin color. Our deep desires for justice are especially compelling when they are empathic, seeking justice for the other as much as for oneself, loving our neighbors as ourselves. When we respond in anger quickly, we don't often distinguish well between the shallow, selfish desires of the moment and the empathic justice that defines civil society.

Perhaps a continuum would help.

---

7. Lomas, "Anger as a Moral Emotion."

Anger as Moral Emotion

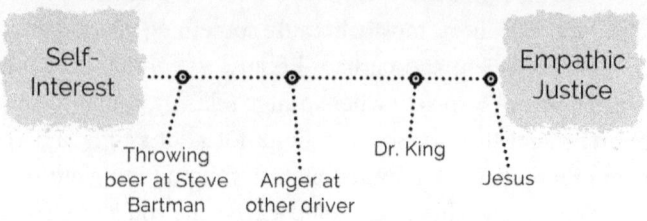

We take Jesus to be the ultimate exemplar of empathic justice, so he shows up at the far end of this continuum. Jesus spoke angry words to and about religious leaders who cared more about their rules than people's welfare, and most famously when merchants and money changers took advantage of weary sojourners coming to worship in the temple. We also see chastisement, maybe a hint of anger, when Jesus' disciples tried to shoo away some parents who came with their children, hoping for Jesus to touch and bless their little ones. These moral matters teach us lasting truths about compassion, empathy, equity, and concern for others.

Most of us can quickly discern that throwing beer at Steve Bartman belongs near the end of the continuum where self-interest rules the moment. One can imagine even more extreme self-interest, so we keep the baseball example a few millimeters away from the edge.

Most often our anger falls somewhere between these extremes. None of us are as pure as Jesus, so our anger is a mixed bag where self-interest and empathic justice get stirred together in varying proportions. Dr. King's anger was mostly directed toward the moral good of society. The long honk at the traffic light likely has a bit more self-interest mixed in.

Today's popular wisdom is that people should discover and express their anger. This seems partly right. It is usually better to admit our anger than to deny it. If we suppress anger, it can have damaging effects on our relationships and our individual health.[8] At the same time, anger can be destructive if experienced too often or if expressed poorly.[9] Locating and

8. Staicu and Cuțov, "Anger and Health Risk Behaviors," 372–75.
9. Suinn, "Terrible Twos."

expressing our anger is probably helpful, but if we set up camp and live there, it won't work out well for anyone.

Popular interpretations of the oft-quoted verse from the apostle Paul to the Ephesians—"Be angry but do not sin" (Eph 4:26, NRSV)—may overstate Paul's intentions, especially if we focus mostly on the first two words. Paul himself seemed to struggle with anger. Before his conversion, he felt rage toward Christians, and then after his conversion, he still experienced deep disagreements that likely evolved into anger, such as his disputes with Barnabas and Peter. Perhaps a better interpretation of the Ephesians verse is that Paul acknowledges anger will happen, but we should be careful with it. It's not so much "be angry" as "do not sin." The New Living Translation makes this clearer: "And 'don't sin by letting anger control you.' Don't let the sun go down while you are still angry, for anger gives a foothold to the devil." Just a few verses later Paul instructs his readers, "Get rid of all bitterness, rage, anger, harsh words, and slander, as well as all types of evil behavior. Instead, be kind to each other, tenderhearted, forgiving one another, just as God through Christ has forgiven you."

At its best, anger can help build moral societies and healthy relationships. At its worst, it can tear them apart.

> **Pause:** Reading about anger can be agitating because the words come alongside personal experiences and poignant emotions. Take a moment to notice any tension you may be feeling. Where do you feel it in your body? What other emotions are stirred as you name and feel your agitation? Sit and feel the emotions stirred without judging or analyzing them just now. Doing so honors the part of you that remembers, feels, and holds pain while also disarming negative emotion that tends to hide in the shadows.
>
> After a moment or two, take a few intentional deep breaths. Inhale God's grace and love. As you exhale, imagine releasing the tensions and the emotions behind them.

The Case for Slow

Anger goes like this: *I am upset about a thing, and something needs to be done.* In its best form we take the urgent emotion of anger and help society become more just, but there are all sorts of ways this can go wrong.

Throwing beer at Steve Bartman does not make the world better. We are walking a tightrope by suggesting that anger be tempered or slowed, knowing that sometimes anger isn't expressed when it needs to be. There is a time and place for moral outrage. But given how much anger is welcomed and encouraged in today's world, our invitation here is to slow down our tendency toward anger and to pursue empathy.

To slow this down, let's parse the two parts of anger and consider them separately. First, *I am upset about a thing*. As already mentioned, it is better to be honest and open to our feelings than to suppress them and pretend they don't exist. If we're upset about something, it's good to pay attention and acknowledge it.

Beyond this lies a dense morass of nuance. Is it best to speak aloud the feeling of anger when we experience it? That depends on circumstance, culture, family systems, how regulated we can be when expressing anger, how the other person might respond, and multiple other variables. There is also the matter of intensity. Given the offense, are we feeling the right amount of upset? Where on the scale between cataclysmic and trivial does this incident fall? There's also the complexity of our own histories and past experiences. Might our feelings of anger be less about this current situation than triggering some previous one we have faced in life? Might we be projecting onto another some of the inner conflicts we face ourselves? If we accuse our friend of being petty and vindictive, it helps protect us from seeing our own history of overreacting to small offenses. It is often easier to be angry at others than to face our own shortcomings. Sometimes we express anger (an outward-facing moral emotion) to protect ourselves from feeling shame (an inward-facing moral emotion). We might show anger at our spouse for not reminding us that their parents were coming for the weekend rather than face our shame at forgetting. The convoluted connections between inward- and outward-facing moral emotions are often challenging to discern and pull apart.

The second part, *something needs to be done*, also carries complexity. What needs to be done, and how quickly, and at what level of magnitude? These decisions need time and wisdom and are rarely evaluated well on the spur of the moment. Consider several examples roiling in the news not so very long ago, during the pandemic, and wonder with us why the *something* that *needs to be done* easily exceeds the magnitude of the offense:

1. A man in his sixties throws a temper tantrum at a grocery store because they don't have the imported cheese he wants.[10]
2. When Chipotle workers announce they need to close the store because of a staffing shortage, a customer pulls a gun out of her bag and says someone needs to make her food or there's going to be a problem.[11]
3. Amid a frustrating pandemic, a twenty-year-old man punches a female flight attendant twice in the face on a flight from New York to Orange County,[12] capping off a year of over five thousand unruly passenger reports on US flights, which resulted in Federal Aviation Administration fines exceeding a million dollars.[13]
4. A parent allegedly slaps her child's school bus driver across the face.[14]
5. A controversy over customers' COVID-19 vaccination status leads to racial slurs and a brawl outside a Manhattan Italian restaurant.[15]

Calling anger a moral emotion is misleading if the reaction turns out to be more outrageous than whatever precipitated the anger in the first place.

Overreacting to anger has always been a problem, and it is amplified exponentially by the speed of electricity. If it weren't for alternating current and all its implications—television, live sports broadcasts, instant replays, the Internet—Steve Bartman might have led a reasonably normal life. A camera operator at the Cubs game chose to zoom in on Bartman after that fateful foul ball, and the producers opted to show that particular camera shot over and over. Online forums erupted, videos popped up everywhere, and a loyal Cubs fan's life was instantly and permanently damaged.

Twenty years later, we still have the speed of electricity to spread our vitriol, and we have progressed to even more effective platforms for accomplishing it. Twitter emerged three years after the Bartman incident and is now—with its new name, X—a prominent way to spread

---

10. Lyall, "Nation on Hold," ¶1–4.
11. 6ABC Action News, "'Give Me My Food,'" ¶1–5.
12. Chen and Schulz, "'One of the worst displays,'" ¶1–3.
13. Federal Aviation Administration, "FAA Fines," ¶1.
14. News8, "Did a Waterbury Parent?," ¶1–2.
15. De Freytas-Tamura, "Footage Reveals," ¶1–5.

moral outrage throughout the world. When researchers evaluated over twelve million tweets, they discovered that moral outrage is shaped by the norms of one's particular social network and then reinforced by that same network.[16] Stop for a moment to mull over how this works:

> Step 1: Our social media followers embrace certain norms around issues such as national debt, environmental sustainability, vaccination protocols, abortion, human sexuality, acceptable social behavior, and so on. The norms of our followers don't necessarily reflect larger social norms or even enduring truths. On many social media platforms we select a personalized network of followers.
>
> Step 2: If any of us express moral outrage on social media, it will likely be consistent with the norms of our particular network.
>
> Step 3: Each of our social networks will then reward us for our outrage by sharing or liking our post.

In one way this seems like common sense for an electronic, social media world. Of course we choose our own social media network, and of course they will be inclined to like what we post. But deliberate on the implications of this. Our anger is being shaped by the norms of the people whose approval we want, and the more outrage we muster, the more approval we gain. Social media multiplies this groupthink, resulting in a massive self-reinforcing circle that further polarizes the world.

The self-perpetuating nature of anger on social media is not lost on its advertisers. When Frances Haugen turned from being a Meta data scientist to a whistleblower providing thousands of documents to the Securities and Exchange Commission in 2021, she disclosed a document showing that when Facebook introduced six ways to react to a post in 2016 ("like," "love," "haha," "wow," "sad," "angry"), their algorithms gave five times as many points for a reaction emoji such as the angry face as for a thumbs-up like. As a result, posts that stirred up big emotions were more likely to show up high in a person's news feed than posts that stirred affection, joy, or empathy. Anger pays. Meta has since changed this algorithm, but it shows how easily we can be influenced and inflamed by the technology lurking behind our screens.[17]

Is it any surprise that we have become such an outraged, angry people? David Brooks, the *New York Times* columnist, once wrote an

---

16. Brady et al., "How Social Learning Amplifies."
17. Merrill and Oremus, "Five Points for Anger," ¶2–6.

article titled "The Cruelty of Call-Out Culture: How Not to Do Social Change." As Brooks suggests, the way we handle anger in today's call-out culture is not a helpful recipe for becoming more just or moral. It makes us worse, not better.

> Even the quest for justice can turn into barbarism if it is not infused with a quality of mercy, an awareness of human frailty and a path to redemption. The crust of civilization is thinner than you think.[18]

Many centuries before David Brooks, James, the brother of Jesus, asked his readers to be slow to anger because "human anger does not produce the righteousness God desires" (Jas 1:20).

Transforming Anger

We could debate for a long time whether anger is good or bad, but let's not, because it has potential for both. Anger happens. We're human beings with amygdalae, presumed to be the nervous system's perception and memory center for processing negative emotions like fear, anger, and sadness and positive ones like happiness, joy, and gratitude. We live in a broken world, so things will be unfair, provoking, and scary sometimes, and our emotions will be stirred. If Gallup poll data hold true, about one in four readers of this paragraph will have been angry yesterday.[19]

When angry, our fight-or-flight instinct will scream, *"Fight!"* with an exclamation point. How we respond to that instinct matters. Our initial impulse may point us toward self-interest, making us vulnerable to rash impulsive choices. Pulling a gun because of unavailable service at Chipotle or striking a flight attendant over frustration with a mask mandate or screaming obscenities at a baseball fan is not how we want to live. If we can slow down the process and be more deliberate about our response, anger can be transformed to a constructive force that improves relationships and societies.

Rather than asking whether anger is good or bad, we invite you toward another sort of question: *How might my responses to anger be transformed so that I think more about the welfare of others and less about myself?* This is an invitation to empathy, solidarity, and kindness, where anger sits boldly amid Christian virtues such as faith, hope, and love.

18. Brooks, "Cruelty of the Call-Out Culture," ¶18.
19. Ray, "2020 Sets Records for Negative Emotions," ¶2.

To regain perspective on anger as a transformative moral emotion, let's return to the deliberate ways of Martin Luther King Jr., who lived and worked before social media or instant replays, and once wrote, "Along the way of life, someone must have sense enough and morality enough to cut off the chain of hate and evil. The greatest way to do that is through love. I believe firmly that love is a transforming power than can lift a whole community to new horizons of fair play, goodwill, and justice."[20]

King certainly experienced anger, and with good reason. He was maligned, attacked, unfairly jailed, and vilified. Many White people rejected his efforts for social justice, and some Black people criticized his nonviolent methods as being too passive or ineffective. Writing about King's anger, Columbia Business School professor Hitendra Wadhwa said, "Great leaders often have a strong capacity to experience anger. It wakes them up and makes them pay attention to what is wrong in their environment, or in themselves. Without anger, they would not have the awareness or the drive to fix what is wrong."[21]

King sometimes snapped at people and showed impulsive outbursts of anger, as most of us do,[22] but what set King apart was the way he challenged himself to do better. He wanted to infuse love into his ministry, which transformed his inner narrative about anger.

In 1955, Dr. King served as spokesperson of a negotiating committee during the Montgomery bus boycott. The committee's goal was to work toward more equitable bus arrangements in Montgomery following the arrest of Rosa Parks. They asked for three things: courteous treatment toward Blacks; seating on a first-come, first-served basis, with Blacks sitting in the back of the bus first and then filling in forward as necessary; and hiring Black bus drivers for routes that contained mostly Black patrons. Over a series of meetings, it became clear that White city leaders were more interested in criticizing King and dividing his negotiating committee than considering his requests. After one difficult meeting, King wrote,

> That Monday I went home with a heavy heart. I was weighted down by a terrible sense of guilt, remembering that on two or three occasions I had allowed myself to become angry and indignant. I had spoken hastily and resentfully. Yet I knew that this was no way to solve a problem. "You must not harbor anger," I admonished myself. "You must be willing to suffer the

---

20. Carson, ed., *Autobiography*, 63.
21. Wadhwa, "Wrath of a Great Leader," ¶5.
22. Greenfieldboyce, "Power of Martin Luther King Jr.'s Anger," ¶20.

anger of the opponent, and yet not return anger. You must not become bitter. No matter how emotional your opponents are, you must be calm."[23]

Notice that King didn't deny his anger, nor did he harbor it or settle into a place of bitterness, but he resolved to hold the anger of others without returning it toward them. He failed at this sometimes, but his desire to move slowly and calmly in times of anger was evident throughout his public ministry.

If we've made this sound easy, it was not. On January 30, 1956, someone threw dynamite at the Kings' home where his wife, Coretta, and daughter Yolanda went about their evening while Dr. King led a church meeting elsewhere. After the dynamite exploded on his front porch, King rushed home to an angry crowd. He calmed the throng, but later that night, lying in bed, his anger rose strong:

> I could not get to sleep. While I lay in that quiet front bedroom, with a distant street lamp throwing a reassuring glow through the curtained window, I began to think of the viciousness of people who would bomb my home. I could feel the anger rising when I realized that my wife and baby could have been killed. . . . I was once more on the verge of corroding hatred. And once more I caught myself and said: "You must not allow yourself to become bitter."[24]

King experienced anger as a moral emotion. He felt it intensely at times, and then talked himself down from the precipice of rage, hatred, and bitterness so that he could help transform the world in positive ways.

King had personal struggles and lapses,[25] but still, the power of his public leadership increased because he learned how to move cautiously amid circumstances that might cause others to unravel in rage. His slow, patient, loving approach to social change has been both lauded and criticized before and after his death. Yet we hold him up as an exemplar of one who understood both the perils and transforming possibilities of anger.

Transforming our experiences of anger from self-interest toward some larger moral good requires slow intentionality as we press ourselves toward seeing from the vantage point of others. When our emotional brain tells us to fight, empathy does not come easily.

23. Carson, ed., *Autobiography*, 70.
24. Carson, ed., *Autobiography*, 80.
25. Preskar, "Adulterous Love Life," ¶3.

An Invitation to Empathy

As a longtime author, I (Mark) seldom encounter anything like writer's block, but I did when I reached this point in the chapter. I tried for days to turn the corner toward an invitation to empathy but couldn't find the words. Lisa could have written about this easily, but I asked her not to because I sensed this related to important work I needed to do. I set the chapter aside for a long time, attending to other chapters instead and taking care of other tasks. I couldn't progress on this chapter because of unfinished business in my own life.

> **Pause:** When it comes to anger, compassion, and empathy for others, does the idea of unfinished business feel familiar? Before reading more about my journey, you might want to take this opportunity to reflect on a relationship that holds complexity and unresolved tension for you. Simply call it to mind for now, and keep it in mind as you read my story.

Empathy wasn't the problem. I became a psychologist, in part, because empathy comes so naturally to me. At times in my career, I've had to work on being *less* empathetic, because too much empathy can be patronizing to others, freezing them in a state of inaction. My problem was anger. Anger woke me almost every night for nearly two years, surging into my thoughts repeatedly through each day.

It's hard to write about anger without slipping into self-protective defense mechanisms. Even now, after showing earlier drafts to Lisa and two caring friends, I wonder how my feelings and these words might be unfair.

Slowly, and with the help of a loving spouse, a gifted therapist, and a compassionate spiritual director, I'm learning to probe around the edges of my anger for greater nuance, to sink more deeply into my own culpability in events that cascaded into a strident reputational attack against me, and to lean toward forgiving. Releasing anger is hard, as is forgiveness, and words can be idealistic things, making arduous journeys seem easier than they are.

This is still unfinished business, at least partly. I write without having fully reached the other side, as one on a journey seeking to forgive. Everett L. Worthington Jr., who does groundbreaking work on forgiveness, distinguishes between *decisional* and *emotional* forgiveness. It took me over a year to decide to release my anger, and I am still working out the emotional complexity of that decision. My words here, which may shine a bit brighter than my lived reality, point toward a few lessons I am learning on this trek from anger back to empathy.

The Magnetic Pull of Self-Interest

The continuum we presented earlier in this chapter ranges from self-interest to empathic concern for justice in the world. One end is all about me, and the other is about the moral welfare of everyone. Who wouldn't want to be on the side of empathic justice when given such a choice, especially when the selfish alternative is presented with extreme examples such as pulling a gun in a fast-food restaurant?

Yes, we want to be people of empathic justice, but one lesson learned during my prolonged season of anger is that self-interested anger is compelling, a magnetic lure into a dark space. Day after day it drew me into fixated obsession with how I had been misunderstood, misrepresented, and maligned.

I had muted interest in the truthful parts of the allegations against me because the untruthful parts felt so unfair. Some days I became so preoccupied with the apology others owed me that I neglected my own need for repentance and change. Thoughts about forgiveness echoed incessantly in my head, but more about how hard it would be to forgive my offenders than about my personal need to be forgiven. David Brooks writes, "The wages of sin are sin."[26] Rather than looking at my own, it seemed so much easier to look at others'. If shame and anger are both moral emotions—one pointing inward and one outward—they were desperately tangled in my heart.

This went on for weeks, which turned into months. Many of them. Most days I could break out of my self-interest well enough to be reasonably attentive as a husband, son, father, grandfather, and friend, but even then, there were always reverberations reminding me how unfairly I had been treated. In the middle of too many nights, I Googled "long-term effects of anger" and read the bad news over and over, but willpower couldn't bring any real change.

The moments I had freedom from anger seemed random at the time, but looking back, I see a theme of kindness. While helping my daughter build a storage shed in her backyard, the two of us needed to

---

26. Brooks, *Second Mountain*, xxi.

lug a 150-pound double door up some outdoor stairs. Two women out for a walk noticed us getting started and offered to help. Likely they have long since forgotten this simple act of kindness, but to me it represented a day of liberation from self-focus as I pondered their generosity. Another day I noticed a "Be kind." bumper sticker in front of me as I sat at a traffic light. I noticed the two words, but especially the period. For a few days I felt freedom as I contemplated the punctuation after those good words: Be kind. *Period.*

On a walk with Lisa, I noticed an oak tree I had walked by thousands of times. This stately old oak seemed to beckon me: "See me. I am steady and old and strong. I am God's gift of kindness to you today." Another time, driving along a steep country road on a sunny winter's day, I turned a sharp corner to behold a gorgeous view of Mount Hood towering high within the Cascade Range. The mountain repeated the words of the oak tree.

An older, wiser friend, one of the kindest humans on earth, noticed my anguish and asked if she could pray for me. She did, as I wept tears of relief and hope. A friend who lives thousands of miles away reached out with resounding kindness. Another friend invited me to ride along in his cart for early morning golf outings, giving up his cherished times of solitude to offer gentle wisdom punctuated by his impressive fairway drives.

Few of these encounters with others involved the details of my situation. Human kindness doesn't require much detail.

These moments and people brought gifts of grace and freedom, and still my mind gravitated toward self-pity after a few hours or days, as if some dark magnet drew me back whenever I dared peek beyond the boundaries of my anger.

Descent and Lament

Sometimes the path back up first requires a downward trek.

We call our little farm Fern Creek because of the small stream that runs along the western edge, lined with forest and ferns. One area along the creek had been long covered with wild blackberries when Lisa found something beautiful beneath the brambles. She cleared away the stubborn foliage and planted hostas and ferns as I dug out steps in the steep hillside with an old, blue-handled shovel, hauling gravel and rock in by the bucketful to create a descending staircase. At the foot of this long outdoor staircase lies a pool, eight feet across and who knows how deep, with a small but steady waterfall from an underground culvert that burbles and splashes, sending its small contribution of underground spring and rain water toward the Chehalem watershed. My eight-year-old grandson and I built a bench at the base of the stairway, next to the fall and the pool, which now provides one of the "pausing benches" for reflection in Lisa's spiritual direction practice. She calls the stairway to the pool the Path of Descent.

Faithful Jews sang the Ascent Psalms in the Hebrew Scriptures as they climbed the road to Jerusalem on their way to celebrate sacred festivals. Maybe we need Descent Psalms too, songs for those times when joy and festivity seem far away. Perhaps the closest thing we have are the songs of lament scattered throughout the Hebrew psalter. Lament involves honestly speaking our pain to God, expressing our anger, revealing our deepest questions and doubts, always in the context of ongoing relationship. Lament is deeply intimate because it assumes God is near enough to hear and hold our sorrows and struggles, even if it sometimes feels like God has abandoned us.

Lisa's vision for a Path of Descent quickly became a place of solace and lament for me. Each time I travel down that path, I remember the long, angry season of life when I shoveled out twenty steps from a rocky hillside, then hauled in two tons of gravel and another ton of split-face cinder blocks. Transforming anger can be like that—arduous and painful and full of rocks that need moving. Then I sit on the bench that Wes and I built, listen to water falling into water, and ponder places of descent in life.

Author Philip Yancey notes how "Christians get very angry toward other Christians who sin differently than they do."[27] That's a fair diagnosis of my anger, and it took a lot of descending before I could see it. My antagonists sinned differently than me, reacting toward me because I sinned differently than them, and then I returned the anger, holding on to it for far too long.

Looking back now, I wonder if I could have found my way to empathy without descending into lament, honestly bringing my anger to God. That downward path prompted me to engage in some new spiritual practices, such as the Daily Examen (see chapter 5) and the Welcoming Prayer (later in this chapter).

---

27. Chellew, "Philip Yancey," 15.

One cold January afternoon I meandered down the Path of Descent, put in my AirPods, and listened repeatedly to a song I hadn't thought of for decades: Chuck Girard's "Lay Your Burden Down."[28] Somehow, I did just that for a few sweet moments. That day I decided to forgive, choosing a healing journey over a life of resentment, a journey that calls me often down that path of descent, where Chuck Girard's simple invitation keeps pointing me toward hope.

The Healing Gift of Empathy

Empathy heals, and not in a straight line. The famous twentieth-century psychologist Carl Rogers believed that therapy clients naturally heal when the therapist offers them empathy, genuineness, and positive regard. Person A is empathetic to person B, and person B prospers as a result. This may well be true, but it is a bit too linear to capture the healing gift of empathy.

Maybe a better image for empathy comes from the pool at the base of the Path of Descent. A steady flow of water falls into that pool, creating a rippling circle of motion. Outward, outward it moves, stirring the entire pool before moving on downstream.

Empathy moves and swirls and heals in multiple directions, and not just in the line from one person to another. As I move away from self-obsessed anger, I experience empathy for my accusers. I don't like what they did, and I can never excuse or condone it, but with empathy I can at least begin to understand. It also occurred to me how much endurance I asked of Lisa during those long months of anger, and I feel empathy for her, too. Getting my eyes off myself and my grievances also helps me remember and notice all the pain in the world around me.

Dr. Worthington's distinction between decisional and emotional forgiveness is just part of his important work on the science of forgiveness. His REACH model involves empathy as one of the first steps in the long, difficult journey of forgiving another:

---

28. Girard was one of the founding members of LoveSong, a well-known Christian rock band associated with the Jesus Movement in the early 1970s. He later went on to do solo recordings, including "Lay Your Burden Down." He has written a memoir in recent years: Girard, *Rock & Roll Preacher*.

R   Recall the hurt

E   *Empathize with the other*

A   Altruistic gift of forgiving

C   Commit to the ongoing work of forgiveness

H   Hold on to forgiveness when it starts to slip away[29]

Numerous studies show how well the REACH model works, and at least one points toward empathy as a key component of its success.[30] When someone brutally murdered Worthington's mother, he decided to forgive. If he can do that, then certainly I can forgive those who blended true and untrue words in constructing a narrative about me.

If empathy swirls rather than moving in a straight line, then empathy is not just about managing our anger toward others. Empathy also helps us understand others' anger toward us. In 1966, King lived and worked in Chicago's Lawndale community, which he described as an "island of poverty amidst an ocean of plenty" and "an emotional pressure cooker." It was there, in the pressure cooker, that King was booed for the only time in his career, and not by White supremacists but by Black men in his own movement:

> I went home that night with an ugly feeling. Selfishly, I thought of my sufferings and sacrifices over the last twelve years. Why would they boo one so close to them? But as I lay awake thinking, I finally came to myself, and I could not for the life of me have less than patience and understanding for those young people. For twelve years I, and others like me, had held out radiant promises of progress. I had preached to them about my dream. I had lectured to them about the not too distant day when they would have freedom, "all, here and now." I had urged them to have faith in America and in white society. Their hopes had soared. They booed because they felt that we were unable to deliver on our promises, and because we had urged them to have faith in people who had too often proved to be unfaithful. They were hostile because they were watching the dream that they had so readily accepted turn into a frustrating nightmare.[31]

---

29. Worthington Jr., *Forgiving and Reconciling*, 73.
30. Vasiliauskas and McMinn, "Effects of a prayer intervention."
31. Carson, ed., *Autobiography*, 302.

Notice in King's account how he felt the full brunt of his anger, initially from a place of self-interest, but then as he moved toward empathy, his anger settled into a larger context of compassion and love.

It's natural to divide the suffering of the world into individual portions where you hold yours and I hold mine and everyone else holds theirs. But what if our suffering is more shared than separate—more like a family-style meal than a plated dinner? As contemplative author Richard Rohr observes:

> When we carry our small suffering in solidarity with the one universal longing of all humanity, it helps keep us from self-pity or self-preoccupation. . . . Almost all people are carrying a great and secret hurt, even when they don't know it. . . . Some mystics even go so far as to say that individual suffering doesn't exist at all—and that there is only one suffering, it is all the same, and it is all the suffering of God.[32]

Perhaps this is what the apostle Paul suggested when he wrote, "We know that all creation has been groaning as in the pains of childbirth right up to the present time" (Rom 8:22). And if our suffering is collective, then maybe our compassion can be also. Compassion means "to suffer with," which hints at the possibility of a pervasive compassion for ourselves and everyone we meet.

Part of laying my burden of anger down involved trying to see from my antagonists' perspective, trying to understand the motivation for their actions toward me. I began to see people in the throes of their own pain, those who also had been misunderstood, misrepresented, and maligned by others. Omid Safi, a Duke University professor, writes in a blog, "When the arc of the moral universe does bend towards justice it is at least in part because some among us vow to see one another fully. We vow to not overlook the fullness of humanity in anyone."[33] The movement from self-interest toward moral goodness begins here, by noticing others and caring enough to see and know them, and by recognizing our common suffering and cries for love.

Empathy saves us from our desperate strivings and obsessions with individualism, reminding us that we are more similar than different, bringing us together in our shared finitude, longings, failings, and sufferings, offering meaning and hope in our times of anger.

32. Rohr, "Nothing Stands Alone," ¶2–3.
33. Safi, "Power of Being Seen," ¶5.

Sometimes empathy even shows up in baseball. Some attentive Cubs executives recognized how terribly Steve Bartman was treated on that October day long ago. In 2016 he was given a World Series ring after the Cubs ended a 108-year drought to win the World Series. Bartman responded with remarkable humility and a call for human kindness: "Although I do not consider myself worthy of such an honor, I am deeply moved and sincerely grateful.... I humbly receive the ring not only as a symbol of one of the most historic achievements in sports, but as an important reminder for how we should treat each other in today's society."[34]

Welcoming Prayer

Trappist monk Thomas Keating once said, "It is Christ in you leading your life," while eulogizing Mary Mrozowski, a spiritual teacher and founder of a contemplative community in New York.[35] Being divorced and Catholic excluded Mrozowski from some opportunities and recognitions, but nonetheless she succeeded in building her life and spiritual teachings around the inclusive love of God. Keating continued in his eulogy of Mrozowski, "I want to see somebody with flesh and blood who's in love with God and says so, and who empowers other people to experience their potentiality with this same romance, this relationship." What a beautiful notion, that our relationship with God can be just as real—maybe even more real—than how we relate to the neighbor across the street, a longtime friend, or a beloved family member. Mrozowski seemed to have this sort of intimate friendship with God and knew how to invite others into a similar sort of authenticity. Someone once wrote of Mrozowski, "I never thought I'd hear God speak with a Brooklyn accent."[36]

Perceiving her yearning to relate deeply with God, find healing for her wounds, and forgive, Mrozowski developed something known as the Welcoming Prayer.[37] Inspired by eighteenth-century Jesuit priest Jean Pierre de Caussade, she developed this prayer of invitation and consent, asking God to be present with us in all our complexity and messiness.

1. *Notice.* Stop and notice whatever it is you're experiencing in this moment. Don't hold back and just give the spiritually acceptable

---

34. Bremer, "Steve Bartman Receives," ¶10.
35. Contemplative Outreach, "In Memory," download 2.
36. Keating et al., *Spirituality, Contemplation*, 42.
37. Contemplative Outreach, "Welcoming Prayer."

answer. If you're feeling angry or envious or lustful or hopeless, notice that honestly. Perhaps you can even locate your experience in a particular part of your body. Does your gut get queasy or your throat or chest tighten? Do you feel tension in your shoulders when you allow yourself to experience the negative emotion you are welcoming?

2. *Welcome.* Offer a simple welcome to whatever it is you're feeling. "Welcome, anger." "Welcome, sadness." Whatever your experience in this moment, welcome it and recognize that God is with you.

3. *Let Go.* Just as you have welcomed your current experience, now let it go. You have welcomed your anger and seen Christ with you in the midst of it, but it doesn't need to control you. Simply say, "I let go of my anger." It will come back eventually, and you can welcome it again, but for now just let it move on through your awareness and go on its way.

This is a brave prayer, inviting God into all our experiences, including the messy pieces. At first this may seem uncomfortable, as if God doesn't want to see these parts of us. Yet God already sees every part of us, whether or not we offer an invitation. By welcoming God, we are acknowledging and consenting to what is already true.

With God's help, we can learn to release the parts of our experience that deeply trouble us. We courageously welcome our anger, our unforgiveness, and our thoughts of revenge and then release them, likely over and over. This practice of releasing is the pivot that comes after the noticing and welcoming.

Slow Ponderings

1. What lessons about anger did you learn in your home growing up? How do these lessons help or hinder you now?
2. How do you respond to the idea of anger as a moral emotion that helps move society toward empathy and justice? How have your own experiences of anger been helpful in making you morally aware?
3. We suggest that anger, at its best, can help build moral societies and healthy relationships. At its worst, it can tear them apart. How have you seen the best and worst of anger?
4. How does social media shape your experience and perception of anger? What sort of social media "best practices" help you in this regard?
5. We have been more personal in this chapter than other chapters of the book, revealing Mark's slow journey from self-interested anger toward laying down a burden, experiencing empathy, and moving toward forgiveness. What personal stories of your own come to mind as you consider this journey?
6. As you contemplate the Welcoming Prayer, how might it help you experience God? What sort of challenges do you anticipate with this spiritual practice?

Chapter 5

Slow to Judge: An Invitation to Humility

You know that moment when you're barreling down the road, making good time, and a traffic light turns yellow? It's decision time. Do you apply the brakes (however abruptly) and stop? Will the light turn red if you decide to power through? What might the consequences be for yourself and others? Judgments like this need to be made quickly, without much time for contemplation.

The two of us have different inclinations in these moments, with Lisa more likely to press the accelerator and Mark to hit the brakes. Whichever of us is sitting in the passenger seat is likely to question the driver's choice in these moments. Two judgments happen here: first the split-second judgment made *by* the driver, then the passenger's snap judgment *about* the driver. The first judgment is essential; the second is optional, and not always welcomed when spoken aloud. In fact, it is usually not welcomed.

Quick judgments are often necessary for safety and efficiency, but not when forming or expressing an opinion about another person's character. In his most famous sermon, Jesus warned against judging others:

> Do not judge, or you too will be judged. For in the same way you judge others, you will be judged, and with the measure you use, it will be measured to you.
>
> Why do you look at the speck of sawdust in your brother's eye and pay no attention to the plank in your own eye? How

can you say to your brother, "Let me take the speck out of your eye," when all the time there is a plank in your own eye? You hypocrite, first take the plank out of your own eye, and then you will see clearly to remove the speck from your brother's eye. (Matt 7:1–5, NIV)

Contrast what Jesus taught about sawdust and planks with this observation from a writer for the British Broadcast Company's (BBC) *Science Focus* magazine: "Outrage has become the defining emotion of the 21st Century, worn righteously, as a finger-pointing badge of honour."[1] We have become finger-pointing people, posting our disapproval and disdain with alarming frequency and vitriol. We do this in the name of virtue, believing we are saving the world from the "bad people," often without considering what loiters in our own hearts.

Jesus calls us toward humility, urging us to appraise ourselves before criticizing others and to use even standards when evaluating ourselves and others. This doesn't come naturally for us, which is probably why Jesus thought to include it in his sermon.

I'm Mostly Okay, You're Basically Flawed

As we walk through each day, we create a moment-by-moment commentary to describe what is happening all around us. In doing this, we consider both *traits* and *situations* when things go bad. Mostly we think of traits when describing others and situations when describing ourselves. If you and another driver have a near accident on the freeway, you might explain your own behavior by looking to a situation: the sun was in your eyes, you were distracted by the child in the back seat, or your phone beeped suddenly. In contrast, we tend to look at dispositional traits when describing the other: "That driver is such an idiot—and a selfish jerk, too." We rarely think she may be rushing her bleeding spouse to the hospital. It could be that.

Stanford psychologist Lee Ross coined the term *fundamental attribution error* in 1977 to describe this propensity to explain others' behaviors based on their character, overlooking factors related to circumstance and situation.

The families of Robert Eric Doyle and Candelario Gonzalez experienced the worst possible outcome of this error on a hot July day in

---

1. Fleming, "Why social media," ¶1.

2015. Both men were driving in Citrus County, Florida—Doyle with his wife, and Gonzalez with his wife, daughter, and granddaughter. And both were recorded on simultaneous 911 calls as they raged at one another, assuming they knew traits about the other rather than taking into account extenuating circumstances or situations. As Gonzalez's wife, Cathi, described Doyle as an idiot to one 911 operator, Doyle described Gonzalez as a maniac to another. It turned into a deadly example of road rage as Gonzalez followed Doyle to his home, where Doyle shot Gonzalez in front of his family.[2]

A road rage shooting is an extreme example, but this shows up in lesser ways every day in our social media feeds. One recent X post declared that "toxic people use unfair tactics to manipulate arguments in their favor." Perhaps. But is the commenter doing the same thing by using a trait ("toxic") to describe others who hold differing perspectives?

Our Christian communities inspire and encourage us to live godly lives, to love as Jesus did. Yet how often do we twist good standards and beliefs into scrutinizing and calling out through plank-blinded eyes the failure of others? We may cite the verse where the apostle Paul instructs his readers to "hate what is wrong" and "hold tightly to what is good," and then cast stones or glances at others, forgetting that "wrong" and "good" can be difficult to discern. In our zeal, we label, demote, and degrade others in our hearts, neglecting the apostle Paul's words about love that surround his instructions about the wrong and the good: "Don't just pretend to love others. Really love them. Hate what is wrong. Hold tightly to what is good. Love each other with genuine affection, and take delight in honoring each other" (Rom 12:9–10).

Love is at the heart of Christianity because love is the heart of Jesus. When we forget to envelop our valuations of right and wrong in the vastness of a loving God, who is patient and does not rush to judgment, we damage ourselves, one another, and our communities.

We long for love. I (Mark) sat at a park with my mother recently, and as we talked, we watched three preschool children play with their Tonka trucks. One little girl, obviously frustrated, called a little boy "mean." His face twisted up in pain (and his heart probably did, too), and he replied through tears, "I'm not mean. I'm nice!" His little heart longed for love, to be seen rather than dismissed or reduced to a derogatory label. So my heart longs, and yours.

2. Valencia and Ellis, "911 calls capture panic." Also, Wagner, "Florida grandfather killed."

From our earliest interactions in life, we judge and pigeonhole others in our disappointment and frustration, labeling their traits rather than the circumstances that may have led to their actions. It's easier to simplify the other and call him mean than to dive into a more complex understanding of how Tonka truck play has proven difficult.

If our natural tendency is to label others, even unfairly, today we can criticize and vilify others with a few keystrokes and post it for any and all to see. GIFs are the animated images that show up on Facebook comments, and at least one website is devoted to providing us with "judgmental Facebook idiots GIFs" so that we can show the world how stupid other people can be.[3]

Make Way for Naive Realism

Early in his long career, Professor Ross coined the term *fundamental attribution error* as part of the tenure process at Stanford, and when a Stanford professor publishes a thing, it's likely to attract attention. The phrase started showing up in psychology textbooks and courses, then in the general media, and soon it was surfacing in sermons, living room conversations, and pop psychology books. Once an idea gets famous, people disseminate it, sometimes distorting it, and it can take on a life of its own.

What most people don't know is that Ross's understanding of the fundamental attribution error changed throughout his career. His evolving thoughts, refined by his conflict negotiation work in Northern Ireland and the Middle East as well as his many laboratory studies, were summarized a few years before his death in 2021.

Ross came to see *naive realism* as the *truly* fundamental attribution error.[4] His later work shows how our inclination to judge others shows up in three easy steps: 1) "I know the truth," 2) "If you know what I know, you'll agree," and 3) "If you still don't agree, then you're an idiot (or worse)."

---

3. Giphy, "Explore Judgmental."
4. Ross, "From the Fundamental Attribution Error."

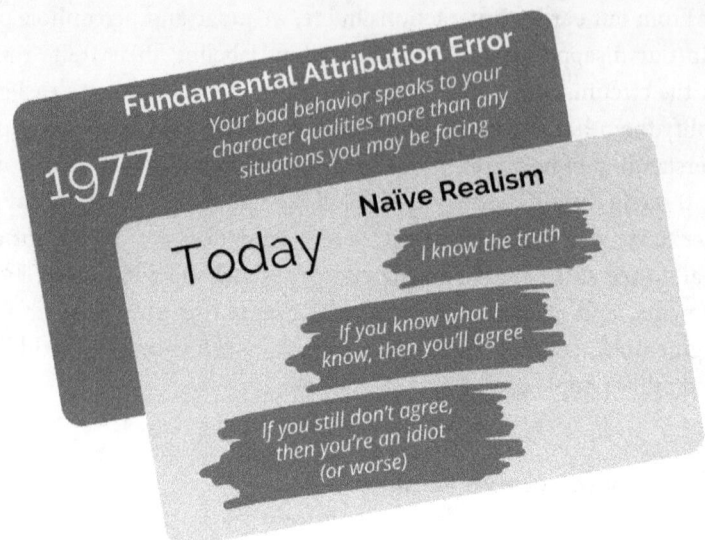

"I Know the Truth"

Some years ago, the Showtime series *Dexter* was recommended to us. The series portrays a likable police analyst who solves crimes during the day and then in the dark of night personally kills the murderers who have avoided prosecution. We only made it through a couple of episodes before putting it on the never-watch-again list. Partly, as Quakers, we find the punishment extreme; partly, as social scientists, we feel ambivalent (at best) about the gruesome display of violence offered as entertainment; and partly, we had a big problem with the main character's hubris. What are the chances that Dexter might make a mistake in his forensic work and then—because he is bypassing our normal jurisprudence process—act as judge, jury, and executioner to an innocent person? The show only works if one assumes that Dexter has complete, infallible, and unquestionable discernment of the truth. And apparently the show *did* work, receiving high acclaim and ratings, probably because we humans walk around most days making this same assumption—that we know all we need to know about people we deem dishonorable.

People are more complex than we think. If you have ever been vilified for mistakes in word, judgment, or action, you know what it is like to have another person assume they know the fullness of a thing. Or to turn this around the other way, if we appraise ourselves honestly, how often have we presumed we know what needs to be known when looking at another person, when, in fact, we know very little, and some of what we "know" is likely untrue? People are more complex than we assume. Here's how this looks in a picture:

People Are More Complex than We Assume

Other Person

What I assume I know about the other person

What I actually "know" about the other person

It's not just people we evaluate harshly but also their ideas: theological, political, and economic ones; expressions of spirituality and sexuality; their parenting; styles, trends, and fads. We carry hubris about knowing the complete and right position on certain matters.

According to Ross's research, we assume not only that we hold the truth regarding objects and events, but we also assume that our thoughts, priorities, feelings, and perceptions are more objective and trustworthy than what others experience. This can make for dangerous hermeneutics and significant troubles in our communities.

Both conservative and liberal Christians believe Jesus would endorse their views about same-sex marriage, taxation, treatment of undocumented immigrants, and abortion, and that Jesus would disagree with the other group's views.[5] In one study, Protestant Christians were more prone to the fundamental attribution error than Catholic Christians.[6] It's a puzzling finding calling for more research, but it has us wondering whether,

---

5. Ross et al., "How Christians Reconcile."
6. Li et al., "Fundamental(ist) Attribution Error."

because we Protestants may think we have full, direct access to an omniscient God, we naively put too much confidence in what we believe, think, say, and feel. One of the reasons for the Catholic-Protestant split in the sixteenth century was that Protestants believed they had direct access to God whereas Catholics saw their access as being mediated by priests.

Even if religion contributes to the problem, having excessive confidence in our version of the truth is not limited to religious folks. Atheists are also prone to assumptions and biases about knowing the truth.[7] It's a human vulnerability, not just a religious one. In 1787, Benjamin Franklin observed, "Most men indeed as well as most sects in religion, think themselves in possession of all truth, and that wherever others differ from them it is so far error."[8] Hold on to Franklin's words for a few moments because we will return to them soon.

"If You Know What I Know, You'll Agree"

We believe ourselves to know the truth, and then we expect others to agree with us. If they don't agree, it's because they don't understand things as well as we do. We assume all we need to do is explain the truth, and then intelligent, reasonable people will certainly agree.

Ross first explored the assumption that others are likely to agree with us in the late 1970s, but a lot has changed since then—the development of the Internet, for example. In pre-Internet days, Ross and his colleagues had Stanford undergraduates consider several situations and then report what they personally would do and what most others would do in the same situation.[9] If they were stopped outside a grocery store, questioned about their experience shopping there, and then asked by the interviewer to sign a release so their comments could be included in a commercial, would they sign it? The researchers didn't care much whether someone said yes or no; they were more interested in knowing whether they thought others would act similarly to themselves. As predicted, those who would sign the release were likely to think others would sign also. In a second situation students were asked if they preferred to be evaluated by writing an individual term paper or by working in a group and submitting a single paper where all group members would

---

7. Amarasingam, "To Err in Their Ways."
8. Benjamin Franklin Historical Society, "Constitutional Convention," ¶2.
9. Ross et al., "False Consensus Effect."

be assigned the same grade. Once again, respondents expected others would share their preference. Third, would a person show up in court to dispute a speeding ticket or just pay the fine by mail? Whatever preference students chose, they expected others would do similarly.

What's more, when asked to give personality ratings of those who agreed and disagreed with them, participants were more critical of those who disagreed with them than of those who agreed. Follow-up studies support the conclusion that we tend to presume people agree with our version of truth or wisdom more than they actually do.

Social media makes the false consensus effect even worse. The two of us are ecology-minded Oregonians, who think and talk quite a lot about sustainability and energy conservation. It's easy, but not correct, to assume others agree with our values. Imagine one of us posts on social media about the strangeness of hurricanes and flooding in the southeast United States while those in the southwest face drought and wildfires. We pose the possibility this is caused by a changing climate and urge people to think about the significance of what we now face. Jared from Scottsdale loves the post and comments about the declining water levels in the Colorado River. James from London likes the post and mentions how things are getting dire on the other side of the Atlantic too. Felicia from Jacksonville comments about the electric vehicle she just purchased, and how wet it is now getting in the shadow of the hurricane. In all we get 102 likes, twenty-three comments, and two shares. Not bad.

But something else is going on here too. We are now networked through social media with a mass of like-minded people that we or they select. It may seem like *everyone* agrees with our post, but this highly filtered version of who "everyone" is gives the wrong impression of how others actually think.

It gets even more complicated because search engines and social media sites use algorithms known as "filter bubbles" to determine our results when making connections for us. Filter bubbles are determined based on past searches, purchases, and websites visited, which means a Democrat and a Republican may get different results when searching for "climate" or "racism" or "gun control." This pushes us further toward false consensus because we are mostly exposed to information consistent with what we already believe. We think we are speaking truth to the masses, but we are merely preaching to the choir.

"If You Still Don't Agree, You're an Idiot (or Worse)"

Because we believe we know the truth and that other reasonable people agree with us, it makes us quick to judge—sometimes quick to pull the character assassination trigger—when we encounter others who are not persuaded by our perspectives.

If given information from peers we agree with on a controversial issue, such as capital punishment, we're likely to regard their reasoning as valid. But if those same people offer arguments contrary to our opinions, we judge their reasoning to be filled with error and bias.[10] Some politicians have taken this to the bank in recent years, convincing their followers that anything untoward coming from the media is "fake news." If we can't get people to agree with us, at least we can disparage them.

An event happens—for example, the world is exposed to a pandemic. Then we tell ourselves a story about what we should do: we ought to rush to develop a vaccine, get emergency approval for it, and then vaccinate everyone. We assume all reasonable people will agree with this understanding of what should transpire. When they do not, it messes with our sense of how things are, and we have difficulty knowing what to do with this surprising information. In our befuddlement, we call them names, assuming our differences are due to their faulty character traits rather than different life situations. Like those children playing with Tonka trucks on the playground, we call them "mean," or worse. During COVID-19, a Facebook friend posted something about those who chose not to be vaccinated, and another friend commented, "You can't fix stupid."

That same day we talked with a man whose twenty-two-year-old daughter had not been vaccinated because she wanted to have children and it wasn't clear to her if the vaccine might affect her fertility. One option is to disparage this woman, proclaiming there is currently no medical evidence that the vaccine causes fertility problems.[11] Another option is to graciously observe this woman's choice is not based on character traits, stupidity, or selfishness but on concern for a child who is not yet conceived. The science on COVID-19 vaccines was young at the time of this woman's choice, while her concern for the welfare of her child is time-honored. These are moments of invitation where we can choose to invite

---

10. Pronin et al., "Objectivity in the Eye of the Beholder."
11. Center for Disease Control and Prevention, "Covid-19 Vaccines," ¶3.

the vastness of God's love, which is patient and does not rush to judgment, to flow in us and from us toward those with whom we interact.

Plato, Philo of Alexandra, and several others through history have been credited with saying, "Be kind, for everyone you meet is fighting a great battle." The words are worth pondering. People want to be seen and understood. People want to be given the benefit of the doubt that suggests there is more to us and more to the battle we are fighting than the observer quick to judge might assume.

Author and researcher Brené Brown has famously suggested that most people are doing the best they can.[12] The little boy on the playground asked to be seen in this merciful way when he cried out, "I'm not mean. I'm nice!" If we could believe such a thing, might it point us toward humility and kindness in our interactions with one another? While our built-in tendencies point us in a different direction—encouraging us to believe we hold more truth than others and that if they don't agree with us, then they are certainly *not* doing the best they can—something is nudging a groundswell of people toward a more humble and gracious way forward. What if that something is the mysterious, redemptive work of God in the world?

The words of Jesus reverberate—words about sawdust and planks. And so do the words of the BBC writer who said that outrage defines our century and that we wear it as a badge of honor. We are prone to judge, but we also have some choice in who we are and who we will become.

> **Pause:** As we move toward an invitation to humility, reflect on one or two people you know to be humble. What is it like to be with them? How do you feel in their presence? What stirs for you just now as you call them to mind?

An Invitation to Humility

Jesus pointed us toward a path of humility in that famous sermon where he noted it's easy to miss the plank in our own eyes as we point out the sawdust in another's. Rather than attacking and criticizing and putting ourselves first, we can learn to listen with curiosity, hold complexity, withhold judgment, accept and care for the other, and help relationships heal. Every moment offers a choice to move toward values of life, dignity, and respect so that we might offer others the same empathy and

---

12. Brown, *Rising Strong*, 111.

compassion we more easily offer ourselves. We're less likely to be judgmental toward others if we engage in meaningful, humble, openhearted conversation with them.

Our invitation, summarized in a table, is to slow our human impulse toward naive realism and press toward a fuller way of being human, one that shows civility and care for one another.

Naive Realism	Inviting Humility
"I know the truth."	"I know some of the truth, though there is much I don't yet know."
"If you know what I know, you'll agree."	"What are our points of agreement and disagreement? I'm curious to understand your perspective."
"If you still don't agree, you're an idiot (or worse)."	"We won't necessarily agree, but I can respect you as one valued and loved by God."

Humility affects both how we see ourselves and our relationships with others. Our default setting is to assume we know the full truth on a matter. Humility allows us to challenge and change that default setting by recognizing that some of our ideas are misinformed or biased.[13] Sometimes we are just wrong. Humility may seem regressive and off-kilter in a time when we are told to trust our gut and stand up for what we believe. Or maybe humility has always been countercultural. Yet Jesus lived—and invites us to join him in living—a countercultural life that moves downward instead of upward, extending grace and forgiveness to our enemies rather than angry, dismissive judgment. Not surprisingly, those highest in humility experience more gratitude, empathy, altruism, and forgiveness than others.[14]

The relational part of humility encourages us to present our ideas fairly, respectfully, and non-defensively while regarding and learning from others' viewpoints. This helps challenge our tendency to think that

---

13. Davis et al., "Distinguishing Intellectual Humility." Also, Van Tongeren et al., "Humility."

14. Leary, *Psychology of Intellectual Humility*, 16.

others will agree with us and that we have a right (perhaps even an obligation) to correct and/or vilify them if they do not.

Humble people care about others' well-being and have strong relationships to show for it. They are liked more than their less humble peers, even after just thirty minutes of contact, and are more inclined to make helpful compromises and negotiate solutions.[15] If a pastor or prominent Christian speaker admits to being wrong, or having been wrong in the past, don't we listen more attentively? Their open humility about past or present error fosters trust and perhaps helps us admit to wrongs of our own.

Franklin's Practice Plan

Life offers a practice field for humility, with ample opportunity for seeing and treating ourselves and others well, growing in compassion, and strengthening connections. Whenever we have an idea challenged, win or lose an award, experience conflict in a relationship, receive feedback, discuss successes or failures, apologize, accept responsibility for words spoken, or assign credit to others for a job well done, we have a chance to practice humility.

When we shared Benjamin Franklin's words about most people thinking themselves as right and thinking anyone who disagrees with them as wrong, we didn't describe the test he faced when writing those words. The Constitutional Convention was held in Philadelphia from May to September of 1787. Fifty-five delegates from twelve of the original states did the work of hammering out how this new country would be governed. Only thirty-nine of these signed the final document. Franklin, at age eighty-one, was the oldest delegate. He wrote a speech for the final day of the convention, which someone else had to deliver because of Franklin's frail health, in which he noted that some parts of the new Constitution didn't seem ideal to him, but he still felt inclined to support it:

> For having lived long, I have experienced many instances of being obliged by better information, or fuller consideration, to change opinions even on important subjects, which I once thought right, but found to be otherwise. It is therefore that the older I grow, the more apt I am to doubt my own judgment, and to pay more respect to the judgment of others. Most men

---

15. Leary, *Psychology of Intellectual Humility*, 16.

indeed as well as most sects in religion, think themselves in possession of all truth, and that wherever others differ from them it is so far error.[16]

Franklin's words speak to humility forged by an imperfect man over the course of a lifetime.

Some fifty-five years earlier Franklin had stopped attending services at his local Presbyterian church—in part because he deemed religion to divide people more than unite them, and in part because he didn't care much for his pastor's preaching. Instead of being a good Presbyterian, Franklin wanted to be a good citizen, so he embarked on an ambitious personal plan to become morally perfect—something that turned out to be more difficult than he imagined.[17] Franklin identified twelve virtues he wanted to develop: temperance, silence, order, resolution, frugality, industry, sincerity, justice, moderation, cleanliness, tranquility, and chastity. He later added humility to the list because a Quaker friend convinced Franklin how overbearing and prideful he could be in conversation. That Franklin believed he could attain moral perfection might argue in favor of his friend's view, and that he would listen to his friend at all and add humility to the list suggests that a deep capacity for humility resided beneath Franklin's pride.

Franklin, a printer by trade, made a little book to monitor his trek toward virtue. Long before spreadsheets, his book was comprised of spreadsheet-like charts to help track how he fell short in achieving moral perfection. Though some might call this obsessive-compulsive, it's a fascinating blend of what we now recognize as self-monitoring and the Ignatian spiritual practice of Daily Examen.

To mention Franklin and virtue together can feel startling to the historically informed because despite his stated intention to become morally perfect, he was a flawed man. It seems harsh to say he abandoned his wife, Deborah, but at least by today's standards, this seems an accurate description of the final half of his long marriage, and the first half may have been filled with contention.[18] Also disturbing is that, like most colonialists in his social class, Franklin owned slaves for a portion of his life. This serves as a tragic example of how blind we can be to the social evils of our day, even for those who set out to find moral

---

16. Benjamin Franklin Historical Society, "Constitutional Convention," ¶2.
17. Franklin, *Autobiography*, 89.
18. Coss, "What Led Benjamin Franklin?," ¶7.

perfection. But perhaps it was being intentional that helped him wake to this profound sin of Western culture, ultimately becoming president of an abolition society in Philadelphia.[19]

At age seventy-nine, Franklin noted that he never arrived at perfection "but fell far short of it."[20] Still, he considered himself a better and happier man than if he had never tried to press toward virtue. Franklin's journey toward humility felt particularly challenging to him:

> In reality, there is, perhaps, no one of our natural passions so hard to subdue as pride. Disguise it, struggle with it, beat it down, stifle it, mortify it as much as one pleases, it is still alive, and will every now and then peep out and show itself; you will see it, perhaps, often in this history; for, even if I could conceive that I had completely overcome it, I should probably be proud of my humility.[21]

These words spoken by an old, flawed man many years ago still capture the paradox of being human: even as we try to inch toward humility we are beset with pride. Self-interest is a survival tactic, after all, one we learn to hone if we are to survive. While some self-interest is necessary, it grows to overblown proportions in our Western societies where competition, achievement, and status are valued more than cooperation, service, and sacrifice.

Franklin's story demonstrates it is possible to notice our propensity toward pride and stand up against it, to move toward humility so that we can listen well and learn from one another. By 1787, when the opportunity to help craft the United States Constitution arrived, Franklin had faced into his pride for many decades and worked to become humbler. And so, by the end of that Constitutional Convention, with all its negotiations and compromises and conversations, Franklin could admit publicly that in many instances he needed better information or fuller consideration, having learned to doubt his own judgment and pay more respect to the judgments of others, even on important topics. He signed the Constitution.

---

19. Benjamin Franklin Historical Society, "Slavery and the Abolition Society," ¶2.
20. Franklin, *Autobiography*, 89.
21. Franklin, *Autobiography*, 92.

Jesus as the Ultimate Exemplar

Christians see the ultimate exemplar of love and humility in Jesus, portrayed clearly in the Christ hymn, an early church anthem:

> Though he was God,
> he did not think of equality with God
> as something to cling to.
>
> Instead, he gave up his divine privileges;
> he took the humble position of a slave
> and was born as a human being.
>
> When he appeared in human form,
> he humbled himself in obedience to God
> and died a criminal's death on a cross. (Phil 2:6–8)

Paul wrote these words to the church at Philippi, urging them to find ways to listen better to one another during conflict. The Philippian church dearly loved Paul, having sent him generous financial support, and Paul also loved the Philippians deeply. The church was twelve to fifteen years old at the time of Paul's letter, and they were experiencing difficulties. Two leaders in the church disagreed about an issue and it was dividing the congregation. By reciting this Christ hymn, Paul entreated the Philippians to hold each other with love, tenderness, and compassion and to take on the humility of Jesus.

Theologians camp out in Philippians 2 for a long while. This is Christology, perhaps the beginning of Christology, as Paul described this great self-emptying—*kenosis*—where Jesus, being in very nature God, emptied himself and became fully human, a baby born in an unseemly place and ultimately executed in one of the most horrific ways conceived. Paul holds up this image of humility to a church experiencing disagreement and dissonance and calls them to love one another out of gratitude for the humble love of God.

Only one could be rightly elevated above the rest of us, and what did that one do? The Word gave up all divine privileges and became God-in-the-flesh, God-with-us, fully human that God might live a humble human life among us, exemplifying love and mercy while pursuing truth and justice. Jesus showed us the face of God, a God willing to be humbled to the point of death on a cross.

And what do we do? Like the Philippians, we insist we know the truth better than others. We build our empires, strive for greatness, and clamor over who is the best at one thing or another.

Jesus is humble, and we're so often not. How then will we be formed in humility?

Growing in Humility

Pastor and author Jared Byas tells the story of a friend who came for advice when his daughter was sleeping with her boyfriend. Byas's friend viewed this as sinful behavior and wanted to know what to say to his daughter, who didn't share his moral perspectives. Byas gave three words of advice: "Love without judgment." His friend teared up in relief and gratitude, because love is exactly what he wanted to offer his daughter. His deep impulse toward love had been covered with layers of Christian obligation to speak the truth, supposing that doing so would bring about change in his daughter's life.

For some, this story may seem unsettling at first glance, as if Byas isn't taking sin seriously, but maybe we have this backward. Perhaps love needs to come from us and we leave the convicting to God. In the Gospel writer Luke's famous parable of the prodigal son, the father wasn't sending letters to his faraway son to convict him of his waywardness. When the son stumbled home in shame, the father didn't meet him with a list of expectations and ground rules but instead with a hug, a kiss, and a feast. Yes, in this story the son confessed the weight of his selfish choices, his disrespect for his father, sins he ultimately recognized as he admitted truths about himself. But the father made no requirement of this. If he had, the story would have an utterly different meaning than what it is: a story of awakening to profound grace.

After telling the story of his friend in *Love Matters More*, Byas writes the passage that has been converted into a social media meme:

> At root is the fear that if we don't tell people they are wrong, and if they don't feel the discomfort of our judgment, they'll have no incentive to change. But that's not how change works—not in the Bible, not in psychology, not in real life. It's amazing to me that we're still convinced that telling people they are wrong is the way to bring about real change in the world, despite it almost never working. I have seen hundreds of lives changed by human beings who have shown up to love without judgment, without

feeling compelled to "speak the truth in love." I have seen almost no lives change when we begin by "speaking the truth in love."[22]

To walk such a path requires humility.

To help his followers walk their faith in humility, Saint Francis of Assisi told them, "We must bear patiently *not* being good . . . and *not* being thought good." And also, "You can show your love to others by *not* wishing that they should be better Christians."[23] It is hard to have an arrogant faith if we accept that we are loved just as we are, imperfect children of God with a limited capacity to be good. When being loved does not depend on our being good—or on our ability to hide our bad so that we are *thought* to be good—the gift of God's mercy opens the way for transformation based on love. Can we, as Francis challenged his followers, extend such love to others? Can we let them also be imperfect as we are imperfect? Doing so requires a humble trust in God for their growth, rather than arrogantly assuming God needs our help to point out their failings and set them aright.

Are you drawn to these words? Do you find them alarming? Perhaps our deepest self, which knows we are imperfect, longs for such words while our ego, which does not want to admit how faulty we are, resists them. They are counterculturual sentiments describing a faith of imperfection. Perhaps letting go of our need to think well of ourselves is a first and essential practice at surrendering to the mercy of God and opening the way for humility.

Maybe embracing a faith of imperfection would lessen our obligation to insist that others be the best Christians they can be. A willingness to face *my* incapacity, *my* failures, the plank in *my own* eye allows me to stay mindful that *I* need God's mercy—and daily—and disinclines me from focusing on why *you* need God's mercy daily.

What kind of world might this be if we could each do so?

The Daily Examen

We mentioned the Daily Examen earlier in this chapter, and it is worth unpacking here as a practice for growing humility. Saint Ignatius developed the Daily Examen for his monks more than four hundred years ago, a practice that invites us to seek God in all moments of our lives. We

22. Byas, *Love Matters More*, 61.
23. Rohr, *Eager to Love*, 101.

examine the day with gratitude for the day's gifts and with humility that asks for help to see our shortcomings. We listen to how God might invite us to make amends, to seek forgiveness, and to make different choices tomorrow. You can find many variations of the Daily Examen, the common theme being to encourage a prayer-led mindfulness that helps us review the day and see where we have met, seen, and responded to God.

Generally done near the end of the day, the Daily Examen includes some version of the steps below (we've added settling in and ending to the typical five steps), with the most time spent in the review. This can be done in five minutes or thirty. If you decide to experiment with this practice, offer ten minutes or so a day to the Examen six days a week for a month before laying it down. As with all spiritual practices, the Daily Examen gains momentum with time, bringing greater mindfulness to the nudges, opportunities, and presence of God throughout the day.

1. *Settling in.* As you begin, become aware of the love with which God sees you. Believing this is true may require some practice itself. If you struggle believing God sees you with love, begin with a few slow, deep breaths. On the inhale, imagine God saying, "I love you, [your name]," and on the exhale, say to God, "I love you, God." Take this affirmation that you want to be true and experience it through breath-filled declarations of love. The intention is to begin by settling yourself in the loving gaze of God.

2. *Gratitude.* Notice what you are grateful for today. Relish these things and recognize them as gifts God has given you—big and small. Thank God for them.

3. *Guidance.* Ask God for insight, for humility, and for courage to review your day honestly, given that we are prone to deny, be defensive, or wallow under the weight of our shortcomings. Ask that God make this Examen a work of grace, fruitful beyond what you could bring to it on your own.

4. *Review and recognize.* With God, review your choices of this day, noting times you were attuned to God and times you failed to be attuned to God. Listen for the stirrings in your heart where you responded with humble openness and allowed your perception to be changed or challenged, where you extended grace, felt joy, and loved. Also take a sobering look for moments revealing empire

building, striving, clamoring for love or attention, or needing to be right. Note what you feel as you recall these moments.

5. *Ask for forgiveness and healing.* Ask for the grace-filled touch of the forgiving God who, with love for you, forgives your sins and removes your heart's burdens. Ask for help to let go of what needs to be released and for discernment in navigating similar challenging moments in the future.

6. *Look toward tomorrow.* Anticipate tomorrow and, with God, consider with some specificity how you might live it in accord with God's loving desire for you and your life. Are there nudges to follow that would bring light and love to someone in your life, amends to be made or forgiveness to be sought?

7. *Ending.* Grateful and aware of God's presence with you, prayerfully conclude your Examen. End as you began, with a loving exchange of prayers as you inhale and exhale.

We recommend beginning and ending the Daily Examen with love, which rests at the center of all the invitations to slow. Humility is choosing love over judgment, one day at a time, recognizing how blind we can be to our own faults, even as we are quick to point out the faults of others. Jesus painted a shocking picture involving sawdust and planks and human eyeballs to drive the point home: loving others involves humility, and humility is not easy.

Anger, blame, anxiety, fear, and judgment flit in and out of our days. Our natural reflex is to respond by pointing out the errors and misdeeds of others, to get others to see the world as we do, because, after all, we know best. We know the truth. This isn't working. In fact, our efforts escalate the polarization and angst. What would it be like to try something different? To look seriously at our own faults and then to show up humbly, in love and without judgment, to our own frail self and also to the frailty of others?

Slow Ponderings

1. How do you respond to the idea that outrage is an honorable stand for truth?
2. Part of this chapter involved exploring the three phases of naive realism. Consider each one in slow motion and think about how these might make you vulnerable to making snap judgments:

    a. "I know the truth."

    b. "If you know what I know, you'll agree."

    c. "If you still don't agree, you're an idiot (or worse)."

3. Name one or two things you might be wrong about, or at least would like more information about. How might you talk in person with someone who holds a different view than you rather than defaulting to getting your information primarily from the Internet?
4. Think of a time when you had a plank in your own eye while pointing out the sawdust in another's. What helped you see this reality?
5. Can you feel God seeing you with love? Your quick answer might be yes, given that this is the "right" answer, but look for what lies beneath the surface. If you "believe" it in your head yet don't experience it in your heart, reflect on that. What might keep you from experiencing God as one who sees you with love? Down the road, you might consider how this foundational piece of our Christian faith is connected to humility.
6. What draws you to the Daily Examen as a practice? What disinclines you from it?

Chapter 6

Slow to Envy: An Invitation to Gratitude

To say a phone is ringing off the hook doesn't make as much sense as it once did, back when mustard yellow handsets were saddled to their rotary dial housings attached to the kitchen wall beside the avocado green refrigerator. But let's imagine it anyway. Your phone is ringing off the hook.

First you hear from a friend who is vacationing in Italy, having the time of her life, enjoying cafés and walks in the countryside and delectable cuisine. Immediately after hanging up, a family member calls to tell you about the new remodel on his house and how beautiful the updated kitchen is turning out to be. Then you hear from an old high school friend who just published her first book with a major publisher, then a colleague who received an amazing promotion at work, then a smitten neighbor who wants to tell you about the bliss of new love.

Welcome to social media, where you can read all the attainments of those you know in five minutes or less. No wall phone required.

Social media connects people, helping us stay in touch with current and former friends, meet new people, and keep up with community events. There is much to be commended about the interconnectivity we're able to foster and experience. At the same time, devouring social media posts can promote feelings of envy as we compare our ordinary existence to the allure and sizzle of others' lives. The comparisons are not realistic because people tend to post the best parts of their lives and leave the mundane and painful parts private, creating the impression that everyone else lives on a higher plateau of excitement and success than we do. Not surprisingly, Facebook envy is a thing.[1] Urban Dictionary describes it compellingly:

> The feeling you get when you come across an old friend on Facebook and realize that their life turned out way better and is more interesting than yours.
>
> Joe: "My wife left me for another woman and my kid should be out on parole next summer. That, and I almost got my mullet grown to the perfect length. So what have you been up to?"
>
> Jim: "I ended up getting married to a supermodel and moving to Monaco after selling my shares in [Microsoft]. Currently doing volunteer work to eradicate poverty. Oh, you may have also seen me in the news recently during my kid's Nobel prize nomination."[2]

Yes, it's a bit exaggerated, but the feeling may be familiar. With envy, we churn inside, feeling the dullness of our lives that makes us feel inadequate, left out, or left behind and coveting what appears to come easily to others. To complicate matters, envy is profitable because marketers fuel social media, sending customized advertisements to our feeds, promising a sparkly life. But the sparkly life never materializes. Instead, envy causes strife, competitive rancor, depression, and divisiveness.

Words are tricky. The Old Testament was mostly written in Hebrew and the New Testament in Greek, but the Hebrew and Greek words for envy can also be rendered as jealousy.[3] This means that some English translations use "jealousy" while others use "envy" when describing the same Hebrew or Greek word. This gets complicated in English, where we distinguish between the two. In English, the word *envy* comes from Latin *invidia*, which is to look maliciously toward another.[4]

---

1. There are many studies of Facebook envy. For example, Alfasi, "Grass Is Always Greener."
2. Urban Dictionary, "Facebook Envy," by brawler_mtl, ¶1. https://www.urbandictionary.com/define.php?term=Facebook%20Envy. Note that this source contains strong language.
3. Sanders, *Envy and Jealousy*, 13–32.
4. Foster, "Anatomy of Envy," 167.

Envy typically involves two people, with one person wanting something about the other's life. In contrast, jealousy usually involves three people, where one person might lose another to the third.[5] For example, Heather and Jorge have been married for two decades. Heather feels threatened by how often Jorge mentions his new coworker, privately wondering if Jorge is developing romantic feelings for someone else. This is jealousy. In contrast, Duncan notices that Neil has been promoted quickly within the company. Feeling threatened by his success, Duncan starts a rumor about Neil to cast suspicion on his character. This is envy.

Jealousy is not always bad because it reminds us of the exclusivity of committed relationships. Even God declared his jealousy in the Old Testament when Israel seemed to be veering off toward other gods. Jealousy can still be a problem and often is, especially when it is highly possessive and demanding, but it emerges from a place of relational yearning that has a seed of good at its core.

In contrast, envy is a covetous longing, wanting something for oneself that another has and often being willing to do damage to the other as a result. Envy is always a dire thing. As the biblical proverb declares, it is "like cancer in the bones" (Prov 14:30).

"Slow to Envy" is different from the other chapters because something good could be said about every other topic in this book. Speaking, grasping, fear, anger, making judgments, consuming, and isolating all have a time and place, but we have nothing good to say about envy. Nor does classic wisdom literature or social science research.

Anti-Love

We hear much these days about the frantic pace of living, the polarization of society, the pressing demands of family and career, oppressive expectations, the prevalence of anger and unrest, the social impact of new and emerging technologies, and the relentlessness of life in the information age. But perhaps the greatest clamor of all comes from within. Maybe all these external manifestations of our frenetic lives emerge from unsettled places in the human heart. If love is the greatest and most enduring Christian virtue, then envy is the great obstacle, interfering with our capacity to love whenever it shows up. Melanie Klein, the Austrian-British

---

5. Smith and Kim, "Comprehending Envy," 47.

psychoanalyst, saw gratitude as the primary marker of love and envy as its greatest hindrance.[6] Envy is anti-love.

The classic Christian list of seven deadly sins isn't in the Bible, but it still goes back a long way—probably to the fourth-century work of Evagrius Ponticus, who identified eight destructive thoughts. Evagrius was part of a thriving intellectual community in Constantinople (now Istanbul) that included Gregory Nazianzen, Melania the Elder, and Rufinus of Aquileia. Trouble struck when Evagrius fell in love with a married woman. Warned in a dream that he must leave town, he departed, became seriously ill, and then—presumably on his deathbed—confessed his struggle to Melania, who was known for her wisdom. Against all odds, Evagrius survived his illness and went off into the desert to pursue the monastic life Melania suggested.[7] A talented thinker and writer, Evagrius ultimately wrote about the eight *logismoi* (thoughts) that cause us problems. His list was then refined by his protégé, John Cassian, and further distilled into seven deadly sins by Pope Gregory the Great. The ominous list includes envy, gluttony, lust, pride, greed, wrath, and sloth.

Some of the topics in this book can morph into one of the seven deadly sins—anger can become wrath if uncontrolled, grasping can cause greed, consuming can lead to gluttony, judging often promotes pride—but only envy stands on its own as a deadly sin.

Deadly

Envy shows up early and often in the Bible, and not with happy endings. Note this quick jaunt through some early Hebrew history.

Just a few chapters after cracking the cover of the Bible, we find the story of Cain and Abel. The Bible doesn't say exactly *why* Cain killed Abel, but postbiblical interpretations lean toward envy and sibling rivalry when Abel received God's favor and Cain didn't.[8] Later in Genesis, fraternal twins—Esau and Jacob—were born to Isaac and Rebekah, resulting in family favoritism and toxic enmity that trickled down for centuries. Jacob's two wives—Leah and Rachel—experienced envy toward one another, leading to animosity, rivalry, and lots of babies. When Jacob played favorites among his many sons, Joseph's brothers were

---

6. Klein, *Envy and Gratitude*, 176.
7. Stewart, "Evagrius Ponticus."
8. Kim, "Cain and Abel."

envious of him, so they threw him into an empty cistern to die before deciding to sell him as a slave instead.

Envy appears in the Ten Commandments, delivered by Moses after a thunderous visit with God on Mount Sinai: "You must not covet your neighbor's house. You must not covet your neighbor's wife, male or female servant, ox or donkey, or anything else that belongs to your neighbor" (Exod 20:17).

Later, King Saul became envious toward David because of his military success, leading to an assassination attempt, a murderous pursuit through the wilderness, and ultimately to Saul's death and David's rise to the throne.

The Persian chief of staff, Haman, was so envious of Mordecai, a Jewish palace official, that he developed an extensive plan to get him executed. But Haman's plan backfired, largely because King Xerxes loved Mordecai's cousin, Esther. Haman ended up skewered on the seventy-five-foot pole that he had built to impale Mordecai.

When Nebuchadnezzar, the Babylonian king, discovered the dream interpretation skills of his Jewish captive Daniel, he promoted Daniel to a place of high authority. Daniel was still in a position of authority after Darius the Mede conquered Babylon, and Daniel continued to grow in favor. Other officials became envious of Daniel's status and tried to bring him down. Through some legislative maneuvering, the schemers were able to get Daniel fed to a den of hungry lions, but, similar to Haman, their plan went badly awry when the lions left Daniel alone and the king fed the envious officials to the lions instead.

Envy shows up in the New Testament also, with the apostle Paul being clear that genuine love is not envious, the apostle Peter admonishing his readers to get rid of all envy, malice, and deceit, and the apostle James pronouncing that envy leads to evil and disorder.

Indeed, it does.

In the quiet, posh community of Santa Barbara, California, George Chen, Cheng Yuan Hong, and Weihan Wang were stabbed to death on May 23, 2014. A few minutes later, Katherine Cooper, Veronika Weiss, and Christopher Michaels-Martinez were shot dead by the same assailant. Another fourteen people were injured.[9] All were victims of one of the most pernicious examples of envy in recent history.

---

9. Woolf, "Chilling Report."

Psychologists who study envy conclude it is a "hostile emotion that often prompts aggressive behaviors."[10] The killer, who also shot himself, was a twenty-two-year-old man who left behind a 137-page manifesto explaining why he would go on a murderous rampage on what he called the Day of Retribution, detailing a headlong dive into the deadly nature of envy:[11]

> My hope that I will one day have a beautiful girlfriend and live the life I desire slowly faded away. . . . I kept thinking about how some boys were easily able to get girlfriends. . . . I couldn't fathom how they did it, and I hated and despised them for it.[12]

> I deserve the love of girls more than the other obnoxious boys of my age, and yet they get girls and I don't. That is a crime that can never be forgotten, nor can it be forgiven. I always wanted to exact my revenge on humanity for forcing me to live such a life.[13]

> I was absolutely livid with envious hatred. When they left the store I followed them to their car and splashed my coffee all over them.[14]

> They were still there, having the time of their lives, and I wanted to ruin it for them. . . . I screamed at them with rage as I sprayed them with my super soaker.[15]

> It was time to plot exactly what I will do on the Day of Retribution. I will be a god, punishing women and all of humanity for their depravity. I will finely [sic] deliver to them all of the pain and suffering they've dealt to me for so long.[16]

> My orchestration of the Day of Retribution is my attempt to do everything, in my power, to destroy everything I cannot have.[17]

One might look at these entries and conclude the shooter felt jealousy toward males in relationships with females, but this isn't quite right. Jealousy implies a relationship already exists between one person

---

10. Smith and Kim, "Comprehending Envy," 46.
11. Nieli, "Santa Barbara Killings," ¶2.
12. Rodger, "My Twisted World," 66.
13. Rodger, "My Twisted World," 82.
14. Rodger, "My Twisted World," 87.
15. Rodger, "My Twisted World," 106.
16. Rodger, "My Twisted World," 131.
17. Rodger, "My Twisted World," 137.

and another, and a third person is perceived to threaten the relationship. The Santa Barbara shooter didn't worry about losing an existing relationship, instead feeling an intense yearning for relationships others seemed to have.

This extreme example of envy offers a vivid illustration of how it can eat away at a person, accelerating as it grows, like cancer in the bones.

> **Pause:** After starting with something as routine as Facebook envy, we moved on to a horrific and intense story. To be clear, we're not suggesting that small envy inevitably leads to murderous rage. Most of us live in the land of minor envies, but even small envy twists our hearts and makes it difficult to love our neighbors as we love ourselves.
>
> Take a moment to reflect on the small envies you carry with you, which we'll talk about next. Name them as yours. Sit with the discomfort of that. After a moment, check in with yourself and ask whether you sense any relief in the naming. You might, and you might not. Either way, take some slow, deep breaths. Imagine breathing in gratitude for God's grace and letting go of your envy with each exhale. If you can, wish the other person well as you end, or perhaps simply name that someday you hope you can wish the other person well.

Schadenfreude and Malicious Envy

Put together the German nouns *Schaden*, which means damage, and *Freude*, which means joy, and we end up with a feature of envy called *schadenfreude*, where the envious person finds joy in the misfortunes of others. Israel's King David cried out in pain about schadenfreude in one of his psalms: "May those who rejoice at my troubles be humiliated and disgraced" (Ps 35:26). Nearly seven hundred years later, Aristotle noted, "The [one] who is delighted by others' misfortunes is identical with the [one] who envies others' prosperity."[18]

A group of international researchers studied this, concluding that *malicious* envy is associated with schadenfreude whereas *benign* envy is not.[19] Both types of envy begin with an upward social comparison. We

---

18. Aristotle, "Aristotle's Rhetoric," ¶1.
19. Van De Ven et al., "When Envy Leads."

look at something desirable about another person and feel inferior or frustrated, watering the seed of envy. Next, we feel motivated to level the playing field. *Benign* envy tries to make things even by catching up with the other person; *malicious* envy tries to do it by bringing the other person down. Six-year-old Tyra is envious of a friend's toy, so she begs her parents to get her a similar toy for Christmas. Evie is also envious of a friend's toy, so she destroys it when the friend leaves the room. Tyra is showing benign envy, and Evie malicious envy. Some languages have separate words for benign and malicious envy (e.g., German, Dutch), but in English we have just one word, so we'll use a drawing to explore the differences.

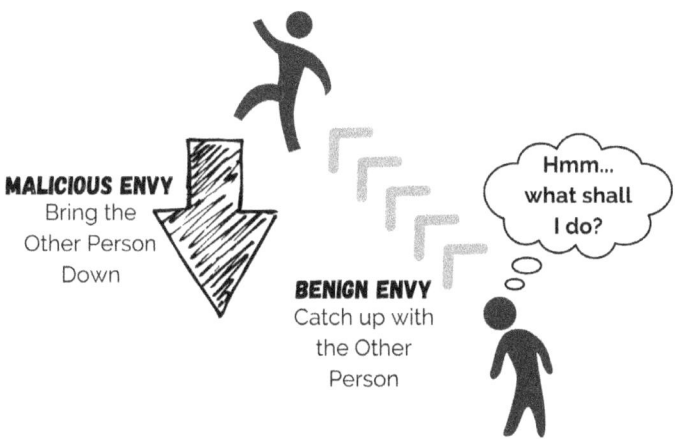

The Santa Barbara shooter, Cain, Joseph's brothers, Haman, Israel's King Saul, and the Babylonian officials trying to ruin Daniel all exemplify malicious envy and slipped into schadenfreude. It turns out schadenfreude happens in smaller ways on social media, too. Some Italian scholars found a way to detect and categorize schadenfreude in X hashtags.[20] Sure enough, it showed up with regularity.

In the New Testament book of James, we find incisive words about how one unfortunate thing can lead to another, spiraling toward death: "Temptation comes from our own desires, which entice us and drag us away. These desires give birth to sinful actions. And when sin is allowed to grow, it gives birth to death" (Jas 1:14–15).

---

20. Cecconi et al., "Schadenfreude."

Negative spirals lead us toward ruin while the positive spiral of gratitude, which we will discuss shortly, leads us toward joy. The negative spiral of malicious envy goes something like this: Envy comes from (1) pain, which drags us away into (2) malicious attitudes. These attitudes give birth to (3) destructive character qualities. And when we allow these character qualities to grow, they give birth to misery and more pain.

Pain

Envy begins with the pain of uncomfortable social comparisons, then progresses from there. Perhaps we could pause there for a moment, and in the recognition that envy begins with pain offer a bit of compassion for our own envy and for the envy of others. Sure, the envy may feel like trivial entitlement on the surface (you make more money than I do, or you have floated the canals of Venice and I haven't, or you have a flawless love life and I don't), but it represents a deep sense of disappointment that life—perhaps especially in the relationship realm—has not turned out the way one hoped, dreamed, and expected it would.

Sometimes the inferior feelings are fleeting, maybe even so quick that we don't notice them at all. But other times feelings of inferiority stick with us, as if a giant "Less Than" symbol is stuck on our foreheads, making us vulnerable to preoccupation, malicious envy, and schadenfreude.

Negative spirals often begin with pain and our coping strategies in times of pain often lead to more pain. In the aftermath of a relationship squabble, one partner heads to the bar to numb the ache, then comes home even more belligerent, deepening the troubles. The person losing at a casino takes even more risks to get the money back and ends up amplifying the losses. Someone feels insecure in a new dating relationship and ends up texting way too much just to see if everything is okay, but the continual contact feels like harassment and drives the other person away.

Feeling inferior is agonizing, so we try to do something about it. Looking to ease our isolation and disappointments in life, we reasonably and wisely turn toward social connections. But if our minds are captured by inferiority, we don't move into these relationships with our best selves. Instead, we bring our wounded, comparative impulses where we size up others, act competitively more than collaboratively, and communicate with criticism and cynicism more than affirmation and hope.

Researchers at Virginia Commonwealth University had participants recall a time when they felt envious, grateful, or neutral, and then a confederate in the study dropped a bunch of pencils in the same room. The researchers wondered whether participants would kneel and help pick up the pencils when given different promptings. Those remembering envy helped less often than others, and when they did help, they picked up fewer pencils.[21]

Add in social media, and the speed of contemporary life gives preoccupation with painful feelings of inferiority easy access to our inner world. We can scroll through social media feeds for hours looking at the accomplishments and delights of our friends as they pop relentlessly into our news feeds. This is especially true for *passive* Facebook users.

Edwin posts frequently on social media, using words and pictures to tell the world what he is doing and interacting with friends about their posts and sending direct messages. Jared lurks more in the shadows, posting occasionally but mostly reading what others post and the comments and discussions that ensue. To researchers studying social media, Edwin is an *active* user and Jared a *passive* user, giving Jared more time for preoccupied inferiority than Edwin. Not surprisingly, passive use of social media is more connected to envy than active use.[22] The lives we have outside of social media complicate this further. Even among active users, those who feel disconnected in real life are likely to have more painful experiences on social media than others.[23]

Malicious Attitudes

Pain caused by social comparison generally subsides quickly,[24] but before it goes it often morphs into destructive attitudes about self and others, attitudes that persist even after emotions subside. Some people veer toward benign envy and imagine making themselves more accomplished, successful, or desirable. Others swerve toward malicious envy, where they imagine bringing the other person down a notch or two (or ten). Neither benign nor malicious envy is helpful or good, but malicious envy leads to greater damage than benign.

---

21. Behler et al., "To Help or To Harm?"
22. Tandoc et al., "Facebook Use."
23. Macrynikola and Miranda, "Active Facebook Use."
24. Lange et al., "Painful Duality of Envy," 589.

Years ago, we bought a Mazda 626, a snazzy four-door sedan that would fit our family while functioning as a good commuter car. Mazda stopped making the 626 twenty years ago, so it's surprising the memory of it being keyed is still fresh. Having a brand-new car with shiny green paint sitting in the parking lot may have provided a way for someone with malicious envy to bring another someone down a notch or two.

It's possible the person who scratched our car didn't recognize it to be an act of envy, but more a statement of defiance or fearlessness. Sometimes malicious envy runs in the background, beneath conscious awareness, which makes it an especially difficult attitude to challenge and correct.

One of the greatest sports scandals in Olympic history occurred around the time we bought that Mazda. On January 6, 1994, Olympic hopeful figure skater Nancy Kerrigan was attacked after practice in Detroit's Cobo Arena when Shane Stant clubbed her right knee with a collapsible baton. Weeks of investigations, confessions, and indictments followed, leading to the discovery that the ex-husband and bodyguard of another world-class figure skater hired Stant. Kerrigan went on to win the silver medal in the 1994 Olympics while her competitor came in eighth. Three weeks later the competitor pled guilty to "conspiracy to hinder prosecution," then in 2018 she admitted she knew something was about to happen and chose not to warn Kerrigan.[25] Is this a tragic example of malicious envy or the sinister side of the high value we place on winning? Or perhaps our value on winning drives malicious envy.

Destructive Character Qualities

Malicious attitudes have a way of sneaking into our character over time. Those who go the way of malicious envy become vulnerable to schadenfreude, finding joy in the misfortunes of others, while those experiencing benign envy are less inclined toward schadenfreude.

One restaurateur smiles privately when the competitor down the street suffers a kitchen fire while another offers sincere condolences. One person feels a spark of inner glee when a glamorous celebrity faces personal tragedy while another feels sorrow. One churchgoer has a sense of moral smugness when a well-known leader is humiliated while another leans toward compassion and grace.

---

25. Pak, "Tonya Harding and Nancy Kerrigan."

If we're honest with ourselves, we experience these sorts of examples less clearly as either-or and more as both-and, shades of gray blending into each other as hints of schadenfreude weave in and out of our otherwise empathic responses. This moral tug-of-war is familiar to most everyone. When we choose to turn ourselves over to the lesser, malignant self who delights in seeing others fail, we poison our relationships as surely as that poison infects our hearts.

> **Pause:** We have made the case that envy is dire and costly. Take stock of your own emotions right now, having read about this deadly sin. Are you eager to move on to something else?
>
> Gratitude eclipses and is the antidote to envy. It is envy's complete opposite. Instead of focusing on what we don't have, gratitude invites us to notice and appreciate the gifts and delights of life.

An Invitation to Gratitude

Spirals move both up and down. Envy spirals downward toward death; gratitude spirals upward toward life abundant. Each of us can look at a person we deem successful or confident or beautiful or godly or lucky and feel envious toward them, but we can also look at that same person and notice a warm and welcoming smile, the lines around dazzling eyes that speak to times of joy and struggle, the spark of personality that makes this person unique and winsome. Envy is a posture of strife whereas gratitude is the stance of love.

Gratitude (1) broadens our attention, helping us (2) notice the good and beautiful things in life. In turn, we (3) recognize our connections and belonging and (4) grow in lovingkindness, which further broadens our attention to notice God's gifts all around.

Broadening Our Attention

The PEP lab sounds like a place where new energy drinks should be tested, but it actually stands for Positive Emotions and Psychophysiology. In the lab in Chapel Hill, North Carolina, Barbara Fredrickson and her graduate students do cutting-edge research on how humans experience emotions. Fredrickson is a leading voice in the science of positive emotions, and what she calls the broaden-and-build theory sits at the core of her work.[26]

To understand broaden-and-build, let's first look at how emotions were typically studied prior to Fredrickson's work. Emotions are associated with *specific action tendencies*. When afraid, our action tendency is to escape. When angry, we want to lash out. If we feel disgusted, we're inclined to withdraw. We don't always do these things—sometimes we need to stick around and clean up the child's vomit even though our action tendency urges us to leave and hope our spouse cleans it up. It's normal to wish to be somewhere else even as we resist the temptation to flee, lash out, or withdraw. But action tendencies narrow our attention and focus, even if we choose to override our natural inclination. This is reasonable, given that intense emotions might indicate a life-threatening situation where we need to concentrate on the danger at hand and respond decisively.

Fredrickson and her colleagues found that studying specific action tendencies didn't work well when looking at positive emotions. What we might do when angry, fearful, or disgusted is predictable, but much less so when we experience love, awe, joy, or gratitude. If you're staring at an angry mama bear in the woods, your thoughts and behaviors are predictable, but if you're enjoying a delightful meal at an outdoor café in late summer, you might be thinking a million different things, which makes it difficult to anticipate what you will do next. The joy of the moment may propel you toward laughter or play or singing or exploring. Who knows what might happen at that café? Threatening emotions narrow our focus while positive emotions broaden our repertoire of potential behaviors.

When hiking with friends recently, we noticed ourselves watching our feet as we moved through a narrow mountain pass rather than looking around at the splendorous waterfalls in Oregon's Columbia Gorge. The threat of a narrow path along a steep cliff constricted our focus even as we longed to look around, broaden our awareness, and notice the stunning beauty of the moment.

A broadened focus builds personal resources. When we are feeling light and happy and spontaneous, we are more likely to meet new people, smile at them, make friends, express ourselves freely, and join in human community. We sense we belong to something bigger than ourselves, bigger than our human community, and discover a sense of being at home in

---

26. Fredrickson, "Gratitude."

ourselves and in the world. We become curious, grow in self-esteem and contentment, and take joy in imagining future possibilities. All the while our brains resound with what Fredrickson calls *positivity resonance*.

Envy narrows our focus, either by evoking cruel desires to inflict misfortune on another (malicious envy) or by compelling us to work harder to catch up with the other (benign envy). Gratitude broadens and builds, moving us out of our smaller selves prone to petty comparisons and strivings and into large spaces where we can appreciate and explore the grandeur of the world around us.[27]

> So gratitude . . . builds and strengthens friendships and other social bonds, it builds and strengthens civil communities, and it builds and strengthens spirituality. Drawing more directly from the broaden-and-build theory, I add to this list that gratitude also builds people's skills for loving and showing appreciation.[28]

Gratitude can show up on social media, too. Posting about a trip to Europe, replete with beautiful pictures, might lead to either envy or gratitude or some mixture of both. But other posts land more squarely in the realm of gratitude, such as reflecting on the genuine wave and smile from the woman standing in the rain holding the construction sign instructing us to Stop and then to go Slow. What if we posted as many (or more) photos of ordinary beauty found in our backyards as those we take from the heights of the Alps? Maybe social media can be broadened and built, too, spreading love, appreciation, and kindness.

As psychoanalyst Melanie Klein observed six decades before Fredrickson's groundbreaking work in the PEP lab, gratitude reflects and shapes our capacity to love.[29]

Noticing the Good and Beautiful

Love starts with slowing and seeing. How can we possibly love without taking ample time to notice others, paying attention to quirks, mannerisms, preferences, hopes, and disappointments? The same applies to loving the natural world to which we belong and the God who created all this magnificence and wonder. We slow to see, and we see to love.

---

27. Xiang et al., "Effect of Gratitude."
28. Fredrickson, "Gratitude," 152.
29. Klein, *Envy and Gratitude*.

Baby Nigerian Dwarf goats frolic in the Fern Creek pasture every spring. Just now, Clara's four little ones race to her udder when she offers the soft nicker that says, "My café is open for business." We sit on downed trees covered in moss and watch them, as Hazel's two little ones dismount from the wood pile with grand twists and spins and hops. Meanwhile, dappled sun comes through the branches of the giant maple over our heads, leafing out, gratitude unfurling leaf by leaf. As Thomas Merton says, "A tree gives glory to God by being a tree."[30] Whether in New York's Central Park or an Illinois suburban forest preserve or rural Oregon, trees and plants of all sorts rise around us, and critters romp in seeming joy, bearing witness to this good creation and its Creator.

Happenings on any particular day are, as Merton would say, a holiness consecrated to God by God's creative wisdom, declaring the glory of God.

So are the sounds of laughter from children on the little farm next door, the playful joy of our own grandchildren when we gather, the sound of our Quaker community's collective voices when we sing in church on Sunday mornings, even the school bus we sometimes get stuck behind as it drops passengers off after a day of school, representing a community that cares for the education and well-being of its children.

Yes, much goes wrong in the world, and yes, much goes right. What goes right is good, beautiful, and plentiful, as it should be. When we broaden our attention, we find tidbits for which to be grateful at every turning. We see much unfolding that gives God glory simply by being what it was created to be.

We learned of Brother David Steindl-Rast through social media. (Of course.) His five-minute reading of "A Good Day" has been paired with various videography and photography to gratifying ends.[31] To watch and listen is a contemplative exercise. Steindl-Rast invites us to notice the good and beautiful surrounding us in the ordinariness of *this* day and to become lovingly present to it.

Steindl-Rast's lifelong emphasis on gratitude gains credibility when one learns that he came of age during the Nazi occupation of Austria in World War II. Being a quarter Jewish, he watched family members seized and sent away to concentration camps. He never saw them again. The Germans drafted him into the army as a youth, and

---

30. Merton, *New Seeds*, 29.
31. While there are many versions, one favorite is Schwartzberg, "Gratitude."

he learned what humiliation felt like and smelled like, how it inhabited and crept into one's sense of self. Yet prior to those years he had been nurtured with a strong sense of human dignity, and he says the most decisive gift his early religious schooling gave him was the joy of life, a joy he has always carried. The capacity to find the good and beautiful amid suffering and ugliness: pale flowers in spring, a blade of grass pushing through concrete, sun breaking through clouds, the met gaze and smile of a fellow suffering soul.[32]

The simple act of noticing the good and beautiful—that is, taking interest in, celebrating, enjoying with awe and wonder what God has made manifest in this created world—fills us with gratitude. Even, Steindl-Rast says, in the presence of pain and suffering.

Recognizing Our Connections and Belonging

What if, when the goodness and beauty of a thing settles into our bones, it happens because we have become aware that we are in a mysterious way connected to and belong to what we recognize as good and beautiful? For Steindl-Rast this began as a child with a sense of wonder and comfort in knowing he belonged to God. It grew into a sense that he was connected to all things because the heart of God contained all things.

As a child his mother taught him the Prayer of the Heart, which held him through the horrors of the World War II years. Whenever he wanted, he had access to God in his heart. He could go there and feel protected, which he referred to as coming home into his heart. "Only because I know that I can always return to my center, am I able to face what confronts me."[33]

We mentioned Julian of Norwich in chapter 3 as an exemplar of courage, but we would not do her life justice if we failed to notice the reason for her courage, which was a profound sense that God's abiding presence and love held everything together. Julian, who lived during the One Hundred Years' War and survived three ravaging visits of the bubonic plague on her village, asserted that there is nowhere we can be where God cannot hold us fast. Even when we feel we are drowning in our circumstances, God encloses us in love.[34] We are not—we cannot

---

32. Sidon, "Gospel of Gratitude."
33. Steindl-Rast, *i am through you so i*, 21.
34. Julian of Norwich, *Selections*, 30.

be—abandoned, however much we may feel as though we have been. As Psalm 139 (which Julian was likely referencing) affirms, there is no place where God is not:

> I can never escape from your Spirit!
> I can never get away from your presence!
>
> If I go up to heaven, you are there;
> if I go down to the grave, you are there.
>
> If I ride the wings of the morning,
> if I dwell by the farthest oceans,
>
> even there your hand will guide me,
> and your strength will support me. (Ps 139:7-10)

Our invitation is to let God do the transforming work for us to be who we are created to be, partnering with God, others, and the created world in order that God might be glorified and that flourishing might abound in a world reflecting the goodness of its Creator.

This begins with gratitude and includes recognizing that we belong to and are part of *all* of it. Not an easy task, that. Yet we know that our individual stories continue a longer story—not only of our ancestors but also of a created world that births and grows new things out of the death or decay of old things, taking and receiving so that life keeps moving forward. We belong to a history and to a future that comes through us, even as we also belong to all that makes up our present life.

Might our sense of belonging deepen if we recognized that our bodies live, think, and act on account of the vegetables, fruits, and animals we eat and the ocean that gets drawn up into clouds that gift the earth with rain and that our bodies eventually also turn back into the stuff of the earth that nourishes new generations of life?

> **Pause:** The conversation about coming from decayed things and being connected to the vegetables you eat might feel a bit out of place, maybe also a bit too, well, *earthy*. Pause a moment, if so.
>
> That we *don't* belong in some biological way to the whole of God's creation would be a hard point to argue, but it doesn't necessarily make it comforting that we do. Reflect on what you are feeling just now. If discomfort, what makes it uncomfortable? What thoughts might be at the root of your discomfort?

SLOW TO ENVY: AN INVITATION TO GRATITUDE 135

> Perhaps your response is neutral. Perhaps positive. If you are willing, try imagining yourself recognizing the depth of your belongingness to a creation held together by Christ. Read Colossians 1:17 and the surrounding verses, and then imagine what it might mean. Respond with gratitude for your life and your chance to live it. Can you imagine such a place, once touched, might give you a greater sense of and comfort in being at home in yourself and in the world?

If envy narrows our attention, beckoning us to unhelpful, petty comparisons with one another, then gratitude does the opposite, expanding our vision, pulling us together into our common creatureliness, all of us and all creation held together by the sustaining love of God, who made it all and then pronounced it good. Gratitude is good for our own well-being,[35] yet perhaps the greater goodness comes when gratitude opens a flow of lovingkindness that blesses those around us.

When Steindl-Rast claims that gratefulness is our only possible response to the gift of life, of this day, of this moment, he does not claim that lightly. After gracing us with example after example of how we might attend to the gifts of this day, he ends his reading this way:

> So these are just a few of an enormous number of gifts to which you can open your heart. And so I wish for you that you would open your heart to all these blessings and let them flow through you, that everyone whom you will meet on this day will be blessed by you; just by your eyes, by your smile, by your touch—just by your presence. Let the gratefulness overflow into blessing all around you, and then it will really be a good day.[36]

Growing in Lovingkindness

Brother Steindl-Rast's words are powerful, and we encourage you to watch the video to get the full effect. As he narrates about the "enormous number of gifts" awaiting our hearts, we see a strawberry in time-lapse, moving from pollination toward a state of delicious red ripeness. Then the video shifts to girls playing hopscotch, the hug of a parent, the beauty of a grand waterfall, a musical family jamming on the front porch around

---

35. We are not discussing all the health benefits of gratitude in this chapter, but the science on this point is robust and compelling. See McMinn, *Science of Virtue*, 71–94.

36. Schwartzberg, "Gratitude," 5:10–6:05.

Grandpa's guitar, some beautiful smiles, and an ice cream party. If belonging is an inherited reality, a gift we acknowledge or not, then the possibility of gratitude unfolds around us in living color with each moment. And if the stuff of envy is comparison and striving, the stuff of gratitude is the lovingkindness made possible when the depth of our belonging and connection to all God has made resonates in our bones. Goodness multiplies as gratitude burbles and flows and cascades all around.

The point of an upward gratitude spiral is not to reach some imaginable or unimaginable pinnacle. Rather, upward spirals connect us more fully to the best version of our ordinary selves, to the life given over to Christ, *who lives in us*.

How do we hold the mystery of Christ living in us as we engage our thoughts, feelings, intuitions, and sensations? How do we hold the mystery of Christ living in us as we engage our partners, friends, children, parishioners, and colleagues? As we live and walk in and among the other members of creation that also belong to and are loved by God? In Paul's letter to the Galatians, he reminds those who live by the Spirit and place their faith in Christ that what is important is not living by the law, but "faith expressing itself in love" (Gal 5:5–6).

Love is the pivot that turns us away from envy and all its small strivings and toward life-giving gratitude. God invites us toward faith expressed in love, toward our *telos*, our ultimate end, toward opening our eyes to see blessings overflowing all around us.

Gratitude Practices

Many gratitude practices have emerged in recent years. Here are a few:

1. *ABCs.* Try going through the alphabet, bringing up some grateful image that begins with each letter.[37] The letter A might cause us to think of Alaska, a place of incredible beauty. B is for blueberries, or maybe blueberries on oatmeal for a morning breakfast. C is for Christmas, a light in the dark winter for those of us in the Northern Hemisphere.

2. *Grateful recounting.* Spend time each week remembering experiences of gratitude. Some do this through journaling, writing about large and small things that call forth gratefulness. Others choose the

---

37. Steindl-Rast, "ABCs."

"Three Things" exercise where they jot down three blessings that showed up during the day. Try one of these or choose your own method for noticing and recounting gratefulness.

3. *Gratitude letter and visit.* Think of someone from your past who has blessed you deeply and write them a letter of thanks. Then, if possible, arrange a visit where you can share your letter and express gratefulness in person.

4. *Grateful posting.* If you post on social media, post a photo that captures something for which you are grateful. Perhaps do this once a week for a year.

None of these are classic spiritual practices, per se, though we would argue that gratitude itself is a deeply faithful and spiritual practice. If you are looking for explicitly faith-based gratitude practices, you can make some adaptations.

For the ABCs exercise, take a moment to thank God after recalling something from each letter of the alphabet. For example, "I am grateful for blueberries. Thank you, God, for creating something as beautiful and delicious as blueberries to cheer our hearts and delight our taste buds." This is much like the gratitude phase of the Daily Examen, described at the end of chapter 5, but more alphabetical.

For the grateful recounting exercise, begin your writing with "Dear God, today I thank you for . . ." This helps you focus your gratitude to God as the giver of the good gifts you are noticing.

For the gratitude letter, write a letter to God expressing your thanks. At first glance this may seem to rule out the possibility of a personal visit where you can share your letter, but then again, maybe that's exactly what quiet prayer is. Find a quiet, spacious place and time to read your letter to God, giving ample time for grateful reflection.

Slow Ponderings

1. Have you noticed social media making you more inclined toward envy? If so, what online practices might help you avoid or minimize envy?

2. Reading through the Old Testament stories about envy, and how badly they ended, can feel quite shocking. How have you experienced the damaging effects of envy in your own life or in those closest to you?

3. We make a distinction between malicious and benign envy in this chapter, noting that some languages have different words for the two experiences, though we don't in English. Recall a time when you experienced benign envy, making you want to catch up with another person whom you perceived to be doing better than you. How did it turn out? What concerns or cautions come to mind for the next time you experience benign envy?

4. Gratitude's upward spiral calls us to broadened attention so that we can notice the good and beautiful gifts of each moment. Recall a recent time when you were able to do that, to set aside the stress of everyday life long enough to notice something or someone you might not have otherwise seen. What stirs just now as you recall that time?

5. If you were to describe your various "memberships," what would they be? To whom do you belong, and how do you experience that belonging? Where is the comfort in that, and where is the discomfort?

6. What is your experience with gratitude practices? Do you sense a nudging or invitation to engage in one, and if so, how are you inspired by those suggested here?

Chapter 7

Slow to Consume: An Invitation to Generosity

The River Tay winds through 117 miles of Scottish landscape, providing a home for salmon, otters, and lampreys, as well as recreation for water sports enthusiasts of all kinds. The largest city on the River Tay hosted the Scottish Horticultural Research Institute in 1969, when Derek Jennings bred a natural hybrid of raspberry and blackberry that became known as the tayberry. Larger and sweeter than its loganberry cousin, the tayberry cannot be machine harvested, so it's not likely to be found anywhere in your local grocery store or in recent memory.

We grow a few tayberries on our little farm because of the generosity of a man named Mike. When we needed to be out of our house for a couple days, we found a charming little Airbnb situated above an equally charming tasting room nestled in the hillside of a boutique vineyard. One afternoon we wandered into the otherwise empty tasting room and met Mike, the host. Mike invited us to the enclosed sun deck where he brought water—in chic glasses for us and in a bowl for our little dog, Oliver—and then visited with us, disappearing periodically to retrieve the next sample of wine offered in the vineyard's tasting. After retiring from an Air Force career and then a second career as a school administrator, Mike settled in Oregon wine country, where he happily works one day a week as a tasting room host. We talked about the Air Force (Lisa's father was also a career Air Force pilot) and the contours of life in Oregon. When we mentioned our little fruit farm, Mike disappeared briefly again and returned with a half-pint of his homemade tayberry jam, which he offered us as a gift. Grateful for his kindness and stunned by the taste of his jam, the next day we ordered a couple of tayberry plants from a local nursery and returned to the vineyard with a pint of our Columbia Star blackberry jam. We exchanged grateful handwritten notes and emails before settling back into our separate lives, but that small encounter on a sunny February day reminds us how life can be lived with hearts open in kindness.

With consuming, we take from the world to fulfill our desires. With generosity, we offer ourselves to the world.

A chapter titled "Slow to Consume" can go in two directions. The first option is to frame the conversation around *big* and *small*. Those of us in Western countries—especially in the United States—live too big. We eat too much (especially too much meat), drive too much, burn too much fossil fuel, build oversized houses, have too many gadgets that end up in landfills, and in the process, we overspend. To be good world citizens, we need to live smaller.[1] We'll start with the *big* and *small* conversation but won't linger there.

The second direction is a conversation around *fast* and *slow*. Later in the chapter, we will notice patterns of *fast* and how they impact our consumption habits, and then we will invite you to consider how *slow* might enhance our way of being in the world—with ourselves, our families, friends and neighbors, distant neighbors whom we may never meet, and the planet itself. We conclude the chapter with an invitation to generosity and suggestions for a spiritual practice of generosity.

Big and Small

In an episode of the vintage show *Columbo*, the famed detective nabs a piece of gum from the villain's garbage to match his tooth print at the murder scene. Looking through people's garbage can be quite revealing, even if ethically and legally complicated.[2]

Each year since 1960, the United States Environmental Protection Agency (EPA) collects data on our garbage, then analyzes the information and releases a thorough report a couple of years later. It's not like anyone is looking for tooth prints on our gum, but they do look at the overall

---
1. Paarlberg, "Over-consumption in America," ¶1–4.
2. Panela, "Is collecting cans?," ¶1. Also, Nosowitz, "Private Eyes Tell Us," ¶3.

weight of our waste along with our landfill and recycling practices. The most recent report, from 2020, which includes data through 2018, shows how our garbage in the United States has increased over the years.

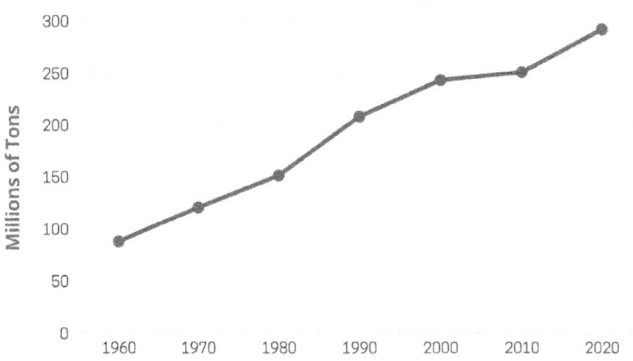

You might rightly push back and argue that the population has also increased since 1960. Yet the per capita waste has also increased, as shown here:

The good news is that we recycle more now than we did in 1960, so per-person waste has not increased much since 1990.[3]

All this recycling material and waste comes from somewhere. Brimming carts roll out of Costco and Sam's Club with new merchandise each day. At the same time pickups with trailers back into transfer centers to unload refuse. Robert Paarlberg, the political scientist who authored *The United States of Excess*, summarizes: "When consumption increases, pure waste increases as well. The wasteful use of both food and energy are now hallmarks of American life."[4]

What drives our excessive consumption? Economists differ on this point. The *consumer sovereignty* school of thought suggests that consumption drives production. If enough people want something, then companies will step up production of it. The more the people want, the more companies produce. Another school of thought, called *structured consumption*, suggests the relationship between supply and demand goes the other way: companies produce goods to make a profit and then convince consumers how important it is to own these new wares. The second view suggests our desires as consumers are molded by the people who make merchandise and the advertisers they hire to convince us to buy it.[5]

It's an ongoing debate. For example, do farmers grow corn because most items in US grocery stores contain corn as an ingredient, or do most items in US grocery stores contain corn because farmers grow so much while distributors, marketers, and policy makers convince us we need it?[6] Of course, there is complexity and truth in both perspectives, but the two of us find the second perspective quite humbling and convicting, especially considering our choices to be environmentally friendly with our consuming.

Because we are concerned about climate change, we have attempted to reduce our impact in multiple ways—we recycle, grow a substantial portion of our food, have a geothermal heat pump, drive an electric vehicle, eat very little meat, and have solar panels sitting above our Energy Star-compliant recycled aluminum roof. From the *consumer sovereignty* perspective, we feel good about these choices—we are voting with our dollars to bring environmentally responsible products into the

3. United States Environmental Protection Agency, "Advancing Sustainable," 2–6.
4. Paarlberg, *United States of Excess*, 3.
5. Stuart et al., "Overconsumption as Ideology."
6. Ferdman, "How Corn Made its Way."

world. But look at this the other way for a moment, from the *structured consumption* perspective. In this view, companies popped up to sell environmentally inclined people like us new products, and we jumped in with our whole hearts. Our old asphalt shingles needed replacing, but now they sit in a landfill somewhere so that our new lifetime aluminum roof can cover our house. The solar companies and geothermal furnace marketers convinced us to give them our money to reduce our dependence on future fossil fuel (*and* our guilt), and Elon Musk and his team persuaded us that buying a Model 3 would help address climate change even as it also helped Musk become one of the world's richest people.[7] So yes, our choices are helping with our environmental footprint, but look at all the consuming we have done to make this happen!

Our point is not to wallow in guilt here, and most days we feel good about our sustainability choices. But notice how complex these issues become when we feel a need to consume more good stuff in order to consume less bad stuff. We can't consume ourselves out of a consumption problem.

We have only scratched the surface, but that's enough of the *big* and *small* conversation. Much has been written about this by others. For the purposes of this book, the *fast* and *slow* conversation offers a different angle, and that's the part of the consumption conversation we'd like to address.

Fast and Slow

Daniel Kahneman, the late, famed research psychologist and Nobel Prize winner, outlines two kinds of mental processing in his book *Thinking, Fast and Slow*. System 1 is automatic, fast, and almost effortless. It allows us to make quick assessments, which are often good ones. We can read the emotions on an angry person's face with incredible speed and accuracy. Children learn language this way, with seemingly little effort and (eventually) incredible precision. System 1 relies on cognitive shortcuts, and they work so well for us that we often fail to recognize our vulnerability to err.

Kahneman gives this example: "Steve is very shy and withdrawn, invariably helpful but with little interest in people or the world of reality. A

---

7. *Forbes*, "World's Real-Time Billionaires."

meek and tidy soul, he has a need for order and structure, and a passion for detail. Is Steve more likely to be a librarian or a farmer?"[8]

Most people will imagine Steve to be a librarian because he fits certain stereotypes in their mind, ignoring the statistical reality that there are twenty times more male farmers than librarians in the United States. Steve is much more likely to be a farmer, though our System 1 processing will lead us toward the faulty conclusion that he is a librarian.

System 2 is slow and effortful, helping us to manage complex situations that involve concentration. If you're working behind the counter when an angry customer approaches with receipt in hand, your System 1 will instantly and effortlessly discern the customer's anger, but listening to the argument, reviewing the receipt, and determining if a refund is appropriate will require System 2.

Because the two of us routinely cook breakfast together, overnight guests often comment on how seamlessly we work in the kitchen. We have done this for many years, so it has been routinized into System 1 processing. One of us slices the vegetables while the other puts oil in the skillet, one starts the three-minute timer for our tea while the other begins steeping it, one finds the spatula in time for the other to flip the eggs, one moves a step back and the other a step forward when we pass in the kitchen. The choreography feels surprising to guests, but to us it is the ingrained movements of System 1 that get played out almost daily. But if we travel and stay at an Airbnb where we plan to cook our normal breakfast, everything changes. Skillets are hard to find, as is canola oil, and passing in the kitchen feels clumsy. System 2 kicks in sluggishly and tediously. There will be inelegance, misunderstandings, and overcooked eggs.

System 1 runs continually. It can't be shut off. System 2 rests frequently. Maybe you've had the experience of driving somewhere and having several minutes go by without much conscious awareness. System 1 knows how to drive your car, and when you get to the toll plaza and remember you left the transponder in your other car, System 2 kicks in. That's a good thing, too, as it keeps you from paying enormous toll fines each month.

> **Pause:** You may be trying to figure out which system is best. Wanting to rank them is normal. Think about it this way: System 1 helps us survive by quickly sifting good

---

8. Kahneman, *Thinking*, 7.

from bad, right from wrong, best from worst, acceptable from unacceptable.

Still, we can't legitimately rank-order Systems 1 and 2 because we need both to navigate the demands of daily life. We make quick, automatic assessments, which calls for System 1, and (hopefully) we recognize our tendency to err when we do so exclusively. This calls us to implement System 2.

Notice and lean into gratitude as you think of an example of each that is occurring right now in your mind.

Both systems impact our consumption patterns. Much of this is determined automatically by System 1, but we can slow down our tendency to consume and invite System 2 into the conversation. When you get in the car each morning to drive to work, or board the train or the bus, you probably don't calculate how much fossil fuel you will be using to get there. You consume unconsciously as you ponder the day ahead. It would be crippling to obsess about pollution and oil reserves every moment of a trip to work. But when it comes time to replace cars or plan this year's vacation or weigh pros and cons of moving an hour away from work, then System 2 becomes essential in helping to make a wise choice.

Fast comes naturally for most of us, but this is a book about slow, so let's look at several ways that System 2's slower processing can help us when it comes to consuming.

A Pathway to Frugality

System 1 can be impulsive. Grab the donut as you walk by the box sitting next to the water cooler. Buy the dress because you love it and you only live once. Venti instead of tall.

Sometimes this works out fine, and sometimes it doesn't. Perhaps you have been part of a sales pitch where you were told the offer is only good today. If you walk out the door, the deal is off. In other words, *don't* think about this. Give System 2 the day off and let impulsive System 1 have what it wants.

When it comes to frugality, the question is how much to let System 2 speak to the impulsive desires of System 1. People differ on this dynamic, which is called *cognitive reflection*. Those high in cognitive reflection invite System 2 into their decisions more than others. Shane Frederick, currently at Yale School of Management, developed something called the Cognitive Reflection Test (CRT).[9] It includes three questions. Notice the answers that come to mind quickly as you glance at the questions.

1. Together, a bat and a ball cost $1.10. The bat costs $1 more than the ball. How much does the ball cost?
2. If it takes five machines five minutes to make five widgets, how long would it take one hundred machines to make one hundred widgets?
3. In a lake, there is a patch of lily pads. Every day, the patch doubles in size. If it takes forty-eight days for the patch to cover the entire lake, how long would it take for the patch to cover half of the lake?

Most people will immediately think the ball costs 10¢, which is the fast System 1 answer. It's also the wrong answer because then the bat and ball would total $1.20 (10¢ plus $1.10). If you allow time for more cognitive processing, you'll find the ball costs 5¢ and the bat $1.05, which totals $1.10. The fast answers to questions 2 and 3 tend to be one hundred minutes and twenty-four days, but both are incorrect. Upon reflection, one can see that it only takes five minutes for one hundred machines to produce one hundred widgets (one widget per machine each five minutes) and forty-seven days to cover half the lake (when it doubles the following day, it will cover the entire lake). Because System 1 thinking is quick, automatic, and often wrong, those employing more cognitive reflection tend to get higher scores on the CRT.

This gets particularly interesting when looking at financial preferences. For example, those with low cognitive reflection (who default to System 1 thinking) tend to prefer immediate reward rather than delayed gratification and are willing to pay more than twice as much for overnight shipping on a new book purchase than those with higher System 2 inclinations.[10]

Slowing down, engaging in more System 2 thinking, helps us to be less impulsive and more frugal with financial choices. Christian philosopher Dallas Willard once wrote, "Practicing frugality means we stay within the bounds of what general good judgment would designate as necessary for the kind of life to which God has led us." Willard goes on

---

9. Frederick, "Cognitive Reflection."
10. Frederick, "Cognitive Reflection," 31.

to suggest, "Frivolous consumption corrupts the soul away from trust in, worship of, and service to God and injures our neighbors as well."[11]

Knowing that frivolous consumption corrupts the soul and causes injury doesn't make frugality easy to practice. For starters, deciding which consumption choices are *frivolous* is subjective. An Apple watch might seem essential to me and frivolous to you, and likewise with a second car, or any car, for that matter. Wrestling with frugality and frivolous consumption is part of living generously.

Marketers—at least the unscrupulous ones—will not appreciate Willard raising the question of good judgment over frivolous consumption. Aggressive sales efforts almost always focus on System 1. Research psychologists refer to the anchoring effect as a way of setting expectations that will then affect perceptions and decisions. If the normal cost of a sweater is $145 but the website is offering a 30 percent off sale today only, the $99 price tag seems good. But notice the System 1 pandering here. The anchor is set at $145, which may or may not be a reasonable anchor value. No one would buy a $100 sweater if the normal price were $50, but by setting it at $145, then $99 seems like a bargain. Also, the time pressure of (presumably) having the sale expire at the end of the day adds urgency. The message is "Don't think about this very much because we want System 1 to make the choice."

We're not suggesting you shouldn't buy the sweater. Rather, we're pointing out how marketing might easily manipulate our buying patterns and that we would be wise to bring System 2 into our internal conversation before clicking the "Purchase Now" button.

During an overnight visit from a grandson who was eight years old at the time, we searched for wooden chess pieces to purchase on Etsy because we no longer had a set and he enjoyed playing chess with Grandpa. He discovered a beautiful board uniquely carved from a slab of olive wood and wanted to spend his entire savings account to buy it for his father. And he wanted to do it *right now*. If we placed the online order, he would hand us the cash next time we came to his house. We saw a lovely, generous, tender heart—and an example of System 1 impulse. We slowed him down and encouraged him to think about it and talk to his mother so he could make the decision with more reflection. We loved his quick, generous heart, even as we saw wisdom in helping him slow down what would be a major purchase, even if for another.

---

11. Willard, *Spirit of the Disciplines*, 168–69.

Fast needs slow to find frugality, godly wisdom, and yes, even generosity.

A Pathway to Relational Connection

Why do we so easily veer toward consumption? It may have more to do with the sociological texture of society than deliberate choice. And this same social texture may influence our relationships with one another more than we imagine.

Thorstein Veblen, an American economist and sociologist, coined the term conspicuous consumption (and conspicuous leisure), which refers to buying and displaying luxury items to show status and wealth. Veblen wrote during the Gilded Age of the late 1800s and aimed his critique at the wealthy, though applications of his theory today consider how both the middle and upper-middle classes participate in conspicuous consumption. We buy an expensive watch, which demonstrates our wealth to those who recognize it as such, when a less expensive watch would have functioned just as well. Our clutches and bags, clothes and shoes, cars, houses, and vacations all give us the opportunity to tell our neighbors, colleagues, and friends of our status and wealth. People, the theory suggests, want to be recognized by their peers as successful, and to achieve a higher social status by being seen as such. While some of this is intentional, much of it has simply become part of System 1 thinking.

Conspicuous consumption has some obvious relational consequences, such as petty competition, envy, and feelings of insecurity, but there are also less obvious relational consequences that show up without any deliberation or malice on our part. Kathleen Vohs studies the psychology of money. In a series of experiments published in the prestigious journal *Science*, Vohs and her colleagues demonstrated that priming people with ideas about money makes them more self-sufficient, less generous, less helpful, and less social than they would otherwise be.[12] For example:

1. Having a pile of Monopoly money nearby made participants less likely to ask for help when solving a difficult puzzle than those doing the same puzzle without the play money nearby.

12. Vohs et al., "Psychological Consequences of Money."

2. Participants who were primed to think about money with a word task were less likely to help with a tedious data coding assignment than those primed to linger on topics other than money.

3. Those primed to entertain thoughts about money offered only half as much time when giving directions to a confused person. And they helped pick up fewer pencils when a confederate in the study "accidentally" dropped a box.

4. Participants were given $2 in quarters as thanks for their involvement. Upon leaving, they were given opportunity to donate some of their earnings to a student fund. Those primed to think about money donated less than others.

5. Some participants were left in a room to wait while a computer screen saver showed images of currency. Others saw fish on their screen saver. All participants were then asked to place two chairs together for a conversation with another person. Those seeing currency on their screen savers placed the chairs farther apart than those seeing fish.

6. Participants were asked if they wanted to work alone or with a peer on an assignment. Those seeing the currency screen saver chose to work alone more than those seeing fish.

7. Participants sitting in a room with a wall poster showing currency were more inclined to choose individual leisure activities than those sitting in the same room with a poster showing a seascape, who were more likely to choose activities involving another person.

These are disturbing findings, especially for those of us living in Western countries largely dependent on and guided by growth economics. Even when we aren't consuming, our values around money encourage us to stay mindful of our retirement funds, stock portfolios, and bank accounts and to keep close count of our pile of money. Charles Dickens seemed to anticipate these findings when penning *A Christmas Carol* in 1843. His leading character, Ebenezer Scrooge, thinks about money constantly and lives an isolated life as a miser. Dickens holds hope for change, even for people like Scrooge, who is visited by ghosts of the past, present, and future and learns to open his heart to others as he loosens his grip on money.

System 1 runs in the background, largely out of our conscious awareness. Vohs's research suggests that every time we focus on money, we shift our balance from one foot to the other, away from relational connection that includes helping others and being generous and toward isolation and self-sufficiency. Shifting back to the other foot requires getting System 2 involved, which is what happened for Scrooge. The slower pace of System 2 potentially yields some good relational questions when facing financial choices.

- Who else should be involved in my decision-making process about this purchase?
- How will this higher-paying job affect my relationships with friends and family?
- Are my anxieties and preoccupations with my investment portfolio interfering with how I relate to others' needs and evoking too strong a sense of self-sufficiency?

Slow thinking allows us to consciously imagine good ways of being in the world, which helps counteract the self-isolating and self-interested tendencies of fast thinking when it comes to money.

A Pathway to Managing Complexity

Choices about money and consumption are challenging and complex, though System 1 will not think so. Kahneman writes, "System 1 is not prone to doubt. It suppresses ambiguity and spontaneously constructs stories that are as coherent as possible . . . the associations that it evokes will spread as if the messages were true."[13]

Simple stories hold allure—people easily comprehend them, they help make the world tidy and predictable, and they show a clear way forward. Holding complexity can be arduous, so System 2 makes managing doubt, uncertainty, and the unexpected possible.

We already mentioned the complexity of our environmental choices and how we have consumed a great deal of green merchandise with the paradoxical goal of being friendlier to the earth. This would be a good time to add the complexity of iPhone conversations in our household.

By disposition, Mark is a technology geek. He writes software for iPhones and iPads, which means he likes keeping up with the latest technology. By disposition, Lisa veers toward Luddism, often reminiscing

---

13. Kahneman, *Thinking*, 114.

about the good old days when a person could buy a $20 wall phone and keep it for life. Oh, and we're both environmentalists of sorts, or at least aspire to be, so we read about things like the human toll of cobalt mining and how our need for lithium-ion batteries affects developing countries.[14] This makes for interesting and complicated conversations when it comes to upgrading phones.

Both of us have our simple, doubt-free, System 1 stories running unconsciously in the background. Lisa's fast thinking tells her phones should last indefinitely. Mark's tells him phones should be replaced frequently to keep up with the latest technology. Clearly, we have a clash to manage, and we can only do so by thinking more slowly. System 2 thinking allows us to enter the complexity and nuance of these conversations, to negotiate and make compromises as needed, and to keep the health of our relationship as a higher priority than our phone purchases.

I (Mark) recently tried to save a few dollars by replacing Lisa's depleted iPhone battery. After ordering the kit online and watching a couple of YouTube videos, I cautiously opened her phone and then carelessly ripped a fragile but critical cable on the inside. The extensive damage meant that our most reasonable option was to replace the phone. As it turns out, it would have been far better to spend a few more dollars to have someone qualified change the battery. Instead, we ended up buying Lisa a new phone. She showed me remarkable grace given that 1) I broke her phone, and 2) she doesn't even like getting new phones. Now I need to figure out how to break my phone, which my System 1 thinking tells me is getting quite old. Lisa thinks we should exchange phones with one another, because my old one suits her just fine. And so it goes.

Consumption choices are complicated, especially when relationships are involved. The slower thinking of System 2 offers a blessing as we learn to navigate the complexity of living in a material world where we constantly balance our needs and wants with the limited resources of our finite existence.

A Pathway to Sabbath

As with *big* and *small* conversations about consumption, discussing Sabbath among Christians can evoke a lot of guilt and uncertainty. The Sabbath commandment leaps off the page with every reading of Exodus

---

14. Frankel, "Cobalt Pipeline."

20, and the reality of contemporary life makes it challenging to shut down our devices, expectations, and responsibilities for a full day each week. Over half of American Protestants still think the commandment applies, but most interpret Sabbath to be Sunday and to satisfy Sabbath commitments by attending church services and spending time with family. Only a quarter of those who observe Sabbath avoid chores, and just one in ten shuns shopping.[15]

In his book *Sabbath as Resistance*, Old Testament scholar Walter Brueggemann offers a peek behind the curtain of legalistic interpretation to see the contextual meaning of the fourth commandment. The Hebrew people had recently escaped slavery in Egypt, where they had been forced to labor nonstop to keep up with Pharaoh's insatiable demands for productivity. When Moses and Aaron asked Pharaoh to release the Hebrew people for a three-day festival, Pharaoh not only said no, but out of vengeance he also increased the slaves' workload by insisting they start gathering their own straw for the bricks they were making. If they didn't produce the same number of bricks as before, they were beaten (Exod 5:1–17). Relentlessly, day after day, Pharaoh insisted on *More! Now! Fast!*

If we remove the significant difference that the oppressed Hebrews had no agency over the relentless and cruel nature of their lives, then our 24-7 culture—with email, texts, and social media posts clamoring for attention; job demands to be productive; and market pressures to earn, consume, and spend—bears a faint resemblance to the life the Hebrew people eagerly left behind. Then and now, God invites us to the countercultural possibility of resisting *More! Now! Fast!* Sabbath, Brueggemann argues, is a countercultural act of resistance to these messages that bombard us every day. The Sabbath is not simply a chance to rest and slow down but an opportunity to reimagine social life away from acquisition and toward neighborly generosity.

Brueggemann says, "Sabbath is a big no . . . to the worship of commodity; it is no to pursuit of commodity. But it is more than no. Sabbath is the regular, disciplined, visible, concrete yes to the neighborly reality of the community beloved by God."[16]

After the Hebrew people escaped slavery and headed into the wilderness, God offered them manna to eat—not enough to store up wealth, but enough to eat for the day, and God asked them to stop and contemplate

---

15. Earls, "Most Churchgoers," ¶15–16.
16. Brueggemann, *Sabbath as Resistance*, 87.

one day each week, to notice the contrast between the old life driven by Pharaoh's demand and the new one founded on God's gracious provision. The Hebrews needed to learn a new way of being in community after four hundred years' living and breathing the oppressive, grasping values of Egypt. Biblical scholar Daniel Erlander suggests the forty years of wandering in the desert provided a "wilderness school" where God taught the Hebrew people a new way of being in relationship with each other, with nature, and with God. Manna provided an early lesson about acquiring and storing food. All food, they learned, is God's, and God provides enough so that hoarding is not only *unnecessary* but leads to rot, decay, and death. A corresponding lesson came through the gift of Sabbath—a reminder that rest is possible and good for humans, animals, and the earth, and allows people to experience and explore the wonder of friendship with God, others, and nature.[17]

The Hebrew people's new way of life would be countercultural, characterized by justice and mercy and founded on God as the one who provides. Slaves and servants, oxen and donkeys were also to be given a day of rest, which gave the land itself rest. Consuming and acquiring of all sorts ceased one day a week and one year of every seven.

The Sabbath offered a corrective to a cultural value that granted the powerful the right to accumulate more than they needed and to use their power to keep and control it. Accumulation of power and stuff and ceaseless work would no longer be valued; rather, mercy and justice, exemplified by rest and by generously sharing what came one's way beyond what one needed, would characterize the people of God.

Brueggemann's and Erlander's works encourage self-examination. How do our lives mirror the ancient Egyptian justification of exploitative consumption, and how can we use this knowledge to understand the radical underpinnings of the Sabbath? How might a true Sabbath perspective invite us to live differently, maybe profoundly so?

We won't suggest what it might look like for you to consider a Sabbath practice. We will suggest that the shift is more than a choice to turn off your phone or computer every Saturday or Sunday or to refrain from shopping one day a week, though it could include these sorts of things.

The larger point, and one we affirm as social scientists, is that the fast-paced, consumer-driven pressure of our day needs to be interspersed with intentional slowness. Stilling of activity gives space for

---

17. Erlander, *Manna and Mercy*, 7–9.

mercy and justice to expand for the sake of our physical and spiritual well-being, for our families and communities, and for other creatures of the earth and for the earth itself.

The *More! Now! Fast!* mentality has become so commonplace that it has embedded itself into our System 1 ways of being. A hurried script is always whirring in the background, prioritizing the up-to-date to-do list, producing and accumulating more than last year, being quicker and more efficient and more profitable. And because these urgent demands are part of our System 1 thinking, we seldom pause to recognize the continual influence they have on our lives and the lives of those around us. If we're not intentional about slowing our consumption and all that entails, we simply won't. We need System 2 to remind us to loosen our tightened grip because we can trust God to graciously provide for our needs, even the needs that cause us anxiety.

The COVID-19 pandemic led to a shutdown as winter eased into spring in 2020 and a slowdown for the following months as industries reduced hours and offerings. People drove less, businesses opened later and closed earlier, and airlines reduced the numbers of flights scheduled. For a season we consumed less than before the pandemic. Air pollution in congested cities like New York dropped by half, and nitrogen dioxide, nitrous oxide, and carbon monoxide levels all dropped strikingly throughout the world, bringing a steep decline in greenhouse gases. Rivers experienced a cleansing, noise pollution dropped in major cities, the color of sea water became bluer in areas made murky by too many tourists, and dolphins returned to the Bay of Bengal and to Venice after a decade's absence.[18] COVID-19 brought negative costs, particularly economic and social-psychological ones, and environmental gains slipped away as life returned to normal. Yet the rest the earth received makes us wonder how a long-term, consistent global Sabbath practice could bring healing and health to individuals, communities, and the planet.

To live we must consume, so we buy and eat food, build houses, clothe ourselves, provide for our children, consult our smartphones (for almost everything), and drive to work in cars that largely depend on fossil fuel. What if we all slowed down—or *shut* down—one day a week? What if we lived a 24-6 life, or something even more spacious? Might it help sustain the fish populations in the oceans, and might our lungs and hearts and our grandchildren thank us someday? What sorts

---

18. Rume and Didar-Ul Islam, "Environmental Effects."

of generosity might emerge from a culture that values what Sabbath-keeping represents?

> **Pause:** Imagine for a moment that you have complete control over your time, money, and schedule (you probably don't, but imagine it). If Sabbath is countercultural resistance to the constant demands for *More! Now! Fast!*, imagine a practice that would bring you pleasure while helping you slow down your pace and pressures to acquire or achieve.

An Invitation to Generosity

Lisa left a twenty-year career in academic sociology (a discipline known for offering curmudgeonly social critiques of just about everything) to return to seminary, where she trained to be a spiritual director. I (Mark) watched this transition with curiosity and interest.

God is love made manifest in a mysterious divine presence among the three persons of the Trinity and poured outward into this universe that God creates, sustains, and loves. The work of a spiritual director is to notice and pay attention to the love of God in all its abundance and generosity.

As the spouse of a spiritual director, I get to observe how God's love is transforming my partner. One of the most practical implications is Lisa's affinity for making and delivering care packages. When she hears of a person going through trouble—a cancer diagnosis, a relational struggle, stressful work—her impulse is to make them a care package. She gathers fresh produce and flowers when we have them, homemade goat milk soap, and baked or preserved goods; writes compassionate words on a card; packages it fetchingly; and then delivers it on someone's front porch.

Her care packages don't cure anyone's cancer or keep a divorce from causing destruction and pain. What they do is lovingly touch something deep inside a hurting person, offering a glimpse of God's generosity and mercy in a world awash with pain and struggle.

The invitation of this chapter is to notice when we are caught up in acquisitive striving and then to open our hands upward, palms exposed in generosity. This sort of liberality involves our money and possessions; our creativity, passions, and gifts; and also, sometimes, our sense of control and power. In pouring ourselves out, we are, paradoxically, filled in return. Relationships grow kinder; humans and communities flourish.

We are not inviting you to superhuman activity or sacrifice that requires more altruism than most people can muster. We're inviting you to live as you have been designed to live: generously. Leading researchers in the science of generosity note, "There is growing evidence that the human brain is wired for generosity,"[19] and for most of us it shows up in various ways every day.

Generosity and its benefits seldom receive as much attention as overconsumption and its consequences, but both transpire regularly. Earlier in this chapter we showed graphs displaying the increasing material waste we've generated in the United States from 1960 to now, both overall and on a per capita basis. That tells part of the story. We would see similar trends if we looked at charitable giving over the same time. Both total and per capita giving have increased sharply, suggesting that as our economy grows and people become more prosperous, we increase in both consumption *and* munificence.[20] It seems fitting to stop, notice, and celebrate this human generosity.

When Mike gave us that tayberry jam, he gifted more than the jam. It also revealed the sort of generous encounter that can happen when human beings slow down enough to notice one another and reach out in lovingkindness. First, Mike took time to 1) see us, offering us a place to sit, engaging with us in good conversation, listening when we revealed our love of growing fruit. Then he cared enough to 2) make connections between our interests and his, noticing a common bond that exists between us. Then he reached out toward us, jam jar in hand, 3) giving a gift that cost him something to make in time, talent, and money. In 4) receiving his gift, we completed the circle, actualizing the sort of generous encounter that makes us all—giver, receiver, and anyone who may witness the exchange—more wholly alive and fully human.

Seeing

When the *Detroit Free Press* broke the story about James Robertson in February 2015, they probably didn't imagine the subsequent outpouring of public generosity. Robertson hadn't missed a day's work in a decade—not since his 1988 Honda Accord died and he couldn't afford to replace it with

---

19. Allen, *Science of Generosity*, 12.

20. *Philanthropy Roundtable*, "Statistics on U.S. Generosity, ¶1. See also Millet, "Numbers are In," ¶1. See also Hadero and the Associated Press, "Americans Gave a Record," ¶1–2.

his $10.55 hourly wage—though it meant a twenty-one-mile walk through Detroit weather and a bus ride each direction.[21] Evan Leedy, a nineteen-year-old university student, noticed the article and started a GoFundMe page to help Robertson raise $5,000 for a new car. In all, 13,248 donors noticed Leedy's page, donated $350,000, and left James kind and encouraging words on the fundraising site besides.[22] Then a car dealer stepped up and donated a Ford Taurus,[23] and employees from financial service companies offered their services pro bono to help James manage his newfound wealth. He kept his job, added health insurance to his monthly budget, and put most of the gift into retirement savings.[24]

Beneath this inspiring story of profligate generosity are a few people who took time to truly see James, to notice his predicament, and to break through whatever indifference they might have initially felt to help a stranger:

- Even before the news story broke, there was an unnamed spouse of the plant manager where James worked who made him a home-cooked meal each day, recognizing his value to the company and his impressive work ethic.
- Blake Pollock was a banker who noticed a man walking in all kinds of weather—and Detroit definitely has all kinds of weather. Pollock started offering Robertson a ride whenever he came across him. Then he brought the story to the *Detroit Free Press*.[25]
- Leedy saw the story, but even more, he saw the humanity of the man in the story. He later said, "God kept tugging at me and all I could think was that it wouldn't hurt to try, and even if I only raised a few hundred bucks, it was better than nothing."[26]

Generosity begins by seeing the other and comprehending their dignity. The new friendship that developed between Evan Leedy, Blake Pollock, and James Robertson is as inspiring as the money raised. Leedy describes it this way: "Before James drove off in his new car to go home,

---

21. Laitner, "Heart and Sole."
22. Leedy, "Help James Robertson."
23. CBS News, "Fundraiser Far Exceeds Goals," ¶4.
24. Stamm, "2015 Recap." Also, *Chicago Defender*, "Detroiter Who Walked 21 Miles."
25. Laitner, "Heart and Sole."
26. Leedy, "Help James Robertson," February 8, 2015 update, ¶1.

he gave me a big hug and said, 'It's not even about the money and the car, it's about random strangers like you and Blake wanting to help a guy like me just doing what I was blessed to do.'"[27]

Jesus once said to his disciples, "Blessed are your eyes, because they see; and your ears, because they hear" (Matt 13:16). The prayer of a generous soul is similar, that we might have eyes to truly see one another, ears to hear the cries of the human heart, and grace to move forward in generosity.

Connecting

Social psychologists have long studied the *just world fallacy*,[28] the belief that people get what they deserve, particularly when they get something bad. System 1, humming along beneath conscious awareness, incorrectly tells us that people warrant the bad fortune they encounter. That unhoused guy on the corner? He must have some deep character flaws that landed him there. Cindy left Alex without warning? Alex must have done something to provoke it. That man who walks twenty-one miles to work every day must have been irresponsible in some way to lose his car. System 1 is often incorrect, but because it operates automatically and beneath full awareness, it carries great authority and power. The just world fallacy is connected to schadenfreude (introduced in chapter 6), finding pleasure in another person's downfall.[29]

Generosity points in a different direction, away from blame and alienation and otherness, reminding us that we are all in this life together and more alike than we are different. We coexist not so much as winners and losers but as fellow pilgrims who navigate the complicated world as well as we can with our wounds, abilities, vulnerabilities, victories, and struggles. At the core of generosity is the capacity to see a common bond between others and ourselves.

Lucy, one of my (Lisa's) spiritual directees, is a woman who has seen and suffered much in her sixty-some years. I had a stable family, and hers was abusive. Her pathway after high school held few opportunities while mine was neat, tidy, and promising. An emergency room doctor telling her a story of a loving judge put her on a God-seeking journey

---

27. Leedy, "Help James Robertson," February 8, 2015, update, ¶1.
28. *Decision Lab*, "Why Do We Believe?"
29. Pietraszkiewicz, "Schadenfreude and just world."

to discover the grace and love she had longed to receive from others. Lucy's life experiences and mine gave us different access to opportunities and shaped almost everything about us. We go to churches that are not alike, we eat differently, we have different sorts of work and recreation. She sized me up at our first meeting as she tentatively shared some of her story and asked me for some of mine. She remarked as she left how very different we are and yet how very similar, too. We connected profoundly in our experience of God, our yearning, our desire, and our trust in God. I am inspired by Lucy and her story of grace, and she says she is drawn to my peace-filled, grounded way of being.

Seeing calls forth a deep sort of connecting that emerges from empathy and solidarity, and Lucy and I have found that in our journeying together.

We can also develop empathy and solidarity for those who will remain mostly strangers to us. What would it be like if I had to walk miles to work and back each day? If I slept under a bridge at night and sat against a building during the day, hoping someone might see, connect, and care for me? What if it had been my spouse to leave unexpectedly? What if I had spent years addicted to alcohol or was addicted still?

The best forms of generosity emerge from recognizing our common bond, connecting our own humanity with the humanity of others.

Giving

Out of solidarity and empathy we offer a gift of kindness—a smile, a word, a donation, help with a project, a gentle nod of understanding, a concerted effort to understand. It may be a $100,000 donation, a few hours of help, or a jar of jam. Generosity is less about the value of the gift than reaching out and giving something of oneself to the other.

Giving is good for us. "By giving ourselves away, we ourselves move toward flourishing. This is not only a philosophical or religious teaching; it is a sociological fact."[30] Generous givers are less likely to be depressed, have a clearer sense of purpose, and experience richer relationships than those who give less.[31] Older adults who volunteer report having better blood pressure and sleep than others, and they live longer.[32]

---

30. Smith and Davidson, *Paradox of Generosity*, 1.
31. Dew and Wilcox, "Generosity and the Maintenance of Marital Quality."
32. Allen, *Science of Generosity*, 19.

Mark embodies generosity. I (Lisa) have had to work at it. I grew up in a home that valued frugality, though my father gave generously to causes and the church. I never thought of myself as *stingy* compared to Mark, just more *frugal*. Mark gives away farm equipment that he could sell, would give away all the fruit we grow (rather than sell it) if I'd let him, volunteers to deconstruct and reconstruct projects for our church, family, and friends. He tips generously, even when tips aren't expected, always looking for how he might give to those who serve us in various ways.

Coming to welcome and appreciate Mark's generosity had as much to do with my shift toward a more invitational and generous way of being as turning from sociology to spiritual direction. I have witnessed how living generously brings Mark joy.

When the Greater Good Science Center at the University of California, Berkeley prepared a report for the John Templeton Foundation, they demonstrated compelling evidence associating happiness and generosity: "While popular culture may imply that happiness comes from focusing on yourself, research suggests the opposite: Being generous can make you happier. This seems to be true even from a young age."[33]

Toddlers often express delight in giving the adults in their lives a toy, a pebble, a smashed bit of peanut butter and jelly sandwich. This tendency toward generosity showed up in research that found toddlers experienced more happiness when giving treats to a puppet than when receiving treats for themselves. Undergraduates who were asked and agreed to help pick up something spilled by a peer reported feeling happier than those who weren't asked to help. Those who offered small acts of kindness to others for six weeks showed increased happiness while those who did small acts of kindness for themselves showed no change in positive emotion. People who volunteer for religious organizations are happier than those who don't.[34]

If you ask people about spending money, they predict that spending on themselves will help their happiness more than spending on others, but the opposite is true: those who spend money to help others report increased happiness while those spending money on themselves report no happiness bump. This connection between giving and happiness is not only true in wealthy Western countries but appears to be universal.

---

33. Allen, *Science of Generosity*, 23.
34. Allen, *Science of Generosity*, 24.

A massive study involving 136 countries showed the same relationship between financial generosity and happiness.[35]

Receiving

If we have made the case that giving helps happiness, so does receiving. Over two thousand Presbyterians throughout the United States responded to a survey about giving and receiving help and their personal health. Both giving and receiving were significant predictors of mental health. Yes, giving was a stronger predictor than receiving, but both mattered.[36]

When offered the tayberry jam, Mark thought about refusing the gift because it felt awkward to receive something from a stranger that required his time and money and also because giving comes easier to Mark than receiving. Mark didn't speak his reservations aloud and recognized later that receiving Mike's gift allowed the circle of generosity to be complete. When James Robertson drove off in his new Ford Taurus after hugging Evan Leedy, he spoke words of friendship in an unexpected culmination of generosity. In gratefully receiving Leedy's gift, Robertson allowed generosity to do its good work in himself, in the thousands of people who gave, and in all those who bore witness as this remarkable story became known.

Generosity thrives in a loop of giving and receiving. When an ice storm took down our beautiful paper birch tree, we offered some of its trunk to our friend, Karl, a woodworking artisan. It seemed both sensible and generous. A couple of months later, Karl surprised us with lovely birch bowls he created on his lathe, redeeming our lost birch and reminding us of Karl's generous heart.[37] This is the same man who once saw potential in a hardworking immigrant without proper documentation and gave him a sizable gift and ongoing mentoring and counsel to help him start his own business. When the man wanted to pay him back, Karl told him to help someone else someday instead. Generosity begins with seeing the other and can have its full impact when it becomes a steady flow of gratitude where generosity received creates space for generosity to be given.

35. Allen, *Science of Generosity*, 25.
36. Schwartz et al., "Altruistic Social Interest."
37. We have each blogged about this. See Lisa's blog at https://www.ferncreekfarm.com/post/when-beauty-breaks, and Mark's at https://www.markrmcminn.com/post/redeeming-birch.

A Generosity Practice

1. *Setting a frame.* Begin by quietly noticing God's generosity for a few moments early in the day. You could do this by enjoying the morning light waking the birds, noticing the face of someone you love, or pondering words from Scripture. For example, reflect on the first words of John 3:16: "For this is how God loved the world: He gave..."

2. *An act of kindness toward another.* Sometime during the day, do something kind for someone else. It doesn't have to be huge, just a small expression of generosity—a word, a card, flowers in a glass jar, a gesture of care, a small gift revealing something of you.

3. *An act of kindness toward the world.*[38] Also, do a small act of kindness for the world today. Consider picking up a stray bit of garbage, altering the heating or cooling a degree or two, choosing to walk instead of drive to the store down the road, or eating a meatless meal.

4. *Review.* As with the Daily Examen described in chapter 5, take a few moments at the end of the day and reflect on your acts of generosity. How did you experience them? What did you notice stirring in you afterward? Is there something you might take and integrate into your life more regularly from this practice?

We hope you read chapter 6 before reading chapter 7, because generosity flows out of gratitude, and both flow from the loving heart of God. As you practiced these small acts of kindness, did you also notice the kindness of others today? Did practicing generosity draw you further into gratitude?

It may not be reasonable to do this generosity practice every day, but consider practicing it regularly, maybe weekly or monthly, as a reminder for how to live with palms open in the world.

---

38. The idea of practicing an act of kindness for others and the world comes from a study exploring the effects of generosity. See Nelson et al., "Do Unto Others or Treat Yourself?"

Slow Ponderings

1. How do you react to the *big and small* conversation when thinking about your consumption patterns? Are there ways you are drawn to live smaller?

2. When you consider particular purchases you have made in the recent past or anticipate making in the near future, what role do you see Systems 1 and 2 playing? What strategies do you find useful in slowing your decisions about major purchases?

3. What reaction do you have about Sabbath as resisting the culture of *More! Now! Fast!*? What ideas come to mind for how you might resist these pressures at least one day a week?

4. Generosity benefits those who receive the gift by addressing a need. How does generosity benefit the one giving the gift?

5. When you consider the four parts of our invitation to generosity—seeing, connecting, giving, receiving—which of these comes most naturally for you? Which is most challenging? Why do you think this is?

6. When you think of generous people you know, what can you learn from them?

Chapter 8

Slow to Isolate: An Invitation to Community

With thirty seconds remaining in the 2020 Famous Idaho Potato Bowl game against the Nevada Wolf Pack, players from the winning Ohio Bobcats team grabbed the Gatorade tub to douse their coach, Frank Solich, except this time it was filled with French fries instead of liquid. Solich responded well, eating a fry, and later saying it was far better than having a beverage dumped on him.[1]

Don't get the Famous Idaho Potato Bowl game confused with the Grand Forks, North Dakota Potato Bowl that occurs near the beginning of the football season each September. North Dakotans grow potatoes, too, and lots of them. The North Dakota Potato Bowl festivities include the world's largest French fry feed each year, which once involved serving up a world-record four tons of fries.[2]

In the United States, the average person eats 110 pounds of potatoes per year, including forty pounds of French fries.[3] This is probably *not* what our parents had in mind when they told us to eat our vegetables.

---

1. Martinelli, "Ohio Players Gave Their Coach a French Fry Bath," ¶4. There were two Famous Idaho Potato Bowl games in 2020, one on January 3 (culminating the 2019 season), and one on December 22 (culminating the 2020 season). The event described here occurred at the January 3, 2020 game.

2. Hamblen, "The State that Hosts an Annual French Fry Festival." Also, Associated Press, "Grand Forks French Fry Feed," ¶1.

3. Smith, "Which Fries are the Best," ¶4.

Sure, potatoes taste good and have a bit of nutritional value, but those golden, tasty spuds don't address the deepest needs of our bodies for wholesome dietary balance. Instead, they may increase our chances of diabetes, obesity, and coronary heart disease. One recent longitudinal study suggests eating fries two or more times per week doubles the risk of death over eight years.[4] But before you post anything on social media about the health hazards of French fries, keep reading.

Another nutrient we need is connection in human community. We yearn to know and be known, to love and be loved, to give and receive in a life-giving rhythm of reciprocity. The importance of this social nutrient was never so evident as during COVID-19 with its deadening isolations of lockdowns and social seclusions and quarantines. The virus rippled through our world with all its variants, and in its wake a deep loneliness settled in, reminding us that we are not made to be alone.

As we have noted numerous times throughout this book, we turn to social media in our loneliness. Americans love social media, with three-quarters of adults under thirty years of age using five or more social media platforms.[5] But heavy social media use may not be much better than eating French fries for our daily vegetables. Frequent Facebook use has been linked to depression, narcissism, neuroticism, loneliness, psychological distress, and other negative mental health markers.[6]

French fries and social media share this in common: both touch a human need, and both provide a partial solution. They brush up against our longings without sating our deepest hunger.

Almost twenty years before the first social media site launched, Richard Foster began *Celebration of Discipline* with "Superficiality is the curse of our age."[7] It still is. Just as our bodies need balanced nutrition, so our souls need the rich interactions offered by deep, caring local communities.

---

4. Veronese et al., "Fried Potato Consumption," 162.
5. Pew Research Center, "Americans' Social Media Use," ¶3.
6. For information on depression, see Yoon et al., "Is Social Network Site Usage?" For narcissism, see Brailovskaia et al., "Addicted to Facebook?" For neuroticism, see Marino et al., "A Comprehensive Meta-analysis." For loneliness, see Reissmann et al., "Role of Loneliness." For psychological distress, see Marino et al., "Associations." For other negative health markers, see Brailovskaia et al., "Comparing Mental Health."
7. Foster, *Celebration of Discipline*, 1.

Slow to Oversimplify

You can probably anticipate where we are heading in this chapter: a) the hazards of isolation and loneliness, b) technology can increase loneliness and isolation, so c) find balance with your devices and d) work to build lasting, meaningful, in-person community. Well, yes, sort of. But things are rarely as simple as they seem—not with social media, and not even with French fries. If we're going to be slow to judge we'll want to avoid oversimplifying.

Real life is more complex than what can be captured in blogs, headlines, and a quotable study or two. Though one longitudinal study suggests eating French fries doubles the risk of death, another larger and longer study didn't find eating French fries connected with increased risk of death at all.[8] We could criticize that huge North Dakota French fry feed because fried foods have health risks, and we could also take a moment to notice how many people come together on those early September days to join in potato sack races, a golf scramble, inflatable games for children, water obstacles, a parade, fireworks, tailgating, and a football game.[9] The joy in the late summer North Dakota air may exceed whatever grumpiness we can muster about the inflammatory omega-6 fatty acids that can come with record-breaking French fry consumption.

Similarly, we might easily oversimplify social media. One scientific review of Facebook use suggests the relationship between depression and social media is too complex to draw simple conclusions,[10] while another shows that viewing grateful posts from Facebook friends can promote one's own satisfaction with life and in-person expressions of gratitude.[11] We've been hard on social media in this book, and we have also acknowledged how it can draw people together. Sometimes Facebook successfully lives up to its mission statement to give "people the power to build community and bring the world closer together."[12]

Our friend Paul has served in various ministry roles throughout his career, including being a pastor and a youth superintendent of his denomination. He now ministers as a school bus driver (Paul himself uses this language, and we think he should write a book about his remarkable

---

8. Hashemian et al., "Potato Consumption and the Risk."
9. Potato Bowl USA, "58th Annual."
10. Baker and Algorta, "Relationship Between Online Social Networking."
11. Sciara et al., "Gratitude and Social Media."
12. Meta, "Our Mission."

encounters with students on his bus, all of whom he knows by name). One spring day, Paul posted the lyrics to "Amazed" by Jared Anderson on Facebook—a song about the sudden realization that God delights in us, singing and dancing over us while we are often oblivious to this reality. His post continued: "For a moment I wondered, 'What if it's really true?' And for a moment it was like it was all new to me. That was a wonderful moment. Then I headed off to drive a school bus."

On the day Paul posted this on Facebook, I (Mark) was heading outside to hoe in the strawberry patch, so I downloaded "Amazed", put in my AirPods, and listened to it a dozen times while dispatching pernicious weeds. I pondered Paul's question, *What if it's really true? What if God dances in delight over me? Over Lisa? Over Paul? Over the children on his school bus? Over all of us?* Joy filled my heart that morning, and Facebook made it possible. I posted a comment thanking Paul for helping me find joy that day and for using Facebook to edify and help his friends.

It should be like that.

Social media offers us the possibility of encouraging, edifying, and bringing people together. When used well, social media brightens our outlook and sharpens our minds. Sadly, these same tools can divide, isolate, and demoralize us, reducing us to the superficiality of our day.

The Hazards of Loneliness

What if social isolation and loneliness are worse for us than French fries? Medical researchers use statistical ratios to determine the mortality risk associated with certain events or behaviors. A ratio of 1.0 means no increased likelihood of dying, 1.25 means 25 percent increased likelihood, 1.50 means 50 percent increased likelihood, and so on. This graph shows mortality ratios for both potato consumption and social isolation, coming from two separate studies.[13]

---

13. Compulsory (but important) small print: Notice that the social isolation/loneliness data can be misleading because it is impossible to determine cause and effect without the impossible task of randomly assigning people to be lonely. Recent polling data suggests that people in poor health are lonelier than others, underscoring how we cannot know how much isolation causes mortality risk and how much mortality risk causes isolation. The two are correlated, and we presume causation goes in both directions, but this is speculative.

Why You Should Eat Your Fries with Someone Else

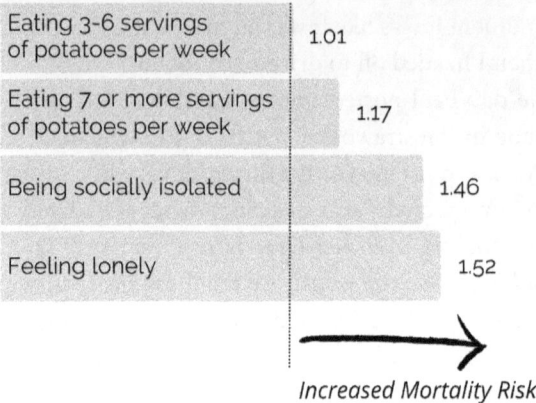

Starting with the top two rows of the graph, imagine you love potatoes and eat them often—French fries, potato salad, mashed, boiled, skillet sautéed—whatever you can get your hands on. You love potatoes so much that you eat them three to six times per week. According to the National Institutes of Health-AARP study, which involved over 400,000 participants, your hazard ratio is 1.01, suggesting you have no increased risk of mortality compared to those who eat potatoes one time per week or less. If you're a Potato Monster (Cookie Monster but with spuds) and eat seven or more helping per week, then your hazard ratio increases to 1.17, indicating a 17 percent increased chance of mortality over those who rarely eat potatoes. How you prepare your potatoes—fries or mashed or whatever else—doesn't seem to make a lot of difference in the hazard ratios.[14] This is good news for potato lovers.

Now move to the third and fourth rows of the graph. Social isolation is based on observable facts about your living situation. If you live alone, have little contact with family or friends, don't interact with colleagues outside work, and don't do much with neighbors, you will score high on social isolation. Loneliness is more subjective, reflecting how you feel about your life circumstances. Examples of loneliness questions include:

---

14. Hashemian et al., "Potato Consumption and the Risk," Tables 1 and 2, data adjusted for age and gender.

- How often do you feel isolated from others?
- How often do you feel you lack companionship?
- How often do you feel left out?

Researchers at Brigham Young University conducted a large meta-analysis of seventy different studies on loneliness, concluding that if you are socially isolated, your mortality risk is 1.46 (46 percent increased risk). If you have feelings of loneliness, your mortality risk is 1.52 (52 percent increased risk).[15] Other researchers have noted that social isolation and loneliness increase our risk of cardiovascular disease, Type 2 diabetes, and dementia.[16] Even prior to COVID-19, Vivek H. Murthy, US surgeon general, called the current situation a "loneliness epidemic," noting that loneliness reduces the lifespan as much as smoking fifteen cigarettes per day.[17]

It's only a slight exaggeration to suggest you can eat as many French fries as you want at the North Dakota French fry feed—just be sure to show up with a friend.

But writing about French fry feeds and hazard ratios seems trite compared to the deeply personal pain of feeling lonely. When you feel lonely, no graph can capture it, and even words trying to describe it fall short. The ache in your heart that wakes you at night or keeps you from falling asleep is an existential alarm system, blaring that things are not right. We are made for connection, for community, and intuitively we have the good sense to be anguished when these relational yearnings go unmet.

The Irish Times once asked readers to tell their stories of loneliness. They heard from the single man who sent out a group text via WhatsApp and didn't get a reply, leaving him to wonder if those on the receiving end were out enjoying themselves without inviting him. A married woman described feeling isolated after moving back home, leaving cherished friends behind. She writes, "I don't know how to go about making new friends; at my age everyone seems to have established their groups of friends." Someone else wrote about the loneliness of being in a marriage with someone who doesn't seem to love you, describing a "constant

---

15. Holt-Lunstad et al., "Loneliness and Social Isolation." As with the potato consumption study, the data are adjusted for age and gender.

16. Christiansen et al., "Loneliness, Social Isolation," Table 2. Also, Sutin et al., "Loneliness and Risk of Dementia."

17. McGregor, "This Former Surgeon General," ¶6.

loneliness that accompanies your every waking—and sleeping—hour." Another person described the inner torture of self-doubt and feelings of worthlessness that pop up whenever he finds himself in social situations. Painful as it is, it's easier to be alone. One woman with lots of friends described the long loneliness that lives in the shadow of a loved one's death. If loneliness were a color, she writes, it would be dark gray. A young stay-at-home mother described the paradox of being home with two children—never alone but desperately lonely.[18]

None of these stories can be graphed or summarized with mortality risks, but each of them reminds us how painful loneliness feels, how ordinary and familiar the circumstances surrounding it sound to us, and how it aches like an empty stomach deprived too long of food. There is no surprise that loneliness is hard on our health. How could it not be?

Even if social science can't capture the deeply personal pain of loneliness, it can help us understand its devastation as it sweeps through contemporary life. On Valentine's Day 2018, the British Broadcasting Corporation launched the biggest ever study on loneliness.[19] Over 46,000 people participated from 237 countries.[20] Various online articles and journal publications emerged, showing the state of loneliness in the early decades of the twenty-first century. Cigna, a large global health service company, reported survey data from 20,000 US participants from 2018 and 2019. Then COVID-19 emerged, bringing more isolation, mask mandates, and lockdowns. More researchers got to work, with many studies now emerging about the effects of social isolation and loneliness.

So, what are we learning about loneliness?

- Those living in individualistic cultures, such as the United States, tend to be lonelier than those living in collectivist cultures, such as Guatemala.[21]
- Men are lonelier than women in adulthood, though in a school-age sample, teenage girls have now surpassed teenage boys in loneliness.[22]
- Loneliness is highest among the young.[23]

18. *Irish Times*, "Lonely People."
19. Gray, "Reading This Alone?"
20. Barreto et al., "Loneliness around the World."
21. Barreto et al., "Loneliness around the World."
22. Cigna, *Loneliness and the Workplace*. Also, Twenge et al., "Worldwide Increases."
23. Barreto et al., "Loneliness around the World." Also, see Hammond, "Surprising

- Among adolescents, loneliness has increased strikingly since 2012. This is true around the world, with the percentage of US fifteen- and sixteen-year-olds who feel lonely rising from 18 percent in 2012 to 37 percent in 2018.[24]

> **Pause:** Do any of these stories and statistics resonate or remind you of one of your own experiences with loneliness? Recall that time. (Maybe it's right now.) If you can, let yourself feel the pain of that loneliness. Name it, feel it, and hold yourself and your memories (or your current situation) in kindness and self-compassion as you notice the thoughts, bodily sensations, emotions, and feelings that come. And then take some deep breaths and keep reading, not because these words will cure loneliness, but because an invitation is coming, and like all invitations, they tend to draw us toward relationship.

Technology and Loneliness

The small things of life, such as our handheld devices, sometimes interfere with the essential things, such as having a rich network of social connections. An arbitrary to-do list transposed onto that handheld device can interfere with meaning-making opportunities when we can't accept an invitation for a walk or coffee with a friend on account of our device dinging at us, reminding us to wash the car or the dog, or mail a package, or clean the garage.

Perhaps you have had the experience of being attuned to your GPS while driving with a friend, trying to navigate the maze of turns and distances and route recalculations, while your friend is simply looking out the window, noticing the surroundings.

You: "It should be right around here somewhere."

Your friend: "Yeah, it's right there. Don't you see the sign?"

You are staring at the small thing—the device or the car display—which is a representation of the real thing that your friend is looking at through the window.

Truth," ¶1.

24. Twenge et al., "Worldwide Increases in Adolescent Loneliness," 261.

Or maybe you have observed a family or group of friends sitting around a restaurant table, poised for good conversation, but instead each one is looking at a smartphone. Each is looking at the small screen—their life one step removed from here and now—instead of the large-as-life possibility of real-time conversation gathered in flesh and blood around the table.

The devices we carry around in our hands or pockets are designed to keep us connected to one another. We call them phones because they have the same talk-and-listen features that phones had in generations gone by, but our phones are rarely used for phoning. We text, post, scroll through websites, watch YouTube videos, scan the news, keep up with sports scores, check the weather, monitor the stock market, shop, play games, and distract our way through life, thinking our "phones" help us stay connected, but mostly, not really.

The devices that connect us to the world don't satisfy our deepest yearning for relationship. They couldn't possibly. Perhaps it says something about our lost sense of connection that we would expect them to. It should concern us that one in four people under the age of twenty-five shows classic signs of addiction to their smartphone, and overusing smartphones is associated with increased risk of depression, anxiety, stress, and poorer sleep.[25] A recent Common Sense Census report shows that teenagers on average now spend almost nine hours per day on screen media, a striking increase of two hours per day from six years ago.[26] And it's not just teenagers. The average US resident spends over seven hours per day on screens, mostly on mobile devices.[27] Not surprisingly, countries with more screen time score lower on the World Happiness Report.[28]

---

25. Sohn et al., "Prevalence of Problematic Smartphone."
26. Rideout et al., *Common Sense Census*, 3.
27. Moody, "Screen Time," ¶1.
28. Oh, the things social scientists do for fun. I (Mark) computed the correlation between screen time and happiness this way: STEP 1. I found 2024 country-by-country data on how much time we currently spend on screens (in the US, it's an average of 7 hours per day), retrieved at Moody, "Screen Time." STEP 2. I found country-by-country data from the 2024 World Happiness Report, retrieved at Helliwell et al., eds., *World Happiness*. STEP 3. Yes, I manually entered all the data into a spreadsheet so I could run a correlation coefficient, which turned out to be -.37. This means that countries with the greatest happiness have the least amount of screen time, and the relationship between the two is reasonably robust. As a reminder, correlation doesn't determine causation. Happy countries may have better things to do than screen time, or screen time reduces happiness, or there could be a thousand other explanations for the correlation.

Such is the paradox of our day, as we trade nutritious food for French fries and genuine human encounter for pixels and TikToks.

One of my (Mark's) Facebook friends whom I have never actually met in real life recently posted, "How do you learn contentment without any friends in real life?" A lively discussion followed, with many of his online friends trying to bring comfort and advice. An hour later he posted, "Blessed are the poor in spirit, for theirs is the kingdom of God." And then, "Blessed are those who mourn for they shall be comforted." And the next day, "I am destined to be alone for the rest of my life. I might as well make the best of it." These posts make my heart ache, knowing that this man is touching something desperately sad about being alone. Having 2,300 friends on Facebook, as he does, will not automatically lead to a rich social life. Facebook is always available on his mobile device and laptop, a place where he recognizes and expresses his loneliness, and vibrant social connection is lost. Rightly, he knows something is not right. Even as I write this paragraph, I hold up into the light of Christ this dear man who lives two thousand miles away. May God bring him comfort, and may it be in the form of a tangible, embodied friend.

Again, we want to be slow to oversimplify the link between technology use and loneliness. Maybe the sad and lonely Facebook friend would be even sadder and lonelier without Facebook. Some research suggests technology that increases social interactions can be helpful, especially among older adults.[29] (Other researchers have questioned this.)[30] Among younger adults, it seems increasingly clear that technology use does *not* help reduce loneliness and may increase it.[31]

Dozens of studies are being published on technology and loneliness each year, with mixed findings. Rather than getting knotted up with meta-analyses, effect sizes, and research methodologies, perhaps we could pause and use common sense to think about how technology shows up in real life. Our friends Karl and Ginny speak with Karl's one-hundred-year-old father once a week on Zoom, along with Karl's siblings. Their scattered family finds a weekly point of connection during this call, technology providing a way for this family to see and talk with one another—something that would have been impossible a few decades ago. Alternatively, we might ask of that family sitting around the restaurant table, each of them staring at their phone displays, phubbing

29. Chopik, "Benefits of Social Technology."
30. Shaw et al., "Evaluation of the Effectiveness."
31. Hunt et al., "No More FOMO."

as they gobble down French fries instead of engaging in real-life conversation, how could this possibly be helpful?

Technology can draw us together or pull us apart.[32]

Finding Balance

The ancient Greek philosopher Aristotle referred to the "golden mean" as that place of moral goodness to be found between two extremes.[33] Rather than scouring your home and removing every technological device you can find (one extreme) or buying each new product Apple and Samsung designers create (the other extreme), how might a path of moderation help us navigate life and loneliness in the information age?

Quakers use queries in times of ambiguity or uncertainty. Queries are questions that prompt self-examination both for individuals and for a gathering of people worshiping together. A good query doesn't have an easy answer but serves as a guide toward clarity and faithful living. Borrowing this practice from our tradition, we offer three queries as we seek balance in a time when technology can easily cast its shadow over our ongoing needs for authentic human connection.

Query 1: How Does My Technology Use Promote and Detract from Meaningful Social Interactions?

Queries are meant to get you thinking, not to cinch down a precise response. Some technology use helps us connect with one another, such as when Paul posted that praise chorus on Facebook, or when Karl and Ginny talk with their family each week via Zoom.

One of our patterns is to do the Daily Mini Crossword on the *New York Times* site together each evening, using one of our phones. We sit side by side on the couch, with our pup Oliver sitting beside us (between us if he can manage it), and commit a few minutes to reading clues, suggesting answers, and racing the silly timer that drives us to move faster than we need to. (Now that we think about it, ignoring the timer may serve our purposes better.) Technology brings us together in those moments, ushering us into a conversation with words and one another while offering us a comfortable ritual that brings us joy.

32. Taylor et al., "Social Media and Close Relationships."
33. Kraut, "Aristotle's Ethics," ¶5.

But sometimes technology tugs us in the opposite direction, keeping our eyes and hearts locked to a display rather than engaging with others around us. Sometimes one of us will ask the other a question and get no reply because the urgency of a mobile device has taken the other into a faraway space.

If you live with others, what is your wake-up routine like? Do you immediately look at your phone, or do you seek connection with the people who share your space? Can you imagine ways to modify your morning routine to enhance connection with those around you?

If you're eating with someone else, where is your phone, and what happens when it comes out during a meal? Is it to share a laugh about a funny YouTube video or to pull you off into the phubbing world of email or text?

When you grab your phone to take a picture for a social media post, to what extent does it pull you away from the moment and those who may be sharing it with you? What helps others feel included at times like this?

Query 2: How Does Technology Affect My Capacity for Solitude?

Fay Bound Alberti is a cultural historian who argues that feeling lonely is a recent invention, at least in the West. The word *lonely* doesn't appear much at all in English writing until 1800, and it meant something different than it does now. Before industrialization, loneliness meant being alone—"oneliness"—which often involved meaningful religious experience. A 1676 English dictionary described loneliness as solitude, without the emotional connotations that we put on the word today.[34] Sadness was not part of loneliness:

> People lived in small communities, they tended to believe in God (which meant they were never really alone, even when they were physically isolated), and there was a philosophical concept of the community as a source of common good. There was no need for a language of loneliness.[35]

With industrialization and urbanization, small communities lost their holding and grounding influence as people relocated for jobs and

---

34. Alberti, *Biography of Loneliness*, 19.
35. Alberti, "Loneliness is a Modern Illness," ¶4.

a better future, which reinforced the budding notion that an individual identity mattered more than membership in one's community. By the time 1900 rolled around, Victorian novels overflowed with the emotional angst we associate with loneliness today as the values and stories of individuals were contrasted with their families and communities.[36] We've now had a couple of centuries to explore the contours of individuality, to dive more deeply into our angst with each generation in the West, and to export our worldview globally with burgeoning social media platforms. Alberti reflects, "The paradox of social media is that it produces the same isolation and loneliness that it seeks to overcome."[37]

Christian contemplatives have long known that solitude allows for connection with God and ultimately for stronger bonds with fellow humans. Solitude and community form a rhythm of the soul, moving inward to experience God's presence, moving outward to be in fellowship with one another, breathing in, breathing out. Lutheran theologian and pastor Dietrich Bonhoeffer wrote of this in *Life Together*: "*Let him who cannot be alone beware of community.* He will only do harm to himself and to the community. . . . But the reverse is also true: *Let him who is not in community beware of being alone.* Into the community you were called, the call was not meant for you alone."[38]

This second query, then, relates to aloneness, to solitude, to the oneliness that was known prior to 1800, to the rhythm Bonhoeffer describes. How is my use of technology affecting my ability to be silent and alone? Am I able to tolerate quiet without reaching for my phone? To wait patiently in a line without distracting myself with my phone? What lessons am I am learning in oneliness, and how is technology helping or hindering these lessons? How could leaning into oneliness help me move and breathe and love in community with others?

Query 3: How Does Technology Contribute to My Being Authentic or Hidden with Those in My Life?

Everyone yearns for belonging. One of the most compelling things about our devices is that they can give us experiences of closeness, but intimacy expressed and experienced with someone in cyberworld sometimes

---

36. Alberti, *Biography of Loneliness*, 32.
37. Alberti, *Biography of Loneliness*, 38.
38. Bonhoeffer, *Life Together*, 77.

lends itself to secrecy or hiddenness with those closest to us in the real world, offering us a false sense of connection without the substance of real relationship. Hiding breeds loneliness.

Perhaps it is the gaming friend or the Instagram acquaintance to whom you feel drawn when communicating with them on your device, or maybe a dating app draws you into the fantasy that the perfect partner is out there looking for someone just like you. Maybe it's the pornography site that soothes moments of loneliness but then deepens isolation over time.

Then again, sometimes our technology can help us experience authentic, in-person closeness. These are not the incognito moments where we want to hide what we have done on our devices, but instead we want to announce what happened to anyone in the room who will listen. I (Mark) recently texted a friend I hadn't seen for several months to let him know I was thinking of him and his family. A warm exchange ensued, including a conversation about the noon basketball games we once enjoyed together. Perhaps it should not have been surprising that the next week he returned to those three-times-a-week hoop games. Technology helped two friends reconnect, and in sharing it, Lisa could celebrate with us too.

When does technology use promote knowing and being known? When and what do I hide from others? Has a virtual relationship—or one that takes place largely in cyberspace—started to feel more compelling than the person sitting next to me in the living room? If so, how do I invite myself back to the living room and engage the people with whom I live?

> **Pause:** This might be a good time to read these three queries slowly, taking a few moments of quiet with each one to consider how your technology choices are affecting you and those closest to you.

An Invitation to Community

Our hearts yearn to belong, to be part of something bigger than ourselves. Humans thrive when in mutually supportive relationship with others. We are not like snow leopards and polar bears, who prefer to live alone and would rather have a tree or chunk of ice for company than another creature.[39] Well, some of us may be more like polar bears than elephants,

---

39. World Wide Fund for Nature, "Self-isolating Animals," ¶3–4.

dolphins, and lions (who all maintain strong social ties), but for the most part, humans experience joy and well-being when embedded in community. We intuitively long for the deep goodness residing there.

Being in a community doesn't guarantee that everyone will flourish or agree or won't be wounded. But it offers a reprieve from our loneliness and a place to belong. Decades before today's research on loneliness showed its devastating effects, Wendell Berry—poet, novelist, and farmer—suggested that loneliness is on a rampage in modern life and that the antidote to loneliness is community.

> A community is the mental and spiritual condition of knowing that the place is shared, and that the people who share the place define and limit the possibilities of each other's lives. It is the knowledge that people have of each other, their concern for each other, their trust in each other, the freedom with which they come and go among themselves.[40]

Recall your best moments from the past month. Most likely these are relational memories that happened in some shared place and touched your mental and spiritual essence.

Berry describes community as "a mental and spiritual condition of knowing that the place is shared." Port William, the small Kentucky farming town where Berry set his fictional short story and novel series, allowed him to contrast values of autonomy, progress, and fast with the slower pace of rural agriculture. Berry covered the lives of Port William's inhabitants from the Civil War to 2021, a time during which independence, mobility, and efficiency came to be valued over the more inefficient, obligatory requirements of community. Berry summarized a key lesson from that history in an address he brought the National Endowment for the Humanities in 2012 titled "It All Turns on Affection." In his lecture, as with his Port William fiction, he punctuates the importance of *place*, lauding those who "'settle, and love the life they have made and the place they have made it.' [They] are motivated by affection, by such love for a place and its life that they want to preserve it and remain in it."[41]

In this community, this place, people motivated by affection "define and limit the possibilities of each other's lives." We belong to one another and have obligations to each other that limit some of our inclinations to grasp and grab. What I do is your business, and what you do is mine,

---

40. Berry, *Long-Legged House*, 71.
41. Berry, "It All Turns on Affection," ¶4.

because our choices impact one another, our children, and our grandchildren.[42] It matters whether I drive slowly in the school zone because it reminds me of (and models for others) our obligation to and hope in a good future for our community's children. It matters if I follow community guidelines and limit my lawn watering in the summer, and pay my taxes, and vote in local elections.

Here in community with mental and spiritual knowing, shared place, and interdependent lives, we find new understandings of *concern*, *trust*, and *freedom*. Berry notes that in small, rural communities, particularly through the mid-twentieth century, people experienced more immediacy in their ways of being. Neighbors embraced *concern* for one another and reached out to ask for and offer help. People assumed a duty to one another, and by carrying out those duties, they established an abiding sense of *trust*. Charity didn't mean giving to a large national organization that then started emailing every week for more money but *freely* and happily giving food or cash or lodging to the neighbor in need or the stranger wandering through town looking for a little kindness and a place to stay.

Berry looks to the "small country town of our agricultural past" as the best model of community,[43] but realistically, most of us do not and cannot live in that sort of town anymore. We can't go back to the fictional Port William of yesteryear. Even so, might there be ways to bring a bit of Port William forward into our contemporary lives?

We belong to a monthly reading group that began several years ago by reading all of Berry's Port William fiction chronologically. Once we made our way through Berry's extensive opus, we decided to keep meeting. Now we read and talk about a non-Berry book each month, though the meal we share and the words disclosed about our own challenges, joys, and opportunities offer the more substantial gift. In creating a chance to be together, we bring a bit of Port William into our lives.

Two members of our group, Maureen and Bill, own Chapters Books and Coffee.[44] Chapters is known in our community as "Newberg's liv-

---

42. In a provocative essay, Berry says sex, like other commonly held necessary parts of society, is everybody's business because the outcomes of sexual choices impact the community. Public and private interests and concerns are best balanced in the context of community—otherwise the public and private interests will destroy each other. See Berry, *Sex, Economy, Freedom*, 119.

43. Berry, *Long-Legged House*, 72.

44. http://www.chaptersbooksandcoffee.com/.

ing room" because Maureen has crafted a welcoming environment that invites people in to browse books and enjoy coffee with friends. People generally don't go to Chapters to get work done because a dozen others who know them will stop by their table for a brief chat, sort of like Jayber Crow's barber shop in Port William. We have our international chain coffee shops in Newberg, too, but the leisurely welcoming ambiance at Chapters offers more than the aroma of good coffee.

If Berry idealizes rural life in Port William, as some have accused him of doing, he stops short of idealizing the church. When a pastor shows up in Berry's fiction, he's likely to be socially clumsy, and when Jayber—trained to be a Baptist pastor—decides to be a barber instead, he becomes a town paragon. Berry describes himself as a "forest Christian," preferring the church of nature to the one with pews, which is evident in his crafting of Port William.[45] Perhaps this adds to Berry's appeal when US membership in faith communities has fallen below 50 percent for the first time.[46]

But to us, admirers of Berry though we are, he misses an opportunity to notice how church may be one of the remaining places to experience rich community. While no church lives up to its aspirations, many are (or aspire to be) shared places of mental and spiritual connection where we willingly define and limit the possibilities of our lives for the sake of mutual concern, trust, and freedom.

Toilet paper is an unexpected example. At the beginning of the COVID-19 crisis, the media partnered with human anxiety to create a toilet paper shortage. We assumed it occurred because of supply chain problems, but panic buying was the real culprit.[47] Store shelves were as bare as . . . well, we'll let you finish that metaphor. But people in vulnerable situations frantically searched their cabinets and closets for one more roll.

One of the pastors in our small Quaker church discovered an unexpected supply of toilet paper and put out an announcement on our LISTSERV offering to personally deliver rolls of this valuable necessity to people's homes. Toilet paper supply is not in our pastor's job description—neither, exactly, is kindness—yet this served as a poignant testimony to the kindred-ness made possible by being part of a faith community.

---

45. Bilbro, "When Did Wendell Berry?," 273.
46. Jones, "U.S. Church Membership Falls," ¶1.
47. Moore, "How the Coronavirus," ¶1.

Someone in our community offered sourdough starter around the same time because a national yeast shortage (also caused by panic buying) made it hard to come by. All of a sudden, a lot of people wanted to make bread. Maybe they simply had more time on their hands with everything shut down. Maybe something stirred in their ancestorial bones reminding them that food can become scarce, and they wanted to ensure they could feed their families. At any rate, we still have our starter, and now five years later, we have a weekly pattern of making sourdough pancakes on Sundays to keep it alive.

Tucked away in the archives of research libraries sit some astonishing studies about life expectancy and church involvement. If you live to age twenty, you will, on average, live another fifty-five years if you never go to church. If you go to church once a week, you will live sixty-two more years.[48] A more recent study among 74,000 female nurses used the hazard ratio statistic we introduced earlier in this chapter. If being lonely renders a hazard ratio of 1.52 (52 percent *increased* chance of death), weekly attendance at religious services yields a hazard ratio of .74 (26 percent *decreased* chance of death) over twenty years.[49]

Few people attend church to enhance their individual health and longevity. Awe and grace draw us to church and our hope that it will be a shared and trustworthy place where we can know and be known, eat together, collectively worship, and care for one another. The earliest followers of Jesus experienced a stunning encounter with community:

> A deep sense of awe came over them all, and the apostles performed many miraculous signs and wonders. And all the believers met together in one place and shared everything they had. They sold their property and possessions and shared the money with those in need. They worshiped together at the Temple each day, met in homes for the Lord's Supper, and shared their meals with great joy and generosity—all the while praising God and enjoying the goodwill of all the people. And each day the Lord added to their fellowship those who were being saved. (Acts 2:43–47)

---

48. Hummer et al., "Religious Involvement," 273-85.

49. Li et al., "Association of Religious Service Attendance." As with hazard ratios discussed earlier in the chapter, we cannot determine cause and effect based on these findings.

Today we are a society of lonely people, yearning for community, with ample evidence that faith communities nurture our individual health and collective well-being.

If you're a churchgoer, we hope that you can offer your own examples of ways your faith community supports and cares for you, as we can. Maybe your faith community sets up meal trains for those facing medical challenges or new family members, has ways to arrange rides to doctor's appointments and airport drop-offs and pick-ups. Faith communities often encourage eating meals together or gathering in smaller groups to play or pray.

Our church's LISTSERV becomes Port William-like when individuals give away tools and furniture they no longer need or request to borrow tools and human ingenuity and labor to help with various challenges of life. We don't eat much meat in our home, but every Thanksgiving I (Lisa) make and can turkey stock for winter soups. So each November, I use our LISTSERV to offer to take a turkey carcass off someone's hands and invariably get multiple offers. Asking a group for a turkey carcass is about as peculiar as offering to deliver toilet paper to people, but all these examples illustrate earthy, practical ways we live in community with one another.

This little Christ-centered country church on the north edge of Oregon's Willamette Valley is a living community, a kinship of friends. We cry with one another in times of loss and lament and pray for one another. We laugh and give thanks together, tear down a pole barn and rebuild it, enjoy potluck meals, play Monday night basketball, have a community garden, together weed around the labyrinth, and work to provide transitional housing for those who need it. We do our best to face our messiness, realizing that none of us reaches our aspirations in our personal or family lives, yet believing we are doing our best to grow in godliness and grace. We strive to be a community, a dynamic collection of complicated people who care for one another and shine the light of Christ into a broken world. If this helps us live longer, all the better, but it's not why we do it.

And yes, opportunities to experience community go well beyond church in our postmodern world. If you're not part of a faith community, we invite you to find other shared places of affection, mutual concern, trust, and freedom rooted in place.

A Community Practice

James Finley—a psychologist and Christian contemplative—recommends that, among other things, we all find our community and enter it.[50] We have suggested various practices throughout these pages and have encouraged you to try some new things. As we reach the end of the book, we encourage you to find or remember your community and enter it.

For some, this may be returning to church after a long hiatus. For others, it may mean entering the center of a faith community where you are now living cautiously at the margins. It could mean becoming more intentional about getting to know and engage with coworkers or neighbors, volunteering to coach youth soccer, or joining the Rotary Club or a local group that cleans up your city parks. Opportunities for local engagement in community abound. Entering a community may require boldly stepping into something new, where—in Berry's words—affection and spiritual knowledge hold you together in a shared place with others.

Community at the level described here might feel foreign and uncomfortable. Western cultural norms and values have encouraged and rewarded autonomy and self-sufficiency, but at the cost of increasing our loneliness. Jumping into a community is risky because it involves being known and trusting others to care for us despite our faults, mistakes, and struggles. Community also involves being willing to let others make a claim on us and asking us to care for them despite their faults, mistakes, and struggles. Take time and move slowly while embracing a step toward meaningful community, if you can.

Slow Ponderings

1. How do times of suffering affect your community involvement? Do you rush toward others in times of pain, do you isolate, or do you choose some other path?
2. Remember a time when social media led you to a sense of joy, connection, and community. What did you learn?

50. Finley, "Summer Symposium Lecture."

3. Remember a time when social media led you to a sense of isolation, loneliness, or pain. What did you learn?

4. Reflect on the Bonhoeffer quote in this chapter (see page 176). What connection do you see between solitude and community?

5. Why do you think churchgoers have a longer average lifespan than others? Consider various possible explanations. For those who don't attend religious services, can you imagine similar sorts of community involvement that might have similar health benefits?

6. Mull over Berry's words about community as turning on affection, that it is a "mental and spiritual condition of knowing that the place is shared, and that the people who share the place define and limit the possibilities of each other's lives." How do you feel about defining and limiting the possibilities of another's life? About others doing that for you? What is frightening about this? What is inviting or appealing?

Conclusion
Railway Stories

Half a century ago, in the library of Neil Armstrong Junior High School, we had the Define the Relationship talk even before DTR was a recognized thing. High school brought its vicissitudes, and the decades have come with some challenges, as we have come to know and love each other deep and long, accumulating a lifetime of stories along the way.

The year before we married, Mark attended Westmont College in California while Lisa trained to be a nurse at Good Samaritan Nursing School in Portland. Phones connected via copper wires, and we paid long-distance rates to hear each other's voices. As students we both counted pennies and took turns calling, talking once a week, those twenty minutes or so a precious pause that allowed us to close the physical distance between us. We sent semiweekly handwritten letters, learning each other's way with words and becoming intimately acquainted with one another's handwriting. Maybe once a month we'd send a cassette tape, which usually included bits of information about us from our roommates and suitemates and allowed us another way of knowing each other with slow and intentional practices.

Describing that feels romantically antiquated and charming and reminds us how vastly more words can be exchanged between people now, with a speedy back-and-forth.

The absence of nuance can be a downfall of written communication—one might not always discern when the other is joking. In 1976, before vinyl was vintage, I (Lisa) bought my first record—Simon and

Garfunkel's *Greatest Hits*. One sunny fall day I left it on my roommate's turntable, located on the windowsill of our dorm room, and it did exactly what plastic does when left too long in the sun—it warped and waved. I bemoaned this in a letter, and Mark responded in his reply that I might try ironing it flat. He told me later he was joking, but even so, it seemed worth a try. After ironing, "The Sound of Silence" became ever so silent.

On the first song from side B of *Greatest Hits*, Paul Simon tells a haunting story of "sittin' in a railway station," moving from city to city in a flurry of performances, all the while yearning to be homeward bound. Railway stations, iconic for their liminality, conjure images of passengers moving from place to place, passing thresholds from now into then. In-between spaces open room for reflection, self-scrutiny, and longing, where life directions get considered and reconsidered, where wistful memories and future ambitions swirl as passengers wait to be transported from here to there. As Simon intimated, train stations capture the glimmer of moving where fast loses its sparkle and we ache to find our way back home to a secure, quiet, loving rest.

We conclude this book by offering a few railway stories, each of them inviting us to slow, pointing toward a quiet, intentional way of being.

Hidden Treasure

Norman Rockwell, the twentieth-century American painter of *Saturday Evening Post* fame, watched all three of his sons leave home in 1954—Jerry to the Air Force and Peter and Tom to school. Rockwell's personal life often showed up in his paintings.[1] The same year his sons left, he painted *Breaking Home Ties*, set in a railway station. Father and son sit on the running board of an old pickup truck, legs touching, cigarette hanging from Dad's mouth as the son—sporting a goofy suit and straddling a suitcase with a State University banner—looks eagerly for an

---

1. For example, in Rockwell's painting *Saying Grace*, one of the young men at the table is Jerry, Rockwell's teenage son who felt delighted to receive a $5 modeling fee, and the other—with cigarette dangling—is Don Winslow, Rockwell's summer intern. The grandson in the painting is Don Hubert Jr., an eight-year-old attending school near Rockwell's studio in Arlington, Vermont, who was so fidgety that Rockwell taped his feet to the studio floor, and the grandmother is May Walker, a widow and Arlington neighbor who died five days before the *Post* cover hit the newsstands, though she did have the privilege of seeing the painting in Rockwell's studio before her death. Rockwell's genius is weaving stories of real life onto a canvas that stands the test of time, that says grace.

approaching train. The collie whose head rests pensively on the son's leg demonstrates the sadness missing from the father's face, though presumably not from his heart.

Donald Trachte—also an artist—and his wife, Elizabeth, moved to Arlington, Vermont, in 1949, where Donald became good friends with his artist neighbor. In 1960 Trachte purchased the *Breaking Home Ties* original from Rockwell for $900, six years after it had been printed as a *Saturday Evening Post* cover.

Life is messy. Donald and Elizabeth divorced, and when Donald got the Rockwell painting in the settlement, he must have felt some anxiety about keeping it on his living room wall or even in his own art studio. Instead, he painted a copy of the prized Rockwell painting and then created an elaborate hiding place behind two sliding walls to conceal the original along with some other valuable artwork.[2] Trachte kept the painting hidden for thirty-two years. Then, after experiencing some memory loss, he died.[3] A year after his death, his sons discovered the secret chamber and sold the Rockwell original at Sotheby's auction house for over $15 million.

The auction price is not the point of the story. This isn't about cashing in on discovered riches but about rediscovering treasures that wait quietly, unobserved, hidden away until we slow down enough to take note of an unexpected bump in the wall or a strange alignment of paneling or a different sort of sound when we pound a nail to hang a picture. It's about letting our attention shift from darting hither and yon long enough to notice subtleties, which sometimes means stumbling upon forgotten treasures.

We hope this book has pointed us all—readers and writers—toward what waits to be rediscovered. Behind our flurrying pace and ubiquitous technologies lies a world of quiet reflection, thoughtful conversation, meaningful faith, and interpersonal connection. The treasures of living slowly easily get walled off with the dinging and ringing and blinging of fastness, with all the expectations, challenges, and disappointments that pop up along the way. The treasures sit there, just behind the wall, waiting to be reclaimed. Their names include *quiet, contentment, courage, empathy, humility, gratitude, generosity,* and *community.*

Or maybe this hidden treasure has one name instead of eight.

2. Goswami, "Windfall from the Walls."
3. Cahill, "Man who Faked Rockwell."

Another of Rockwell's most popular paintings is *Saying Grace*, crafted for the 1951 Thanksgiving issue of *Saturday Evening Post*.[4] Inspired by a real story, Rockwell paints a crowded café where an old woman and her grandson have situated their trays on an already-occupied table and then pause to say grace. The two young men at the crowded table lean in to observe this event in a café teeming with people. They look curiously at the familiar yet perhaps personally unpracticed religious ritual occurring just beyond the condiment tray. Maybe also they wonder about and yearn to enter such a grace-filled space in the midst of chaos.

If one looks closely at Rockwell's *Saying Grace*, through the dim glass window where bold letters pronounce "RESTAURANT" in mirrored backwardness, a railway station stands. Rockwell effectively depicts the bustle of life in the café, and adding the busy, noisy movement of a railway station in the background syncopates the painting's meaning—our longing for quiet spaces of grace in a world that moves too fast and is too loud.

The caption beneath Rockwell's Thanksgiving *Post* cover reads, "Our world is not the happiest place today." The caption, like the painting, still fits seventy-plus years later. We still yearn for a quiet, slow grace to fill our senses and guide our paths through troubled times.

Both these Rockwell paintings feature railway stations. Life contains comings and goings, clamor and din, hellos and goodbyes. And occasionally an old woman and her grandson pausing to offer a slow, grateful thank-you for food, for a place to sit, for family and life and love. They say grace, because in the end, grace may be our greatest treasure.

Grace. If we wrapped together every invitation in this book and every treasure in the long history of the church, in the natural world around us, in human civility and goodness and resilience and hope, in the enduring and pervasive love of God, it might all come together in the shape of grace.

One More Train to Ride

Trains captivate me (Lisa). Seeing them snake along the Washington side of the Columbia Gorge from the Oregon side stirs something akin to that which draws unattached wanderers who ride the rails, like those whose

---

4. Norman Rockwell Museum, "Saying Grace."

stories, poetry, photos, and drawings my once-colleague Cliff Williams collected over the years and published in *One More Train to Ride*.[5]

Besides short jaunts riding trains from the western suburb of Wheaton into Chicago during the years we lived in Illinois, my most significant train rides occurred during the weeks it took my father's body to let go of life. Mom and Dad lived in Pennsylvania, about a thirteen-hour train ride from our Wheaton home, and when we thought he had only a few weeks to live, my sister Pamela and I arranged to pass in the night—on trains, it turned out—to accompany Mom and Dad on this final journey so that Dad could die at home. The plan was for me to follow Pamela's ten-day stint with six days, and if he lived still, she would follow for the next six days, and so on, though we didn't imagine there would be a "so on." But his dying stretched into six lingering weeks, and two more trips east after the one when I thought I had said goodbye.

Riding the Amtrak from Chicago to Harrisburg helped slow me down, to leave the fast pace of the end-of-semester rush characteristic of a full-time academic job, so that I could enter the slow, sacred space that long dying requires. I'd like to say I had deep thoughts about life and death on the train, and maybe I did, but I most remember grading term papers, trying to sleep in an uncomfortable sitting posture, and worrying about Mom and Dad and what I'd find when I arrived in Pennsylvania.

Because I journal, I have access to my experience of those days. Mom and I traded off falling into the bed in the basement, emotionally and physically exhausted after moving beds, cabinets, sofas, and chairs to accommodate Dad's increasing losses, and the energy of grieving those losses, for his sake and also for ours. The other slept fitfully on the couch near Dad so one of us could assist him in the night as he grew restless or needed relief from pain or simply the reassurance of our presence. As we alternated this task, every night we imagined—we hoped—that in the morning Dad's battle would be over. I remember waking up on the couch some mornings to his quiet weeping, Dad's own grief that he had awakened to live another day.

I never regretted the choice to step aside from my career for a season to attend this sacred, once-in-a-lifetime passage. Doing so offered gifts that have nourished me in the years since Dad's death.

Dad's and my relationship had grown rocky in my adulthood, as I made decisions to pursue graduate education and a full-time career that

---

5. Williams, *One More Train to Ride*.

he could not reconcile as being God's will for me. My choice to not let that career limit my ability to be present to him and Mom opened the pathway for significant healing in our relationship.

He would gaze outside for hours, watching hummingbirds feed on the columbine or just gazing. "It's a beautiful day outside," I said one morning.

"Yes, it is," he said. After a pause he added, "And you are such a beautiful person. You are such a comfort to me. You have sacrificed so much time with your own family to be with me. You are so patient and care so gently for me. I could never have been as patient." These were the sorts of words I had ached to hear from him for years. He said other things as well, all of them written down in my leather-bound travel journal. I stored them up and treasure them still.

Choosing to walk this slow journey that took the time it took gifted Dad and me with a good ending. Choosing to step away from the urgency of *fast* and *now* that always characterizes a semester's last weeks also contributed to Mom and Dad having the goodbye they both wanted, given the givens. It allowed Pamela and me to draw nearer to each other in our care for our parents, a bond that we have shared now for nearly twenty years.

That Pamela and I traveled by train offers a rich metaphor for what we have tried to communicate in this book. For the first visit, I did, in fact, fly and realized it saved me very few hours in the end. Besides, it made for a hurried sort of travel experience versus the slow rumbling of a train across the countryside that fostered the dropping away of a hurried pace and entering into a necessary slow one. A pace that more easily allowed grace to waft in, quietly filling the crevices and holding us in our shared grief.

The Nameless Stranger

When Howard Thurman, the American minister and author we introduced in chapter 1, published his autobiography in 1979, he dedicated it to a nameless stranger he encountered sixty-five years earlier at a railway station.

Being Black in Florida in the early 1900s meant Thurman had no funding for public education past seventh grade. His teachers and family could see his intellectual gifts and encouraged him to attend private high school, though it meant earning money for his tuition, room, and board. Thurman worked extraordinarily hard to pay for his dream. The day finally came to take the train from his home in Daytona to Florida Baptist Academy in Jacksonville, crossing a threshold from boyhood to adulthood. He arrived at the train station with train fare, a borrowed trunk, and one spare dollar in his pocket. Because train tickets were always attached to luggage handles and Thurman had no handles on his trunk, the station master asserted that his trunk would need to be shipped to his destination in Jacksonville. With no money to ship the trunk, fourteen-year-old Thurman sat hopelessly, weeping on the station steps, suspended in liminality, trapped in the sort of quandary Jim Crow laws created.

Then a stranger showed up—a Black man dressed in railroad work overalls who rolled a cigarette while asking Thurman to explain his situation. After the tale was told, the stranger declared that if Thurman still wanted an education to follow him. He walked Thurman back to the station agent, took out a money bag, and paid for the dilapidated trunk to be shipped to Jacksonville. The stranger took the receipt from the agent, handed it to Thurman, then disappeared without saying another word.[6] Thurman never saw him again.

Thurman went to high school in Jacksonville, where he graduated as valedictorian, then to college, where he also became his class valedictorian, then to seminary, and on to a notable career as a minister, educator, contemplative, and visionary writer.[7]

Our various biddings throughout *An Invitation to Slow* reverberate in this story about a Black railroad worker in 1915 who paused enough to notice a boy quietly weeping on a rail station stairstep. He listened as he *quietly* rolled that cigarette, demonstrated *empathy* for Thurman's dream housed in a Black body, practiced *humility* and *contentment* by putting Thurman's needs ahead of personal financial grasping with no need for recognition or fanfare, showed *courage* in accompanying Thurman back to the agent who had likely made a decision based more on a passenger's skin color than the condition of his luggage, exhibited the sort of radical *generosity* that spawned a lifetime of *gratitude* for Thurman, and revealed the solidarity of *community* in the process.

In *Meditations of the Heart*, Thurman's words provide a fitting benediction to this book:

---

6. Eisenstadt, *Against the Hounds of Hell*, 70.
7. Eisenstadt, *Against the Hounds of Hell*, 76.

> It is good to make an end of movement, to come to a point of rest, a place of pause. There is some strange magic in activity, in keeping at it, in continuing to be involved in many things that excite the mind and keep the hours swiftly passing. But it is a deadly magic; one is not wise to trust it with too much confidence.[8]

And so we end as we began, boldly claiming that the grace we long for persists, available to us in any moment. The magic of our activity is less real and less satisfying than the mystery we encounter in the pauses. God's grace endures, present in all things: peopled interactions and solitary moments, in blooming flowers and dying ones, in morning birdsong, the rotating of our planet that brings sunrises and sunsets, and our journey around the sun bringing winter, spring, summer, and fall. God stays lovingly present in the interstitial spaces. There is nowhere God is not. We embrace the comfort of this truth when we slow down, pause, and enter the moment.

---

8. Thurman, *Meditations of the Heart*, 29.

Bibliography

6ABC Action News. "'Give Me My Food:' Woman Pulls Gun While in Line at Philadelphia Chipotle." September 23, 2021. https://6abc.com/chipotle-gun-woman-pulls-firearm-cottman-avenue-philadelphia-guns/11038216/.

ABC13 Eyewitness News. "Shopper Opens Fire, Killing One, Over Parking Spot." November 25, 2016. https://abc13.com/shopper-shooting-road-rage/1625048/.

Abernathy, Kenneth, et al. "Alcohol and the Prefrontal Cortex." *International Review of Neurobiology* 91C (2010) 289–320.

Adolphs, Ralph. "The Biology of Fear." *Current Biology* 23 (2013) R79–R93.

Alberti, Fay Bound. *A Biography of Loneliness : The History of an Emotion*. Oxford: Oxford University Press, 2019.

———. "Loneliness is a Modern Illness of the Body, Not Just the Mind." *The Guardian*, November 1, 2018. https://www.theguardian.com/commentisfree/2018/nov/01/loneliness-illness-body-mind-epidemic.

Alfasi, Yitshak. "The Grass Is Always Greener on My Friends' Profiles: The Effect of Facebook Social Comparison on State Self-esteem and Depression." *Personality and Individual Differences* 147 (2019) 111–17.

Allen, Summer. *The Science of Generosity*. University of California, Berkeley: Greater Good Science Center, 2018. https://ggsc.berkeley.edu/images/uploads/GGSC-JTF_White_Paper-Generosity-FINAL.pdf.

Amarasingam, Amarnath. "To Err in Their Ways: The Attribution Biases of the New Atheists." *Studies in Religion/Sciences Religieuses* 39 (2010) 573–88.

American Academy of Audiology. "Levels of Noise." Reston, VA: American Academy of Audiology, 2010. https://audiology-web.s3.amazonaws.com/migrated/Noise Chart_Poster-%208.5x11.pdf_5399b289427535.32730330.pdf.

American National Election Studies. *Time Series Cumulative Data File (1948–2020)*. American National Election Studies, 2024. https://electionstudies.org/data-center/.

Aristotle. "Aristotle's Rhetoric, Book 2, Chapter 9" (350 BCE/2011). https://kairos.technorhetoric.net/stasis/2017/honeycutt/aristotle/index.html.

Arjava, Antti. "The Mystery Cloud of 536 CE in the Mediterranean Sources." *Dumbarton Oaks Papers* 59 (2005) 73–94.

Associated Press. "Grand Forks French Fry Feed Set Record with 4 Tons of Spuds." *The Seattle Times,* September 8, 2017. https://www.seattletimes.com/nation-world/grand-forks-french-fry-feed-sets-record-with-4-tons-of-spuds/.

———. "Two People Shot at Tallahassee Walmart Over Parking Space: Cops." *6 South Florida,* November 23, 2012. https://www.nbcmiami.com/news/local/two-people-shot-at-tallahassee-walmart-over-parking-space-cops/1913330/.

Baker, David A., and Guillermo Perez Algorta. "The Relationship Between Online Social Networking and Depression: A Systematic Review of Quantitative Studies." *Cyberpsychology, Behavior and Social Networking* 19 (2016) 638–48.

Bao, Ruiji, et al. "Dispositional Greed Inhibits Prosocial Behaviors: An Emotive-Social Cognitive Dual-process Model." *Current Psychology* (2020) 1–9.

Barreto, Manuela, et al. "Loneliness around the World: Age, Gender, and Cultural Differences in Loneliness." *Personality and Individual Differences* 169 (2021) 110066.

Behler, Anna Maria C., et al. "To Help or To Harm? Assessing the Impact of Envy on Prosocial and Antisocial Behaviors." *Personality & Social Psychology Bulletin* 46 (2020) 1156–68.

Benjamin Franklin Historical Society. "Constitutional Convention." *Benjamin Franklin Historical Society.* http://www.benjamin-franklin-history.org/constitutional-convention/.

———. "Slavery and the Abolition Society." *Benjamin Franklin Historical Society.* http://www.benjamin-franklin-history.org/slavery-abolition-society/.

Bermudez, Esmeralda, and Ruben Vives. "Store Reopens after 2 Killed." *Los Angeles Times,* November 30, 2008. https://www.latimes.com/archives/la-xpm-2008-nov-30-me-toysrus30-story.html.

Berry, Wendell. "It All Turns on Affection." The Jefferson Lecture (2012) National Endowment for the Humanities. https://www.neh.gov/about/awards/jefferson-lecture/wendell-e-berry-biography.

———. *The Long-Legged House.* Berkeley: Counterpoint, 2012.

———. *Sex, Economy, Freedom and Community.* New York: Pantheon, 1993.

Bilbro, Jeffrey. "When Did Wendell Berry Start Talking Like a Christian?" *Christianity & Literature* 68 (2019) 272–96.

"Black Friday Death Count." http://blackfridaydeathcount.com/.

Bonhoeffer, Dietrich. *Life Together.* New York: Harper & Row, 1954.

Bourgeault, Cynthia. *Centering Prayer and Inner Awakening.* New York: Cowley, 2004.

Brady, William J., et al. "How Social Learning Amplifies Moral Outrage Expression in Online Social Networks." *Science Advances* 7 (2021) eabe5641.

Brailovskaia, Julia, et al. "Addicted to Facebook? Relationship between Facebook Addiction Disorder, Duration of Facebook Use and Narcissism in an Inpatient Sample." *Psychiatry Research* 273 (2019) 52–57.

Brailovskaia, Julia, et al. "Comparing Mental Health of Facebook Users and Facebook Non-users in an Inpatient Sample in Germany." *Journal of Affective Disorders* 259 (2019) 376–81.

Bremer, Shelby. "Steve Bartman Receives Cubs World Series Ring." *5Chicago,* July 31, 2017. https://www.nbcchicago.com/news/sports/chicago-baseball/chicago-cubs-bartman-world-series-ring/20919/.

Brooks, David. "The Cruelty of the Call-Out Culture: How Not to Do Social Change." *New York Times,* January 14, 2019. https://www.nytimes.com/2019/01/14/opinion/call-out-social-justice.html.

———. *The Second Mountain: The Quest for a Moral Life*. New York: Random House, 2019.
Brown, Brené. *Rising Strong: The Reckoning. The Rumble. The Revolution*. New York: Random House, 2015.
Brueggemann, Walter. *Sabbath as Resistance: Saying No to the Culture of Now*. Louisville: Westminster John Knox, 2014.
Byas, Jared. *Love Matters More: How Fighting to Be Right Keeps Us from Loving like Jesus*. Grand Rapids: Zondervan, 2020.
Cahill, Timothy D. "The Man who Faked Rockwell." *The Christian Science Monitor*, April 14, 2006. https://www.csmonitor.com/2006/0414/p11s01-alar.html.
Carson, Clayborne, ed. *The Autobiography of Martin Luther King, Jr*. New York: Grand Central, 1998.
CBS News. "Fundraiser Far Exceeds Goals for Detroit Man with 21-mile Walk to Work." February 9, 2015. https://www.cbsnews.com/news/fundraiser-tops-350000-for-james-robertson-detroit-man-with-21-mile-walk-for-work/.
Cecconi, Christian, et al., "Schadenfreude: Malicious Joy in Social Media Interactions." *Frontiers in Psychology* 11 (2020) 558282.
Center for Disease Control and Prevention. "Covid-19 Vaccines for People Who Would Like to Have a Baby." August 11, 2021. https://www.cdc.gov/coronavirus/2019-ncov/vaccines/planning-for-pregnancy.html.
Chapman University. "Top 10 Fears of 2023." https://www.chapman.edu/wilkinson/research-centers/babbie-center/_files/2023%20Fear/23csaf-9-top-10-list-2023.pdf.
Chen, Eve, and Bailey Schulz. "'One of the worst displays of unruly behavior': American Airlines Bans Passenger after Flight Attendant Injured." *USA Today* (November 1, 2021). https://www.usatoday.com/story/travel/airline-news/2021/10/28/american-airlines-flight-forced-divert-after-flight-attendant-hurt/8580912002/.
Chellew, Candace. "Philip Yancey: Amazed by Grace | Interview." *Whosoever*, May 1. 2004. https://whosoever.org/amazed-by-grace-an-interview-with-author-philip-yancey/.
Chicago Defender. "Detroiter Who Walked 21 Miles to Work Gets Restraining Order Against Girlfriend to Keep $350,000." *Chicago Defender*, March 16, 2015. https://chicagodefender.com/detroiter-who-walked-21-miles-to-work-gets-restraining-order-against-girlfriend-to-keep-350000/.
Chittister, Joan. *The Rule of Benedict: Insights for the Ages*. New York: Crossroad, 1992.
Chopik, William J. "The Benefits of Social Technology Use Among Older Adults Are Mediated by Reduced Loneliness." *Cyberpsychology, Behavior and Social Networking* 19 (2016) 551–56.
Christiansen, Julie, et al. "Loneliness, Social Isolation, and Chronic Disease Outcomes." *Annals of Behavioral Medicine* 55 (2021) 203–15.
Cigna. *Loneliness and the Workplace: 2020 U.S. Report*. Wilmington, DE: Cigna, 2020. https://legacy.cigna.com/static/www-cigna-com/docs/about-us/newsroom/studies-and-reports/combatting-loneliness/cigna-2020-loneliness-report.pdf.
Cohen, Kelly. "Timeline of Lance Armstrong's Career Successes, Doping Allegations and Final Collapse." *ESPN*, May 22, 2020. https://www.espn.com/olympics/cycling/story/_/id/29177227/line-lance-armstrong-career-successes-doping-allegations-final-collapse.

Contemplative Outreach. "In Memory of Mary Mrozowski: An Exemplar of a Lay Contemplative." June 19, 2020. https://www.contemplativeoutreach.org/2020/06/19/in-memory-of-mary-mrozowski-an-exemplar-of-a-lay-contemplative/.

———. "Welcoming Prayer." https://www.contemplativeoutreach.org/welcoming-prayer-method/.

Contemporary Christian Music Magazine Staff. "The Healing Mission of the Porter's Gate." *CCM Magazine,* November 13, 2019. https://www.ccmmagazine.com/features/the-healing-mission-of-the-porters-gate/.

Coss, Stephen. "What Led Benjamin Franklin to Live Estranged from His Wife for Nearly Two Decades?" *Smithsonian Magazine,* September, 2017. https://www.smithsonianmag.com/history/benjamin-franklin-estranged-wife-nearly-two-decades-180964400.

Covington, Dennis. *Salvation at Sand Mountain: Snake Handlers and Redemption in South Appalachia.* Boston: Addison Wesley, 1994.

Cowen, Alan S., and Dacher Keltner. "Self-report Captures 27 Distinct Categories of Emotion Bridged by Continuous Gradients." *Proceedings of the National Academy of Sciences—PNAS* 114 (2017) E7900-9.

Crusius, Jan, et al. "Dispositional Greed Predicts Benign and Malicious Envy." *Personality and Individual Differences* 168 (2021) 110361.

Davis, Don E., et al. "Distinguishing Intellectual Humility and General Humility." *The Journal of Positive Psychology* 11 (2016) 215–24.

De Freytas-Tamura, Kimiko. "Footage Reveals New Details in Tourist Melee at N.Y.C. Restaurant." *New York Times,* September 18, 2021. https://www.nytimes.com/2021/09/18/nyregion/carmines-vaccination-fight.html.

The Decision Lab. "Why Do We Believe that We Get What We Deserve?" The Decision Lab. https://thedecisionlab.com/biases/just-world-hypothesis/.

Dew, Jeffrey, and W. Bradford Wilcox. "Generosity and the Maintenance of Marital Quality." *Journal of Marriage and Family* 75 (2013) 1218–28.

Drehs, Wayne. "Almost Famous: How One Man Came Inches Away from Saving Steve Bartman From Himself." ESPN: Outside the Lines. http://www.espn.com/espn/eticket/story?page=110927/PatLooney.

Dubner, Stephen J. "Who Killed Jdimytai Damour?" *Freakonomics,* December 2, 2008. https://freakonomics.com/2008/12/who-killed-jdimytai-damour/.

Earle, Mary C. *Julian of Norwich: Selections from Revelations of Divine Love—Annotated & Explained.* Woodstock, VT: Skylight Paths, 2013.

Earls, Aaron. "Most Churchgoers See Sabbath as Sunday." *Lifeway Research,* December 4, 2018. https://research.lifeway.com/2018/12/04/most-churchgoers-see-sunday-as-sabbath/.

Eisenstadt, Peter. *Against the Hounds of Hell: A Life of Howard Thurman.* Charlottesville: University of Virginia Press, 2021.

Erlander, Daniel. *Manna and Mercy: A Brief History of God's Unfolding Promise to Mend the Entire Universe.* Minneapolis: Augsburg Fortress, 1992.

Fainaru-Wada, Mark, and T. J. Quinn. "Not as Great: Assessing Barry Bonds, Roger Clemens without the PED Factor." ESPN, December 10, 2021. https://www.espn.com/mlb/story/_/id/32806209/barry-bonds-roger-clemens-far-less-great-subtract-ped-factor.

Federal Aviation Administration. "FAA Fines Against Unruly Passengers Reach $1M." Federal Aviation Authority, August 19, 2021. https://www.faa.gov/newsroom/faa-fines-against-unruly-passengers-reach-1m.

Felitti, Vincent J., et al. "Relationship of Childhood Abuse and Household Dysfunction to Many of the Leading Causes of Death in Adults: The Adverse Childhood Experiences (ACE) Study." *American Journal of Preventive Medicine* 14 (1998) 245–58.

Ferdman, Roberto A. "How Corn Made its Way into Just about Everything We Eat." *The Washington Post,* July 14, 2015. https://www.washingtonpost.com/news/wonk/wp/2015/07/14/how-corn-made-its-way-into-just-about-everything-we-eat/.

Finley, James. "Summer Symposium Lecture." Albuquerque, NM: Program of the Center for Action and Contemplation, The Living School (July 2019).

Fleming, Amy. "Why social media makes us so angry, and what you can do about it." *Science Focus,* April 2, 2020. https://www.sciencefocus.com/the-human-body/why-social-media-makes-us-so-angry-and-what-you-can-do-about-it/.

Forbes. "The World's Real-Time Billionaires." https://www.forbes.com/real-time-billionaires/#29f050fb3d78.

Ford, Bradden. "Artist Profile The Porter's Gate." https://www.newreleasetoday.com/artistdetail.php?artist_id=6395.

Foster, George M. "The Anatomy of Envy: A Study in Symbolic Behavior." *Current Anthropology* 13 (1972) 165–202.

Foster, Richard J. *Celebration of Discipline: The Path to Spiritual Growth.* San Francisco: HarperSanFrancisco, 1978.

———. *Prayers from the Heart.* San Francisco: HarperOne, 1994.

Frankel, Todd C. "The Cobalt Pipeline: Tracing the Path from Deadly Hand-Dug Mines in Congo to Consumers' Phones and Laptops." *The Washington Post,* September 30, 2016. https://www.washingtonpost.com/graphics/business/batteries/congo-cobalt-mining-for-lithium-ion-battery/.

Franklin, Benjamin, *The Autobiography of Benjamin Franklin.* New York: P. F. Collier & Son, 1909.

Frederick, Shane. "Cognitive Reflection and Decision Making." *The Journal of Economic Perspectives* 19 (2005) 25–42.

Fredrickson, Barbara L. "Gratitude, Like Other Positive Emotions, Broadens and Builds." In *The Psychology of Gratitude,* edited by Robert A. Emmons and Michael E. McCullough, 145–66. New York: Oxford University Press, 2004

Friends Bulletin Corporation. *North Pacific Yearly Meeting of the Religious Society of Friends Faith and Practice,* third ed. Corvallis, OR: Friends Bulletin Corporation, 2018.

Frykholm, Amy, *Julian of Norwich: A Contemplative Biography.* Brewster, MA: Paraclete, 2010.

Futagi, Yasuyuki, et al. "The Grasp Reflex and Moro Reflex in Infants: Hierarchy of Primitive Reflex Responses." *International Journal of Pediatrics* 2012 (2012) 191562.

Gallup. *Gallup Global Emotions.* Washington, DC: Gallup, 2024. https://www.gallup.com/analytics/349280/gallup-global-emotions-report.aspx.

Gibbons, Ann. "Why 536 was 'The Worst Year to Be Alive.'" *Science,* November 15, 2018. https://www.science.org/content/article/why-536-was-worst-year-be-alive.

Giphy. "Explore Judgmental Facebook Idiot GIFS." https://giphy.com/explore/judgmental-facebook-idiots.
Girard, Chuck. *Rock & Roll Preacher: From Doo-Wop to Jesus Rock.* Houston: Worldwide, 2021.
Glacial Lake Missoula. "The Short Story." https://www.glaciallakemissoula.org.
Godspace. "Focus—Welcome—Let Go—With Help from Thomas Keating." Godspace, June 18, 2015. https://godspacelight.com/focus-welcome-let-go-with-help-from-thomas-keating/.
Goswami, Neal. "Windfall from the Walls." *Bennington Banner,* December 1, 2006. https://www.benningtonbanner.com/local-news/windfall-from-the-walls/article_bb68e692-5032-5a5d-a847-1874c5a48ab9.html.
Gray, Alex. "Reading This Alone? Recent Surveys Reveal the Curious Truth About Loneliness." *World Economic Forum,* October 9, 2018. https://www.weforum.org/agenda/2018/10/loneliness-survey-research-findings-bbc-2018/.
Gray, Katti. "Black Friday Pepper Sprayer Elizabeth Macias Threatens to Sue Walmart." ABC News, December 10, 2011. https://abcnews.go.com/US/black-friday-pepper-sprayer-threatens-suit-walmart/story?id=15128509.
Gray, Kurt, et al. "Paying It Forward: Generalized Reciprocity and the Limits of Generosity." *Journal of Experimental Psychology. General* 143 (2014) 247–54.
Gregory I. *The Dialogues of Saint Gregory, Surnamed Dialogus and the Great, Pope of Rome and the First of that Name.* New York: Fordham University, 1608/1911/1995. https://sourcebooks.fordham.edu/basis/g1-benedict1.asp.
Greenfieldboyce, Nell. "The Power of Martin Luther King Jr.'s Anger." *CodeSwitch,* February 20, 2019. https://www.npr.org/sections/codeswitch/2019/02/20/691298594/the-power-of-martin-luther-king-jr-s-anger.
Guardado, Maria. "Bonds Misses HOF in Final Year on Ballot." MLB, January 25, 2022. https://www.mlb.com/news/barry-bonds-misses-hall-of-fame-in-10th-year-on-ballot.
Hadero, Haleluya, and the Associated Press. "Americans Gave a Record $471 Billion to Charity in 2020." *Fortune,* June 15, 2021. https://fortune.com/2021/06/15/americans-gave-a-record-471-billion-to-charity-in-2020-pandemic/.
Hamblen, Amy. "The State that Hosts an Annual French Fry Festival." Mashed, February 28, 2021. https://www.mashed.com/344030/the-state-that-hosts-an-annual-french-fry-festival/.
Hammond, Claudia. "The Surprising Truth about Loneliness." BBC Future, September 30, 2018. https://www.bbc.com/future/article/20180928-the-surprising-truth-about-loneliness.
Harvard University Center on the Developing Child. "ACES and Toxic Stress: Frequently Asked Questions." https://developingchild.harvard.edu/resources/aces-and-toxic-stress-frequently-asked-questions.
Hashemian, Maryam, et al. "Potato Consumption and the Risk of Overall and Cause Specific Mortality in the NIH-AARP Study." *PloS One* 14 (2019) E0216348.
Helliwell, J. F., et al., eds. *World Happiness Report 2024.* Oxford: University of Oxford Wellbeing Research Centre, 2024. https://worldhappiness.report/ed/2024/.
Holt-Lunstad, Julianne, et al. "Loneliness and Social Isolation as Risk Factors for Mortality: A Meta-Analytic Review." *Perspectives on Psychological Science* 10 (2015) 227–37.

Hummer, Robert A., et al. "Religious Involvement and U.S. Adult Mortality." *Demography* 36 (1999) 273–85.

Hunt, Melissa G, et al. "No More FOMO: Limiting Social Media Decreases Loneliness and Depression." *Journal of Social and Clinical Psychology* 37 (2018) 751–68.

The Irish Times. "Lonely People—Your Stories: 'The Kind of Loneliness that Makes My Heart Ache.'" *The Irish Times*, September 7, 2015. https://www.irishtimes.com/life-and-style/people/lonely-people-your-stories-the-kind-of-loneliness-that-makes-my-heart-ache-1.2343121.

Janela, Mike. "Kansas City Chiefs Fans Reclaim Record for Loudest Crowd Roar at Sports Stadium." Guiness World Records, October 2, 2014. https://www.guinnessworldrecords.com/news/2014/10/kansas-city-chiefs-fans-reclaim-record-for-loudest-crowd-roar-at-sports-stadium-60872.

Jones, Jeffrey M. "U.S. Church Membership Falls below Majority for First Time." Gallup, March 29, 2021. https://news.gallup.com/poll/341963/church-membership-falls-below-majority-first-time.aspx.

Joye, Yannick, et al. "A Diminishment of Desire: Exposure to Nature Relative to Urban Environments Dampens Materialism." *Urban Forestry & Urban Greening* 54 (2020) 126783.

Julian of Norwich. *Selections from Revelations of Divine Love*. Edited by Mary C. Earle. Woodstock, VT: SkyLight, 2013.

Kahneman, Daniel. *Thinking, Fast and Slow*. New York: Farrar, Straus and Giroux, 2011.

Kaufman, Scott Barry. "The Pressing Need for Everyone to Quiet Their Egos." *Scientific American*, May 21, 2018. https://blogs.scientificamerican.com/beautiful-minds/the-pressing-need-for-everyone-to-quiet-their-egos/.

Keating, Thomas. *Intimacy with God: An Introduction to Centering Prayer*. New York: Crossroad, 2009.

Keating, Thomas, et al. *Spirituality, Contemplation, & Transformation: Writings on Centering Prayer*. New York: Lantern, 2008.

Kershner, Jon. "The (Com)Motion of Love: Theological Formation in John Woolman's Itinerant Ministry." *Quaker Religious Thought* 116 (2011) Article 3.

Kim, Angela Y. "Cain and Abel in the Light of Envy: A Study in the History of the Interpretation of Envy in Genesis 4.1–16." *Journal for the Study of the Pseudepigrapha* 12 (2001) 65–84.

Klein, Melanie. *Envy and Gratitude and Other Works 1946–1963*. New York: Free Press, 1975.

Kleinfeld, Rachel. *Polarization, Democracy, and Political Violence in the United States: What the Research Says*. Washington, DC: Carnegie Endowment for International Peace, 2023. https://carnegieendowment.org/files/Kleinfeld_Polarization_final_3.pdf.

Kodell, Jerome. "St. Benedict Teaches Us to Welcome All as Christ Does." https://wau.org/resources/article/st_benedict_teaches_us_to_welcome_all_as_christ_does/.

Kraus, Michael W., et al. "Social Class, Contextualism, and Empathic Accuracy." *Psychological Science* 21 (2010) 1716–23.

Kraut, Richard. "Aristotle's Ethics." *Stanford Encyclopedia of Philosophy*, July 2, 2022. https://plato.stanford.edu/entries/aristotle-ethics/.

Lacey, Rebecca E., and Helen Minnis. "Practitioner Review: Twenty Years of Research with Adverse Childhood Experience Scores—Advantages, Disadvantages and Applications to Practice." *Journal of Child Psychology and Psychiatry* 61 (2020) 116–30.

Laitner, Bill. "Heart and Sole: Detroiter Walks 21 Miles in Work Commute." *Detroit Free Press*, January 31, 2015. https://www.freep.com/story/news/local/michigan/oakland/2015/01/31/detroit-commuting-troy-rochester-hills-smart-ddot-ubs-banker-woodward-buses-transit/22660785/.

Lange, Jens, et al. "The Painful Duality of Envy: Evidence for an Integrative Theory and a Meta-Analysis on the Relation of Envy and Schadenfreude." *Journal of personality and social psychology* 114 (2018) 572–98.

Lapidot-Lefler, Noam, and Azy Barak. "Effects of Anonymity, Invisibility, and Lack of Eye-contact on Toxic Online Disinhibition." *Computers in Human Behavior* 28 (2012) 434–43.

Leary, Mark R. *The Psychology of Intellectual Humility*. West Conshohocken, PA: John F. Templeton Foundation, 2018. https://www.templeton.org/wp-content/uploads/2020/08/JTF_Intellectual_Humility_final.pdf.

Leedy, Evan. "Help James Robertson Get a Car." GoFundMe, February 8, 2015. https://www.gofundme.com/f/getthisguyacar.

Li, Shanshan, et al. "Association of Religious Service Attendance with Mortality Among Women." *JAMA Internal Medicine* 176 (2016) 777–84.

Li, Yexin Jessica, et al. "Fundamental(ist) Attribution Error: Protestants are Dispositionally Focused." *Journal of Personality and Social Psychology* 102 (2012) 281–90.

Little, Becky. "The Worst Time in History to be Alive, According to Science." History.com, December 3, 2018. https://www.history.com/news/536-volcanic-eruption-fog-eclipse-worst-year.

Lomas, Tim. "Anger as a Moral Emotion: A 'Bird's Eye' Systematic Review." *Counselling Psychology Quarterly* 32 (2019) 341–95.

Lyall, Sarah. "A Nation on Hold Wants to Speak with a Manager." *New York Times*, January 1, 2022. https://www.nytimes.com/2022/01/01/business/customer-service-pandemic-rage.html.

Macrynikola, Natalia, and Regina Miranda. "Active Facebook Use and Mood: When Digital Interaction Turns Maladaptive." *Computers in Human Behavior* 97 (2019) 271–79.

Marino, Claudia, et al. "The Associations between Problematic Facebook Use, Psychological Distress and Well-being among Adolescents and Young Adults: A Systematic Review and Meta-analysis." *Journal of Affective Disorders* 226 (2018) 274–81.

Marino, Claudia, et al. "A Comprehensive Meta-analysis on Problematic Facebook Use." *Computers in Human Behavior* 83 (2018) 262–77.

Martinelli, Michelle R. "Ohio Players Gave Their Coach a French Fry Bath after Famous Idaho Potato Bowl Win." *USA Today Sports*, January 4, 2020. https://ftw.usatoday.com/2020/01/ohio-players-gave-their-coach-a-french-fry-bath-after-famous-idaho-potato-bowl-win.

McCall, Jeffrey M. "Media Spread Fear, Americans Listen." *The Hill*, May 30, 2021. https://thehill.com/opinion/technology/556160-media-spread-fear-americans-listen/.

McFadden, Robert D., and Angela Macropoulos. "Wal-Mart Employee Trampled to Death." *New York Times*, November 28, 2008. https://www.nytimes.com/2008/11/29/business/29walmart.html.

McGregor, Jena. "This Former Surgeon General Says There's a 'Loneliness Epidemic' and Work is Partly to Blame." *The Washington Post*, October 4, 2017. https://www.washingtonpost.com/news/on-leadership/wp/2017/10/04/this-former-surgeon-general-says-theres-a-loneliness-epidemic-and-work-is-partly-to-blame/.

McMinn, Lisa Graham. *The Contented Soul*. Downers Grove, IL: InterVarsity, 2006.

McMinn, Mark R. *The Science of Virtue*. Grand Rapids: Brazos, 2017.

Merrill, Jeremy B., and Will Oremus. "Five Points for Anger, One for a 'Like': How Facebook's Formula Fostered Rage and Misinformation." *The Washington Post*, October 26, 2021. https://www.washingtonpost.com/technology/2021/10/26/facebook-angry-emoji-algorithm/.

Merton, Thomas. *New Seeds of Contemplation*. New York: New Directions, 1961.

Meshi, Dar, and Morgan E. Ellithorpe. "Problematic Social Media Use and Social Support Received in Real-life versus on Social Media: Associations with Depression, Anxiety and Social Isolation." *Addictive Behaviors* 119 (2021) 106949.

Meta. "Our Mission." https://about.facebook.com/company-info/.

Miller, Jonas G., et al. "Roots and Benefits of Costly Giving: Children Who Are More Altruistic Have Greater Autonomic Flexibility and Less Family Wealth." *Psychological Science* 26 (2015) 1038–45.

Millet, Brandon. "The Numbers are In: American Generosity Hits an All-Time High During COVID." *Philanthropy Roundtable*, July 15, 2021. https://www.philanthropyroundtable.org/the-numbers-are-in-american-generosity-hits-an-all-time-high-during-covid/.

Mishel, Lawrence, and Jori Kandra. *CEO Pay Has Skyrocketed 1322% Since 1978*. Washington, DC: Economic Policy Institute, 2021. https://www.epi.org/publication/ceo-pay-in-2020/.

Moody, Rebecca. "Screen Time Statistics: Average Screen Time in US vs. the Rest of the World." *comparitech*, March 20, 2024. https://www.comparitech.com/tv-streaming/screen-time-statistics/.

Moore, Andrew. "How the Coronavirus Created a Toilet Paper Shortage." *College of Natural Resources News*, May 19, 2020. https://cnr.ncsu.edu/news/2020/05/coronavirus-toilet-paper-shortage/.

Moore, Calvin Conzelus, and John B. Williamson. "The Universal Fear of Death and the Cultural Response." In *Handbook of Death and Dying*, edited by Clifton D. Bryant and Dennis L. Peck, 3–13. Thousand Oaks, CA: Sage, 2003.

Moulton, Phillips P., ed. *The Journal and Major Essays of John Woolman*. Richmond, IN: Friends United, 1989.

Nelson, Katherine S., et al. "Do Unto Others or Treat Yourself? The Effects of Prosocial and Self-Focused Behavior on Psychological Flourishing." *Emotion* 16 (2016) 850–61.

News8. "Did a Waterbury Parent Slap a School Bus Driver? Police Investigating Alleged Altercation." *News8*, September 20, 2021. https://www.wtnh.com/news/connecticut/new-haven/waterbury-police-investigating-alleged-altercation-between-parent-school-bus-driver/.

Nieli, Russell. "The Santa Barbara Killings: When Envy Becomes the Deadliest Sin." *Public Discourse*, August 8, 2014. https://www.thepublicdiscourse.com/2014/08/13555/.

Norman Rockwell Museum. "Saying Grace." *Saturday Evening Post* cover, November 24, 1951. https://prints.nrm.org/detail/261014/rockwell-saying-grace-1951.

Nosowitz, Dan. "Private Eyes Tell Us about Digging through People's Trash." *Atlas Obscura*, March 18, 2016. https://www.atlasobscura.com/articles/private-eyes-tells-us-about-digging-through-peoples-trash.
Oliver, Mary. *Thirst*. Boston: Beacon, 2006.
Paarlberg, Robert. "Over-consumption in America: Beyond Corporate Power." OUPblog, May 31, 2015. https://blog.oup.com/2015/05/over-consumption-america-corporate-power/.
———. *The United States of Excess: Gluttony and the Dark Side of American Exceptionalism*. New York: Oxford University Press, 2015.
Pak, Eudie. "Tonya Harding and Nancy Kerrigan: A Complete Timeline of Kerrigan's Attack and Aftermath." Biography, February 8, 2019. https://www.biography.com/news/tonya-harding-nancy-kerrigan-attack-photos.
Panela, Rhea. "Is collecting cans from curbside bins legal in Oregon?" News Channel 21, January 1, 2020. https://ktvz.com/news/2019/12/31/is-collecting-cans-from-curbside-bins-legal-in-oregon/.
Pew Research Center. "Americans' Social Media Use." Report, January 31, 2024. https://www.pewresearch.org/internet/2024/01/31/americans-social-media-use/.
Philanthropy Roundtable. "Statistics on U.S. Generosity." https://www.philanthropyroundtable.org/resource/statistics-on-u-s-generosity/.
Pietraszkiewicz, Agnieszka. "Schadenfreude and just world belief." *Australian Journal of Psychology* 65 (2013) 188–94.
Piff, Paul K. "Wealth and the Inflated Self." *Personality & Social Psychology Bulletin* 40 (2014) 34–43.
Piff, Paul K., et al. "Having Less, Giving More: The Influence of Social Class on Prosocial Behavior." *Journal of Personality and Social Psychology* 99 (2010) 771–84.
Piff, Paul K., et al. "Higher Social Class Predicts Increased Unethical Behavior." *Proceedings of the National Academy of Sciences—PNAS* 109 (2012) 4086–91.
Piff, Paul K., et al. "Awe, the Small Self, and Prosocial Behavior." *Journal of Personality and Social Psychology* 108 (2015) 883–99.
Piff, Paul K., and Jake P. Moskowitz. "Wealth, Poverty, and Happiness: Social Class Is Differentially Associated with Positive Emotions." *Emotion* 18 (2018) 902–5.
Piff, Paul K., and Angela R. Robinson. "Social Class and Prosocial Behavior: Current Evidence, Caveats, and Questions." *Current Opinion in Psychology* 18 (2017) 6–10.
Potato Bowl USA. "58th Annual Potato Bowl USA." *Potato Bowl USA*. https://www.potatobowl.org/.
Preskar, Peter. "The Adulterous Love Life of Martin Luther King Jr." *Lessons from History*, July 27, 2021. https://medium.com/lessons-from-history/love-life-of-martin-luther-king-jr-193f19db839.
Pronin, Emily, et al. "Objectivity in the Eye of the Beholder." *Psychological Review* 111 (2004) 781–99.
Public Religion Research Institute. "Dueling Realities: Amid Multiple Crises, Trump and Biden Supports see Different Priorities and Futures for the Nation." Public Religion Research Institute, October 19, 2020. https://www.prri.org/research/amid-multiple-crises-trump-and-biden-supporters-see-different-realities-and-futures-for-the-nation/.
RadioLab. "Worst. Year. Ever." January 7, 2022. https://www.wnycstudios.org/podcasts/radiolab/articles/worst-year-ever?fbclid=IwAR2Ptmnc4v3mHXjlxf3I5_3cpG4Z5xVzYdoPo2vg1AZ_gshGw5UEUvH2auU.

Rapoport, Robyn, et al. *Methodology Report: American Fears Survey*. Orange, CA: Chapman University, 2023. https://www.chapman.edu/wilkinson/research-centers/babbie-center/_files/2023%20Fear/23csaf-wave-9-methodology-report.pdf.
Ray, Julie. "2020 Sets Records for Negative Emotions." *Gallup*, July 20, 2021. https://news.gallup.com/poll/352205/2020-sets-records-negative-emotions.aspx.
REI Co-op. "OptOutside." *REI Co-op*. https://www.rei.com/opt-outside.
REI Staff. "REI History: It Started with an Ice Axe." https://www.rei.com/blog/camp/rei-history-it-started-with-an-ice-axe.
Reissmann, Andreas, et al. "The Role of Loneliness in Emerging Adults' Everyday Use of Facebook—An Experience Sampling Approach." *Computers in Human Behavior* 88 (2018) 47–60.
Rideout, Victoria, et al. *The Common Sense Census: Media Use by Tweens and Teens*. San Francisco: Common Sense, 2021. https://www.commonsensemedia.org/sites/default/files/research/report/8-18-census-integrated-report-final-web_0.pdf.
Rodger, Elliot. "My Twisted World: The Story of Elliot Rodger." https://www.documentcloud.org/documents/1173808-elliot-rodger-manifesto.
Rohr, Richard. *Eager to Love: The Alternative Way of Francis of Assisi*. Cincinnati: Franciscan Media, 2014.
———. "Nothing Stands Alone: It Can't Be Carried Alone." *Center for Action and Contemplation*, January 2, 2022. https://cac.org/it-cant-be-carried-alone-2022-01-04/.
Rolheiser, Ronald. *The Holy Longing: The Search for Christian Spirituality*. New York: Doubleday, 1999.
Ross, Lee. "From the Fundamental Attribution Error to the Truly Fundamental Attribution Error and Beyond: My Research Journey." *Perspectives on Psychological Science* 13 (2018) 750–69.
Ross, Lee, et al. "The 'False Consensus Effect': An Egocentric Bias in Social Perception and Attribution Processes." *Journal of Experimental Social Psychology* 13 (1977) 279–301.
Ross, Lee, et al. "How Christians Reconcile Their Personal Political Views and the Teachings of Their Faith: Projection as a Means of Dissonance Reduction." *Proceedings of the National Academy of Sciences—PNAS* 109 (2012) 3616–22.
Rume, Tanjena, and S. M. Didar-Ul Islam. "Environmental Effects of COVID-19 Pandemic and Potential Strategies of Sustainability." *Heliyon* 6 (2020) E04965.
Safi, Omid. "The Power of Being Seen for Who We Are." *OnBeing*, July 5, 2017. https://onbeing.org/blog/omid-safi-the-power-of-being-seen-for-who-we-are/.
Salary.com. "Browse Executive Salaries." https://www.salary.com/personal/executive-salaries/.
Sanders, Ed. *Envy and Jealousy in Classical Athens: A Socio-Psychological Approach*. New York: Oxford University Press, 2014.
Schurr, Amos, and Ilana Ritov. "Winning a Competition Predicts Dishonest Behavior." *Proceedings of the National Academy of Sciences—PNAS* 113 (2016) 1754–59.
Schwartz, Carolyn, et al. "Altruistic Social Interest Behaviors Are Associated with Better Mental Health." *Psychosomatic Medicine* 65 (2003) 778–85.
Schwartzberg, Louis. "Gratitude: The Short Film." Gratefulness.org, February 19, 2017. https://gratefulness.org/resource/gratitude-a-film/.

Sciara, Simona, et al. "Gratitude and Social Media: A Pilot Experiment on the Benefits of Exposure to Others' Grateful Interactions on Facebook." *Frontiers in Psychology* 12 (2021) 667052.

Seuntjens, Terry G., et al. "Defining Greed." *British Journal of Psychology* 106 (2015) 505–25.

Seuntjens, Terry G., et al. "Dispositional Greed." *Journal of Personality and Social Psychology* 108 (2015) 917–33.

Shaw, Syed Ghulam Sarwar, et al. "Evaluation of the Effectiveness of Digital Technology Interventions to Reduce Loneliness in Older Adults: Systematic Review and Meta-analysis." *Journal of Medical Internet Research* 23 (2021) E24712.

Sidon, Rob. "The Gospel of Gratitude According to Brother David Steindl-Rast." Grateful Living, November 2017. https://grateful.org/resource/gospel-gratitude-according-brother-david-steindl-rast/.

Slaughter, Thomas P. *The Beautiful Soul of John Woolman, Apostle of Abolition.* New York: Hill and Wang, 2008.

Smith, Aaron. "Which Fries are the Best." Department of Agricultural and Resource Economics, March 1, 2023. https://asmith.ucdavis.edu/news/which-fries-are-bes.

Smith, Adam. *The Money Game.* New York: Open Road Media, 2015.

Smith, Christian, and Hillary Davidson. *The Paradox of Generosity: Giving we Receive, Grasping We Lose.* New York: Oxford University Press, 2014.

Smith, Richard H., and Sung Hee Kim. "Comprehending Envy." *Psychological Bulletin* 133 (2007) 46–64.

Sohn, Sei Yon, et al. "Prevalence of Problematic Smartphone Usage and Associated Mental Health Outcomes amongst Children and Young People: A Systematic Review, Meta-analysis and GRADE of the Evidence." *BMC Psychiatry* 19 (2019) 356.

Solzhenitsyn, Aleksandr. "A World Split Apart. Commencement address at Harvard University (June 8, 1978)." https://www.solzhenitsyncenter.org/a-world-split-apart.

Staicu, Mihaela-Luminița, and Mihaela Cuțov. "Anger and Health Risk Behaviors." *Journal of Medicine and Life* 3 (2010) 372–5.

Stamm, Alan. "2015 Recap And Updates: Gifts to 'Walking Man' James Robertson Pass $350,000." *Deadline Detroit,* December 30, 2015. https://www.deadlinedetroit.com/articles/11460/2015_recap_and_updates_gifts_to_walking_man_james_robertson_pass_350_000.

Steindl-Rast, David. "The ABCs of Grateful Living: A Practice." Gratefulness.org. https://gratefulness.org/resource/the-abcs-of-grateful-living-gratitude-alphabet-practice/.

———. "A Good Day." https://www.ousd.org/cms/lib/CA01001176/Centricity/Domain/3765/A%20Good%20Day.pdf

———. *i am through you so i.* New York: Paulist, 2017.

Stellar, Jennifer E., et al. "Class and Compassion: Socioeconomic Factors Predict Responses to Suffering." *Emotion* 12 (2012) 449–59.

Stephan, Rick, et al. "Meta-analysis of Clinical Neuropsychological Tests of Executive Dysfunction and Impulsivity in Alcohol Use Disorder." *The American Journal of Drug and Alcohol Abuse* 43 (2017) 24–43.

Stewart, Columba. "Evagrius Ponticus and the Eastern Monastic Tradition on the Intellect and the Passions." *Modern Theology* 27 (2011) 263–75.

Stuart, Diana, et al. "Overconsumption as Ideology." *Nature and Culture* 15 (2020) 199–23.
Stuart, Jaimee, and Riley Scott. "The Measure of Online Disinhibition (MOD): Assessing Perceptions of Reductions in Restraint in the Online Environment." *Computers in Human Behavior* 114 (2021) 106534.
Suinn, Richard M. "The Terrible Twos—Anger and Anxiety—Hazardous to Your Health." *The American Psychologist* 56 (2001) 27–36.
Suler, John. "The Online Disinhibition Effect." *Cyberpsychology & Behavior* 7 (2004) 321–26.
Sutin, Angelina R., et al. "Loneliness and Risk of Dementia." *The Journals of Gerontology. Series B, Psychological Sciences and Social Sciences* 75 (2020) 1414–22.
Syme, Rachel. "Mary Oliver helped us stay amazed." *The New Yorker*, January 19, 2019. https://www.newyorker.com/books/page-turner/mary-oliver-helped-us-stay-amazed.
Tandoc, Edson C., et al. "Facebook Use, Envy, and Depression among College Students: Is Facebooking Depressing?" *Computers in Human Behavior* 43 (2015) 139–46.
Tangney, June Price, et al. "Moral Emotions and Moral Behavior." *Annual Review of Psychology* 58 (2007) 345–72.
Taylor, Samuel Hardman, et al. "Social Media and Close Relationships: A Puzzle of Connection and Disconnection." *Current Opinion in Psychology* 45 (2022) 101292.
Thurman, Howard. *Meditations of the Heart*. New York: Harper and Row, 1953.
Tickle, Phyllis A. *Greed: The Seven Deadly Sins*. New York: Oxford University Press, 2004.
Tippett, Krista, and Mary Oliver. "I Got Saved by the Beauty of the World." *On Being Podcast* (original February 5, 2015, updated March 31, 2022). https://onbeing.org/programs/mary-oliver-i-got-saved-by-the-beauty-of-the-world/.
Tolkien, J. R. R. *The Two Towers*. Boston: Houghton Mifflin Company, 1954.
Twenge, Jean M., and Thomas E. Joiner. "U.S. Census Bureau-assessed Prevalence of Anxiety and Depressive Symptoms in 2019 and during the 2020 COVID-19 Pandemic." *Depression and Anxiety* 37 (2020) 954–56.
Twenge, Jean M. et al. "Worldwide Increases in Adolescent Loneliness." *Journal of Adolescence* 93 (2021) 257–69.
United States Environmental Protection Agency. "Advancing Sustainable Materials Management: 2018 Fact Sheet." Washington, DC: United States Environmental Protection Agency, 2020. https://www.epa.gov/sites/default/files/2021-01/documents/2018_ff_fact_sheet_dec_2020_fnl_508.pdf.
Valencia, Nick, and Ralph Ellis. "911 calls capture panic of alleged road rage killing." CNN, July 27, 2015. https://www.cnn.com/2015/07/27/us/florida-road-rage-killing/index.html.
Van De Ven, Niels, et al. "When Envy Leads to Schadenfreude." *Cognition and Emotion* 29 (2015) 1007–25.
Van Tongeren, Daryl R., et al. "Humility." *Current Directions in Psychological Science*, 28 (2019) 463–68.
Vasiliauskas, Sarah, and Mark R. McMinn. "The effects of a prayer intervention on the process of forgiveness." *Psychology of Religion and Spirituality* 5 (2013) 23–32.
Veronese, Nicola, et al. "Fried Potato Consumption Is Associated with Elevated Mortality: An 8-y Longitudinal Cohort Study." *The American Journal of Clinical Nutrition* 106 (2017) 162–67.

Vohs, Kathleen D., et al. "The Psychological Consequences of Money." *Science* 314 (2006) 1154–56.

Wadhwa, Hitendra. "The Wrath of a Great Leader: How Martin Luther King, Jr. Wrestled with Anger and What You Can Learn from His Example." *Inc.*, January 12, 2015. https://www.inc.com/hitendra-wadhwa/great-leadership-how-martin-luther-king-jr-wrestled-with-anger.html.

Wagner, M. "Florida grandfather killed in front of family during road rage clash as victim and attacker both call 911." *New York Daily News*, July 27, 2015. https://www.nydailynews.com/news/crime/fla-man-killed-front-family-road-rage-clash-article-1.2305371.

Whyte, David. *Consolations: The Solace, Nourishment and Underlying Meaning of Everyday Words.* Langley, WA: Many Rivers, 2014.

Willamette Valley Wine. "Facts & Figures." https://www.willamettewines.com/trade-resources/facts-and-figures/.

Willard, Dallas. *The Spirit of the Disciplines: Understanding How God Changes Lives.* San Francisco: HarperSanFrancisco, 1988.

Williams, Cliff. *One More Train to Ride: The Underground World of Modern American Hoboes.* Bloomington: Indiana University Press, 2009.

Woolf, Nicky. "Chilling Report Details How Elliot Rodger Executed Murderous Rampage." *The Guardian*, February 20, 2015. https://www.theguardian.com/us-news/2015/feb/20/mass-shooter-elliot-rodger-isla-vista-killings-report.

Woolman, John. *A Word of Remembrance and Caution to the Rich.* London: The Fabian Society, 1897. https://www.jstor.org/stable/10.2307/community.29886594.

World Wide Fund for Nature (WWF). "Self-isolating Animals: 8 Species That Have Mastered Social Distancing." *The Guardian*, April 15, 2020. https://www.theguardian.com/environment/gallery/2020/apr/15/self-isolating-animals-species-social-distancing-wwf.

Worthington, Everett L., Jr. *Forgiving and Reconciling: Bridges to Wholeness and Hope.* Downers Grove, IL: InterVarsity, 2003.

Xiang, Yanhui, et al. "Effect of Gratitude on Benign and Malicious Envy: The Mediating Role of Social Support." *Frontiers in Psychiatry* 9 (2018) 139.

Yoon, Sunkyung, et al. "Is Social Network Site Usage Related to Depression? A Meta-analysis of Facebook–depression Relations." *Journal of Affective Disorders* 248 (2019) 65–72.

Zeelenberg, Marcel, et al. "When Enough Is Not Enough: Overearning as a Manifestation of Dispositional Greed." *Personality and Individual Differences* 165 (2020) 110155.

www.ingramcontent.com/pod-product-compliance
Lightning Source LLC
Chambersburg PA
CBHW020838160426
43192CB00007B/699